D0521789

THE COMPLETE GUIDE TO

Consulting Success

Howard Shenson
Ted Nicholas

Paul Franklin, Consulting Editor

THIRD EDITION

Upstart
Publishing Company
Specializing in Small Business Publishing
a division of Dearborn Publishing Group, Inc.

This publication is designed to provide accurate and authoritative information in regard to the subject matter covered. It is sold with the understanding that the publisher is not engaged in rendering legal, accounting, or other professional service. If legal advice or other expert assistance is required, the services of a competent professional person should be sought.

Executive Editor: Bobbye Middendorf
Managing Editor: Jack Kiburz
Project Editor: Karen A. Christensen
Cover Design: The Publishing Services Group
Interior Design: Lucy Jenkins
Typesetting: Elizabeth Pitts

Published by Upstart Publishing Company,
a division of Dearborn Publishing Group, Inc.

Printed in the United States of America

98 99 10 9 8 7 6 5 4 3

Library of Congress Cataloging-in-Publication Data

Shenson, Howard L.
     The complete guide to consulting success / Howard L. Shenson, Ted
Nicholas ; consulting editor Paul Franklin.—3rd ed.
         p.   cm.
     Includes bibliographical references and index.
     ISBN 1-57410-055-6 (paper)
     1. Business consultants.   2. New business enterprises—Management.
I. Nicholas, Ted, 1934-   .—II. Title.
HD69.C6S516   1997
001'.068—dc20   96-36016
                                                                    CIP

Upstart books are available at special quantity discounts to use as premiums and sales promotions, or for use in corporate training programs. For more information, please call the Special Sales Manager at 800-621-9621, ext. 4384, or write to Dearborn Financial Publishing, Inc., 155 N. Wacker Drive, Chicago, IL 60606-1719.

Contents

Figures

Chapter 7

Chapter 8

Chapter 9

Appendix

Preface

Looking to the Future

As a consultant, you are part of the fundamental and pervasive changes affecting the American free enterprise system, and yours is one of the most challenging businesses in the American economy. This is a book about the future of consulting in that economy and about the future of your business in consulting.

Although addressed primarily to consultants who are developing and building a practice, this book can be extremely valuable to those who are just starting a consulting business or are already well established.

Most new consultants have plenty of experience in their specialization, but they are generally new to being in business for themselves when they start out. Suddenly, they have to handle all the details of a business. As their business grows, consultants face the challenges of change and increased management responsibilities. Chapter 1 will look at some of the basics of the consulting business. It will be of greatest interest to the beginning consultant, and it may contain some valuable points of information for the developing or established consultant.

Building your practice demands a solid understanding of the special financial arrangements and billing procedures used in consulting. Those who leap into consulting without planning soon find themselves bankrupt and out of business. Many beginning consultants fail to take overhead, expenses, and profits into account. Like any business, a successful practice requires financial planning and sound accounting procedures. Special accounting techniques for consulting practices will be reviewed in Chapter 9 on fees and finances.

However, there is more to running a consulting practice than balancing the books and allocating resources. As a consultant, you have to look to the future, anticipating changes in your market and areas of specialization, and predicting new trends. If you don't, you become part of the past. Chapters 4 and 5 on finding and using opportunities demonstrate how to assess future directions and take advantage of them.

As a consultant, you also look to the future by marketing. Just getting a contract, no matter how big, will not guarantee continued success. You win by building and managing your practice. Chapter 6 on marketing will show you how to avoid the periodic famines that result from inconsistent or ineffective sales efforts.

Another reality of business life is competition. Consultants who fail to update their practice and evaluate their market position end up wondering why they aren't getting new contracts. You need an edge in competition, and you need to keep that edge sharp. Chapter 3 on skills inventory shows you how to stay ahead of your competitors.

A successful consultant is professional. When a professional consultant is retained by a client, the relationship that follows is handled as a business contract. A flamboyant nod and a handshake are not enough. Chapter 10 on contracts and client relationships covers the subtleties of this important area.

Success in consulting calls for more than just expertise in your chosen field. To be successful, you must be able to build a strong reputation, publicize your abilities, have prospective clients see the need for your service, and handle contracts. Besides being a good technician, you need to be a marketer, manager, and planner. Most of all, you have to be willing to work for your fee by rendering a valued service. The simple truth is that a consulting practice is a business like any other, and its success depends on your ability to manage it.

We owe an enormous debt of gratitude to Paul Franklin, editor of *The Professional Consultant,* for his invaluable advice and contribution to this revised edition.

CHAPTER 1

The Business of Consulting

Small business, the backbone of the American economy, is still alive and well. The entrepreneur's spirit of adventure and risk is a compelling idea to many Americans. In *How to Buy a Business* (see the bibliography), the authors show that small business is indeed big business: "Taken in the aggregate, small privately held businesses make up a major portion of our economy. . . . Since 1982, the United States has been creating new businesses at the rate of 600,000 to 700,000 per year." Our country and economy have made fundamental shifts from the stable military-industrial complex anchored by large corporations that flourished following World War II to one in which small businesses provide the economic backbone.

As we are about to enter a new millennium, all trends point to an even greater role for small businesses in our economy. Corporations have and will continue to downsize, breaking down the sense of security that used to come with working for someone else. Widely accessible and affordable technological tools allow small businesses to produce what only large businesses could afford to do less than a decade ago. The continual changes that come with an information-based, technologically driven society mean that businesses must be able to respond quickly and adeptly—a factor that works to the advantage of "small and rapid" over "big and cumbersome."

Consultants have been in the 1990s, and will remain, an important part of this growth in small enterprises. Most consultants start out as sole practitioners, and many stay that way throughout their careers. Fewer than one in four, for example, work in consulting firms of three or more professionals.

In *The 100 Best Jobs for the 1990s and Beyond* (see the bibliography), Carol Kleiman looks ahead to the changing demographics of America in the next century: "Because of the influx of foreign workers and the need to upgrade the skills of all workers, employment opportunities for management and training consultants will increase. The need for a better-educated, more technically trained work force will be apparent at every level." In fact, Kleiman cites management consulting services as one of the fastest-growing industries whose biggest responsibility is "training a diverse work force and helping firms meet employee's work and family needs."

But it is not just in management consulting where growth has and will continue to occur. Growth—in some cases phenomenal growth—is also occurring in many other consulting specialties. In particular, consultants who have a technical specialty are in increasing demand and can expect to be so into the next century. From Internet specialists through mechanical engineering packaging design experts to telecommunications and environmental consultants, tremendous growth has occurred in many technical specialties in the 1990s.

This growth, however, doesn't guarantee success for those entering the profession, irrespective of their background. In fact, the entry of more and more individuals into the consulting profession and across specialties makes it more difficult to characterize the "typical consultant" today than it was in the early 1990s. There is a great disparity, for example, between the fees charged by consultants in many specialties today, and fees charged in years past. It is not uncommon, for example, to find top consultants in a specialty field charging two to four times as much for their services as many others in the field. As a result, it's not surprising to find great disparities in the money earned by the top consultants in a field when compared to their less financially successful peers.

Even though the most recent study of consultant billing rates and earnings was conducted in 1991, experience suggests that the data and its implications remain accurate. Figure 1.1 shows a breakdown of fee and income information gathered in the 1991 study on over 7,000 consultants. The table shows only a few of the multitude of consulting specialties, but they are representative of the range of fees and income.

Both the median daily billing rate and income of consultants provide measures of how healthy the field is. The income figures represent income after business expenses and before taxes. You can see that, on the average, consultants are well paid for their services.

The median fees and average incomes for all consultants and all consultants in a specialty have not changed much since these data were collected. But you can see from the differences between the median billing rates of all consultants and those of the "Top 10 Percent" the disparity we are talking about. And this disparity is believed to be more pronounced today between the average income of the top consultants of any given specialty and the income of their peers. As we examine how the consulting business works, you will learn how the top 10 percent of consultants make the most of their business.

The Demand for Consultants

The increasing complexity and sophistication of business call for the expertise and special skills that a consultant can deliver. Increased competition means that an organization needs employees with more skills and knowledge than it can either find or afford to hire full time. As companies downsize, their needs for skills and knowledge doesn't go away with departing staff. They rely on consultants and other "outsourced service providers" to impart the necessary skills and knowledge at critical times.

FIGURE 1.1   Median Daily Billing Rate and Average Annual Income of Consultants by Selected Specialties

Field of Consulting	All	Top 10%	Average Income Before Taxes
All Consultants	$1,102	$1,994	$104,188
Advertising	1,113	2,513	105,482
Aerospace	1,116	1,490	110,375
Banking	1,119	1,756	100,026
Broadcasting	993	1,595	99,902
Business Acquisition/Sales	1,022	1,891	103,348
Chemical	1,069	1,955	97,454
Data Processing	1,087	1,715	92,290
Dental/Medical	1,202	1,993	111,098
Education	821	1,306	66,023
Engineering	1,277	1,723	109,343
Export/Import	1,182	1,678	103,285
Finance	1,148	2,231	110,772
Fundraising	877	1,456	75,311
Graphics/Printing	781	1,451	79,660
Health Care	1,230	2,142	113,458
International Business	1,147	1,974	105,440
Marketing	1,109	2,034	104,920
Personnel/HRD	901	1,986	78,997
Psychological Services	761	1,446	88,778
Public Relations	883	1,552	80,048
Purchasing	1,102	1,629	93,383
Quality Control	1,107	2,088	103,885
Research & Development	1,261	2,211	121,349
Scientific	1,299	2,256	125,092
Security	881	1,486	93,860
Training	914	1,652	84,818

Source: *Economics of the Consulting, Training & Advisory Professions, Consulting Fees, Incomes, Operating Ratios, Marketing Strategies,* May 1991. Reprinted by permission of National Training Center.

Consultants provide companies the talent and flexibility needed to "win" in an increasingly competitive and global marketplace. The old image of a consultant as an ivory-tower expert no longer applies. Consultants offer a wide range of services that have become an integral part of the American economic system.

Consultants also offer valuable services to government agencies and nonprofit organizations. These groups, which cannot afford to employ all the skilled workers they need, are turning to consultants in increasing numbers to buy these services. New legislation, the need for operating capital, and proposal writing are only some of the sources of opportunity for enterprising consultants in the public and nonprofit sectors of the economy.

Consulting is no longer a part-time diversion from golf for restless retirees. It is a rapidly growing, even trendy, business enterprise that is having a major impact on the American economy. New consulting firms are on the cutting edge of innovation. Consultants work in every area of the economy, from planning for government agencies to developing new products for the latest high-tech companies.

Consulting Is Unique

Several qualities set the consulting practice apart from other businesses. First, consultants tend to work in rather small entrepreneurial environments, including more and more frequently from well-equipped home offices. Because they often worked for large companies before entering business for themselves, consultants must face withdrawal from the infrastructure, "perks," and staff support of the corporate world. Now in business for themselves, they have to go out and find work, arguably the most difficult-to-grasp, yet most important, element of consulting success.

One of the purposes of this book is to help you master marketing strategies that should help generate from 70 to 90 percent of your business opportunities through referrals and build your reputation as an expert. Even though many consultants sit in their offices waiting for the telephone to ring or for a stream of walk-in business, they, and most others, know that business is usually the result of carefully structured marketing plans. In short, success—theirs or yours—doesn't happen by accident.

Second, consultants have to love problem solving and creative challenges. They are frequently asked to look at a complex situation, define it, isolate its most relevant parameters, and develop and often implement practical approaches or solutions.

Third, consultants are loners. They work in a vacuum. In most cases, they do not have a big staff to implement their solutions or assess their strategies. Almost three-fourths of all consulting practices consist of one or two professionals with limited clerical support. Unlike people working for large organizations, they don't have colleagues to consult with. Most of their interactions are with their clients. Because of the client-professional relationship, they usually can't just float an idea to their clients and hash it out as they could with their peers.

Finally, consultants are self-starters. No one tells them to get up in the morning—they do that themselves. They get to work on time because they decide to. They set their own schedules, decide their goals, and create their own businesses. These factors make consulting unique in the free enterprise system.

The Successful Consultant

What sets successful consultants apart from those who are struggling to stay afloat? One outstanding characteristic of successful consultants is their ability to market their skills. They are good at getting out and selling themselves. This isn't the hard sell we often associate with the classical used-car salesperson.

Successful consultants know how to "sell without selling," a concept that will be dealt with in detail in Chapters 6 and 7. Successful consultants understand the purpose and goals of a consulting practice. They serve the interests of their clients. No interest comes before that of the client—not even the consultant's self-interest. Successful consultants avoid any conflict of interest. They are attentive to clients; they pay attention to clients and hear them; they don't offer pat answers or give the impression that they know it all.

Prosperous consultants are architects of reality. Their solutions are often not the optimal solutions that could be found with unlimited time and funds. However, their solutions are workable and effective; they get the job done for the client in a timely fashion.

Successful consultants are disciplined. They keep their business in order and set aside time for marketing and management as well as actual consulting. Those who can develop the habits and approaches of a successful consultant stand a good chance of becoming one—given that they have a marketable skill, are competent in their field, and have the motivation and desire to succeed.

The Importance of Motivation

Motivation and desire drive every successful consultant. The need to succeed and get the job done makes consulting worthwhile. One consultant started with the cushion of a year's severance pay that he used to cover living expenses while he got his practice off the ground. He spent the first month picking a name. He devoted the next month to designing a logo and a letterhead. The third month he looked for office space. The fourth month he undertook a thorough search for a good secretary. The next month he sent out promotional materials. This slow start led to failure. The necessary hunger to succeed was missing. It was not until his fifteenth month, when he was out of funds, that he began to get serious and started on the road to his eventual success.

Getting off to a good start in consulting doesn't require large amounts of capital. If anything, too much capital can be detrimental. Successful consultants are those who yearn to succeed. One consultant lost his job unexpectedly on a Friday afternoon. He vowed that he would never again work for a corporation and put his fate in the hands of other people. He decided to go into business for himself as a consultant. He woke up on Monday morning and said to himself: "I cannot go to bed tonight until I have made $600 in personal income." He went to bed at 4 AM—after he made that $600. When he got up at 9 AM on Tuesday, he repeated his goal. He was a bit more successful because he got to bed at 2 AM after making another $600. On Wednesday, he repeated his goal and was even more successful because he got to bed that night at 11 PM. Within a week's time, he figured out how to make $600 each day in personal income and get to bed at a reasonable hour. He met his objective because he had to—he was motivated.

The Three Big Myths

Consultants are as much the victims of stereotyping as other professionals. In the world of romantic dreams, consultants render sophisticated and desired services at very high fees. They live a life of abundance, working a few days a week and spending much of their time enjoying the fruits of their labors. While their clients vie with one another for their services, these consultants become fully self-sufficient, perfectly self-confident, and completely self-actualized.

The reality is that most consultants are working hard, some are struggling to get by, and the successful ones work so hard that they have little time for a life of leisure.

This dream world is founded on the "Expert Myth," one of the three myths that cause most of the confusion about consulting and keep people from seeing the profession as it really is. The other two myths are the "No Security Myth" and the "Big Competitor Myth."

The Expert Myth

Believers of this myth think that being an established expert is all you need to start and succeed in consulting. They assume that experts just have to open their doors for business and clients will flock to them. The fact is that clients don't come to you simply because you're good at what you do. Even when potential clients are aware of your talents and skills, they don't necessarily see how you can be of service to them.

A successful consulting practice requires all the skills and talents that any other business needs. Technical expertise is just one requirement for success. The experience of countless successful consultants confirms this finding: Successful consultants sell clients results, not expertise, because results hold meaning for clients.

The top experts in most fields are usually too specialized to handle the demands of a real business. The nitty-gritty fact is that you may spend most of your time doing the necessary research to be an expert, which will not leave much time for starting a business and making it succeed. As a result, very few consultants are the world's leading authorities in their specialty. Instead, they are active, practical, energetic people who put theory to work and make it pay. You should not feel unqualified just because you do not rank as number one in your field. Clients want results, not theory.

The No Security Myth

Every consultant—even a highly successful one—can expect to be told that there is no security in independent consulting. Again and again you will hear that the only real security is in getting a regular salary.

Poor business practices and ineffective marketing can make this prediction come true. If potential clients don't see your services as valuable, then your consulting practice is certainly less secure than a salaried position. However, if you can make yourself indispensable to clients who see the need for your services and can pay for them, you have a far more secure position than the typical employee. An employee has only one "client," and the loss of this "client" can be catastrophic. The typical consultant may have as many as seven clients simultaneously, so the loss of one or two is far less devastating.

The Big Competitor Myth

This myth insists that an individual consultant is bound to lose when competing with large consulting firms. The truth is that if you are competing with large firms in their own fields, you won't automatically lose, but you may be in for a good fight. Large firms' size and vast experience often work very much in their favor.

On the other hand, big competitors are usually slow and ponderous. Because their overhead is higher, they are often more expensive. The expense of thicker carpets on the higher floors of expensive office buildings, sabbatical leaves for top personnel, libraries, internal staff managers, and other embellishments are passed on to the client.

Because of high overhead, a large firm often has to offer more generalized, "one-size-fits-all" services to generate enough business, giving the smaller consulting practice an opportunity to offer customized and specialized services at a competitive fee. Clients often see the specialist as offering quality work that they can't get from a larger consulting firm. And they prefer the special attention afforded their "account" by the principals of smaller firms.

It is also difficult for large firms to enter new areas. It may take a large firm a year or more to discover that you are in competition with them, and 18 months or so before they plan any response to your challenge. By that time you will have established yourself firmly in your area and be in control. Big firms may even want to subcontract to you when their clients need assistance in your specialty.

The fact that you are small and flexible gives you an added advantage. You can anticipate changes in technology and economic conditions and respond rapidly, whereas a large corporation, beset by bureaucratic inertia, is often slow to respond to change.

A Successful Transition

Lloyd attended a seminar on building a consulting practice. During a break, he shared his personal goals and fears. Because of bad business fortunes and a subsequent downsizing, he had been suddenly and involuntarily laid off by the firm for which he had served as personnel director for eight years. He enjoyed being a personnel director but was having difficulty finding another job. He wasn't sure he wanted to be a consultant, so he asked for advice. It was clear that Lloyd was worried about the possible lack of security in consulting. He was used to receiving a regular salary and wasn't sure he could compete with large firms. He also had doubts about his expertise. He had been a good personnel director, but he wasn't a noted authority on the subject.

We suggested that he start a consulting practice that would allow him to have the security and income of consulting while continuing to do what he loved best—being a personnel director. We told him that he could compete effectively if he "set up shop" as a personnel department for several small businesses that could use his service but couldn't afford a $65,000-a-year personnel director. By contracting with several companies, he could have security in numbers. If he lost one or two contracts, he had others to fall back on. Six months later, Lloyd called to let us know that he had followed our advice. He had eight clients paying between $1,500 and $2,500 for an average of $2,000 a month for him to be "the outside personnel director." He had overcome the three big myths that prevent consultants from being successful and was reaping the benefits.

The Consultant's Orientation: Task or Process?

Many consultants limit their opportunities for success by being task oriented rather than process oriented. *Task-oriented consultants* seek out consulting opportunities that are almost identical to the tasks they carried out for their last employer. For example, a consultant who has worked successfully with lasers may decide to establish a practice limited to laser applications. The practice concentrates on what tasks the consultant can perform instead of looking at the marketplace to find out what is needed that matches the consultant's wide range of talents. Because we all have many potential and realized talents, concentrating on a limited range of tasks can severely limit our opportunities for growth and financial success.

Process-oriented consultants take a much broader view of the marketplace. Instead of looking at their past organizational achievements, they consider all their skills in determining how they can best meet their clients' needs. They seek opportunities to apply their skills in ways that are valuable to their clients. This added flexibility greatly enhances their chances of success.

Being process oriented rather than task oriented requires looking beyond the knowledge and skills learned in a class or from a book. The skills that make a difference in consulting often come easily and naturally, and may have been evident even in childhood. Successful process-oriented consultants offer the ability to negotiate, build a consensus, analyze a problem, and handle many variables simultaneously as well as various other skills that may have nothing to do with formal "book learning" or training.

Process-oriented consultants are not unreasonably concerned with the specific nature of a task or with the working environment. They are comfortable in a factory, a laboratory, or an office, depending on what the job calls for. Process-oriented consultants are not limited by their past experience. Indeed, their past experiences serve as a springboard for new opportunities. Although they may seem to be different specialists to their various clients, they are actually generalists who are applying a wide variety of skills in meeting each client's needs.

Suppose Tom is in charge of planning for a hospital's critical care unit and decides to become a consultant. If he is task oriented, he will seek consulting opportunities related only to planning for critical care units at hospitals. On the other hand, process-oriented consultants will realize that they can find numerous areas in hospitals where their skills are valuable. They will also see that their skills are applicable in organizations other than hospitals. By emphasizing their process skill, which is planning, they will find a larger market.

Even consultants operating in highly specialized technology-based fields can resist the temptation to be totally task oriented and extend their value to clients. Earl, for example, is a mechanical engineering consultant who specializes in packaging design for electronics equipment. If all he did for clients was conceptualize a design and draw it, his value would be narrowly defined.

But Earl does more. He gets involved with his clients in conceptualizing an entire electronics product so that he can advise them on the most cost-effective, efficient, and environmentally sound packaging alternative. He coordinates with and manages the outside vendors who take his drawings and make prototypes of a package. He works with a client's staff to make the electronic equipment "fit" more efficiently in a designed package, making the overall product less costly to produce. He then works with the production staff—in-house or outsourced—to see that the production standards included in the final design are, in fact, achieved.

Earl and other successful consultants like him have learned that their value to clients can be extended well beyond conducting a specific task. Obviously, your market is broader and your prospects will be brighter if you take this process-oriented approach.

Competing

Competition is what makes the free enterprise system work. Consultants who don't face the need to compete are failing themselves and their clients. You need to develop your abilities just as an athlete does. Winning athletes are aware of what they can do and what they can't. They know their abilities and work hard to develop them. In basketball it is an advantage to be tall, but plenty of basketball players aren't. In Chapter 3, we will go through a skills inventory. The first part of the inventory deals with business skills, and the second part covers consulting skills. Getting away from concentrating on just one or two tasks that you are good at enables you to see the larger picture and become process oriented. By becoming familiar with the consulting process, you will no longer be limited by what you have done in the past, and you will be able to explore your potential to its fullest.

The sport of handball is a good example of how concentration on the process gives an edge in competition. The best players don't have unbeatable serves; they aren't the hardest volleyers. The best players know strategy: They are in the right place so they don't have to run to make a shot; they make their opponents do the running. Older players are often the best because they have integrated their skills and have the experience to make the best moves.

Protecting Your Turf

After you have developed your skills, both in business and consulting, and have acquired some clients, you want to make sure that you keep those clients and continue to build your practice. An inventor is allowed to patent a new product, and a writer can copyright a novel. The law grants writers and inventors a legal monopoly on the product of their minds for a certain time period, but consultants have no such protection. Anyone can imitate your work. The only recourse you have is to protect yourself by identifying your unique skills and matching them to what a given market needs. That means you can't be complacent. You have to update your approaches and stay in touch with your clients' needs so that you have a jump on the competition. And you can be certain that if you are successful, plenty of competition will materialize.

Protecting your market position involves two basic steps: First, you must choose an area in which you can achieve quick recognition. Second, you must thoroughly and quickly channel your resources toward being identified as the consultant with the unique skills needed in that area. Your purpose is to offer a service—or better yet, results—that few or no other consultants can provide so that you are seen as the one who can best meet your prospective clients' needs.

Successful consultants are perceived by their clients as uniquely qualified individuals who are accessible and informed authorities. Perhaps it is a consultant's ability to meet clients' needs in a rare or unique way. Maybe the consultant was the first to establish himself or herself as the authority. Or the consultant may have deliberately chosen and perfected a service that clients cannot get elsewhere. You should not feel squeamish about planning to protect your market position—such planning is not only important, it is essential.

If you plan for exclusivity, you have every reason to expect success. If you do not, you can expect failure or mere survival. The profitability of your business hangs directly on the degree to which your clients see you as the exclusive provider of an essential service. If you offer a service that they can get anywhere, your fee is subject to negotiation and compromise—even if you have a large market. As your talent gets closer to being unique—or to being perceived as unique—your fee becomes less of a consideration in the decision to retain your services. Then your supply of services becomes scarce in comparison with the demand for them. The price of your services can naturally rise, and success is certainly within reach.

Look at defining and defending your market position as a way of getting a patent or copyright on your skills and ideas. Just remember that whatever you call it, *defending your turf is the key to your success in consulting.*

☞ Tips

The word *consultant* often conjures up the image of a lifestyle that bears little relationship to reality. Consulting is like any other business. Make sure that you want to be a business owner and manager before you decide to become a consultant.

Any number of books on the market can help you analyze your readiness for the entrepreneurial venture in general. Unfortunately, some consultants are like inventors who work out of a garage. They may have discovered a good idea, but because they don't know how to sell it, they barely survive. Chapter 6 on marketing will help you avoid that pitfall.

All consultants at some point have to decide whether they are running a real business or simply being an inventor working out of a garage. Do they remain the same in size and scope or expand and grow? This decision seems to be more difficult for consultants than for owners of other types of businesses.

Consultants probably enjoy the "doingness" of the consulting business more than the management and marketing of their practices—that is just the nature of the beast. Most consultants would rather spend time and energies on client projects. They view efforts toward expansion and growth as diverting precious time and energy from doing what they enjoy most. A larger and more complex operation is viewed as needing an inordinate amount of maintenance. Yet failure to expand limits income and opportunity. The ability to handle larger, more complex assignments and clients is reduced; there is less economic insulation in the event of illness or disability. This situation can create unhealthy stress.

It is not the work itself that creates the stress but the consultant's attempts to take on more responsibilities without a corresponding expansion in operations. The practice becomes more difficult, more complex, and lacks the necessary support systems.

By being aware of these issues as you enter the profession, you can prepare yourself to handle the challenges and changes that come your way. On the basis of your abilities and interests, you can decide what kind of practice is right for you. If you take a businesslike approach from the start, you will develop the skills you need for a long, successful career.

CHAPTER 2

Starting Your Practice

This chapter is devoted to the basics of getting a consulting practice off to a businesslike start. Those who have been in consulting for a while may want to skim this chapter and go on to Chapter 3 on developing your personal skills inventory. However, even those who have been practicing for several years may find a useful pointer or two, particularly in the section on writing a capabilities statement.

Reviewing Your Business Skills

This section is aimed at the entry-level consultant. As you undertake the challenge of beginning a practice, you can benefit greatly from a review of your business skills. You already have extensive skills in business, but you may not associate them with the enterprise of consulting. Some of those who have been successful at consulting have learned from painful experience that no practice succeeds without the application of basic, practical business skills.

Business Skills Inventory

To succeed as a consultant you need practical business skills. In reviewing your business skills, keep in mind that you already have plenty of business experience. You are really trying to relate what you already know to your consulting practice. To assess your level of ability in each area, list related tasks that you have handled, then draw up a second list of the skills that you used in carrying out each task. For example, some of us are better at handling money than others. With an accurate estimate of your ability in this and other areas, you can plan your business to use your strongest skills and supplement the areas in which you're weak.

The following six areas are of prime importance in building and maintaining a consulting practice:

1. Basic business knowledge
2. Financial management
3. Marketing
4. Sales
5. Trend prediction
6. Human resources management

As you review each kind of business skill, use the worksheet on business skills provided in Figure 2.1. Write down your experiences in the left-hand column and your skills in the right-hand column. Be absolutely honest with yourself, as you need an accurate picture of your business ability to be a success in consulting.

Don't confuse the skills you use in consulting with business experience. If you are an engineer, you will be selling your skills in engineering—that is your product. Selling that product is a business skill. You may well learn more about business by managing a hamburger stand for three months than you could studying engineering for four years in college.

Basic Business Knowledge

You need information about business licenses, taxes, drawing up an operating plan, forecasting profits and losses, and the like. The skill involved in this area is knowing where to go to get the information you need. You have a number of resources at your disposal: books; periodicals; seminars; business courses; other businesspeople; small business development centers; and federal, state, and local government agencies, such as the Small Business Administration and state and local economic development departments.

Financial Management

List your experience in handling monetary forecasting and planning. You are looking for skills and for areas where you have difficulty. In business it's just as important to know what you can't do as to know what you can.

Marketing

You will be marketing yourself. Have you had experience in setting up marketing plans? Are you skilled at making contacts? You may have worked for a volunteer agency and helped put together a publicity campaign. Pay particular attention to your networking ability because making and using contacts is the most important avenue to getting requests for your services.

FIGURE 2.1 Business Skills Worksheet

Activities	Skills
Business Knowledge	
Business Knowledge	
Business Knowledge	
Sales	
Price Trends	
Human Resources Management	

Sales

If your self-marketing is successful, you'll have the opportunity to make sales. Making a sale in consulting is a matter of being credible and persuasive. Usually, the hard sell doesn't work. List your experiences in sales and in persuasion. Skills you want to look for are your ability to gain the confidence of others and to get them excited about a project.

Trend Prediction

Consultants need to predict trends in their fields of specialization as well as for business and society in general. If you're doing just one kind of work and the market changes, you may be out of business. Think of times when you have successfully anticipated future trends in your specialty and in other areas.

Human Resources Management

Most consultants start out in business by themselves or with one or two other people. First and foremost, this involves skill at managing yourself. It will also require the skill to manage any clerical, bookkeeping, and other support you will need, either full-time, part-time, or outsourced.

With time you'll face the choice of expanding your business or staying small. Expanding may involve working with partners and/or hiring workers. You may also outsource projects or parts of projects to experts or lease or engage a temporary employee through an employment agency. These last three options—outsourcing, leasing workers, or hiring "temps"—allow you to avoid setting up payroll accounts and paying payroll taxes and workers' compensation while allowing you to use specific talents only as long as you need them. But regardless of how you acquire needed assistance, it means coordinating efforts, motivating workers, scheduling activities, and managing time.

Carefully assess your ability to handle time. Is your schedule smooth or messy? Can you work comfortably and effectively with others? Can you get yourself and others motivated and interested? Knowing your strengths and weaknesses in these areas is important when starting out and later when you face the choice of expanding.

Reviewing Your List

Don't be discouraged if you find some areas where you lack ability. In an area like basic business knowledge, you can learn what you need. In other areas you may need to supplement your skills. Those who succeed in business either have the necessary skills, hire someone who does, or acquire these skills on their own. If you regularly mess up your checkbook, get a part-time accountant or bookkeeper who can organize your finances while you merely oversee the work. If you aren't a good manager, hire one or work with a partner who is. With experience you'll learn more about scheduling and time management. Chapters 6, 7, and 8 will show you how to set up a marketing plan and handle sales.

An honest appraisal of your business skills is a guide to planning your career. By relying on your strengths, you can increase your effectiveness.

Beginnings

There are certain down-to-earth business realities to consider when opening a consulting practice. One of the first decisions is the appropriate form of business for you. You may also decide to

- choose a lawyer,
- contract with an accountant,
- establish a working relationship with a banker, and/or
- become a member of one or more professional associations.

Once you have established an ongoing practice, you'll want to periodically re-evaluate your arrangements and make changes.

The Form of Business

You can choose from one of several forms of business for your consulting practice:

1. Sole proprietorship
2. General or limited partnership
3. Corporation—either a C corporation or an S corporation
4. Nonprofit corporation
5. Professional corporation
6. Limited liability company

Your choice depends on whether you are working alone or with others, the size of your business, the anticipated risks, and your personal tax situation. If you have considerable personal assets to protect, for example, you may be less interested in entering a proprietorship or partnership in which you may be responsible for all liabilities.

Law and current business practices influence your choice. You may start out in one form, then change as conditions and legal requirements change. One important consideration in choosing a form for your business is the tax rate you'll pay. Changes in tax laws should be taken into consideration as they may affect the relative advantages of each form. For example, many people who found it advantageous to incorporate converted back to a proprietorship in response to changes in federal tax laws.

Sole Proprietorship

A *sole proprietorship* is a business owned outright by one person. Typically, the success of the business depends completely on the skill and active involvement of the owner, or proprietor. Forming a sole proprietorship is simple and inexpensive, which is probably why it is the most popular form of business among consultants. Most states simply require you to obtain an assumed business name, a process that varies from state to state.

A sole proprietorship has two drawbacks: (1) The business usually folds if the owner dies or is incapacitated by illness, and (2) the proprietor is personally and wholly responsible for any liability of the business. You can protect yourself with insurance against some types of business-related legal claims, but insurance does not cover bad debts or business losses.

Some consultants operate as sole proprietors when the prospect of incurring a large liability is either very remote or easily covered by insurance. Nevertheless, sole proprietorships can entail a high degree of risk.

General and Limited Partnership

In a *general partnership,* two or more parties contribute assets to the business and share in the profits. These partners may be responsible for the liabilities of the business to the extent of their assets. In a *limited partnership,* the partners are personally liable for all business debts to the extent of their participation in the business. The extent of responsibility for general and limited partnerships varies from state to state; a lawyer's advice may be needed at this point.

Partnerships assume several different forms. If a partnership interests you, first discuss the possibility with your accountant and lawyer.

A partnership is much like a marriage: You can spend as much time with a partner as you do with a spouse. And like marriages, when partnerships work well, they are beautiful. When they don't, they can be hell on earth.

While contingent liability is the biggest problem for all partnerships, consultants who go into partnership face an even greater danger. If partners disagree strongly, in most businesses they do not destroy the assets. If two partners in a shoe store have an argument and decide to break up, they haven't destroyed the assets, which are the stock and equipment. One partner can continue to sell the shoes. In the case of a consulting practice, however, the consultants *are* the assets. Their synergy and ability to work together—the major assets of the business—are destroyed if they are fighting and undercutting each other. The business may be unable to survive with only one of the partners.

Most people enter partnerships for the wrong reasons. A partnership works because of the absolute dependency of the partners on each other to run the business. However, many partnerships are entered into because people want someone to talk to and commiserate with. You can socialize with friends for much less trouble and risk than by entering a partnership.

Consultants can work together, which is valuable and beneficial, in other ways. Consultants can associate with each other and work on projects while each has an independent business. They can share offices, split the rent, go 50–50 on a coffeemaker, hire a secretary, subcontract with each other, and discuss a variety of matters—all without entering into a partnership.

Corporations—Either C or S

In law a *corporation* is defined as a legal person. Although a business may be your creation, it becomes a separate legal entity. You may be an officer in the corporation, become its employee, or even consult with your own company, but you are not legally the company itself as in the case of a proprietorship.

Incorporating offers several advantages. The foremost is that the business is liable for its own debts. Creditors may empty the firm's treasure chest, but they cannot take your home away. There are exceptions—for example, if you are found guilty of fraud or, as corporate treasurer, of neglect in withholding taxes. Savvy creditors, however, are increasingly requiring personal guarantees, which negates the protection of a corporation for that transaction.

The tax advantages of a corporation may or may not pertain to your financial situation. The essential question is: At what point do corporate tax rates help me more than individual tax rates? Your accountant can advise you on this point. Your accountant is also the person to walk you through the decision of whether a C or S corporation is best for your business and personal tax situation. Both offer similar benefits but have different filing requirements.

Perhaps the chief drawback of incorporating is the increased reporting requirements. A corporation's tax obligations and its legal requirements are more complex than those of other forms of business. As a result, there is more need for accounting and legal assistance. Also, you can't always control a corporation as easily as a proprietorship or a partnership.

Give serious thought to whether you want to incorporate. If you want to protect your personal assets from being attached as a result of a lawsuit, talk to a lawyer about the option of placing your assets in a trust and operating your consulting practice as a proprietor.

If you do decide to incorporate, you must then decide whether the C or S form is most appropriate in your situation.

Nonprofit Corporation

A *nonprofit corporation* has several advantages. First, the cost of doing business is less than it is for profit-making firms. Suppose Roberta Riggs, a consultant who is incorporated in California, wants to give a seminar in Texas. If she has set up a profit corporation, she would pay a fee each year for the privilege of doing business in Texas. A nonprofit corporation based in California would pay a one-time flat fee to the State of Texas and continue to give the seminar the rest of its corporate life. Nonprofit corporations are often eligible for a significant number of government and foundation grants, whereas profit-making corporations rarely are.

Incorporating as a nonprofit organization does not necessarily mean that you cannot make any profit. Under the law in many states, nonprofit corporations are permitted to engage in incidental profit-making activities. However, most state laws are not very specific about what is meant by incidental. You can make some profits, but you are not usually allowed to withdraw them through dividends. Most members of a profit-making corporation don't withdraw profits as dividends anyway. They simply retain profits in the corporation, with outlays going for salary and various fringe benefits. If you are not planning to distribute dividends, you should consider establishing a nonprofit corporation. Consult a lawyer who has worked with nonprofit corporation proceedings before. Those who have not tend to avoid recommending nonprofit corporations (perhaps because they aren't familiar with the procedures).

The chief disadvantage of a nonprofit corporation is that in most states its board of directors must consist of three or more people. The board members of a profit-making corporation don't affect your control because you hold the stock and thus have the final say on everything. But a nonprofit organization does not issue stock, and thus each board member has a say that could affect your control of the business. Unless you can fill the board positions with people you trust, you may want to avoid the nonprofit corporation. For more information, see *The Complete Guide to Non-profit Corporations* by Ted Nicholas cited in the bibliography.

Professional Corporation

A *professional corporation* is a for-profit business entity formed for the purpose of providing one or more specific types of professional services. All the shareholders must be licensed to render one or more of the services offered. Obviously, this type of business formation is not universally appropriate, but it does deserve consideration when applicable.

Limited Liability Company

A newer type of business formation, the *limited liability company* (LLC), is an unincorporated association that has two or more members. But unlike a partnership, members of an LLC are not personally liable for its debts. For federal income tax purposes an LLC may be classified as a corporation, depending on whether it has the corporate characteristics of centralization of management, continuity of life, free transferability of interests, and limited liability. Or it may be classified as a partnership if it has no more than two of the above-mentioned characteristics.

Reviewing Your Choice

As your business grows and changes, you'll want to evaluate the form you have chosen. After starting out as a sole proprietor, you may decide to enter into partnership with other consultants to offer a broader range of services. If you find that your liability risks have increased, you may choose incorporation to protect your personal assets.

Depending on circumstances, you may want to switch your corporate status from profit to nonprofit. If there are rapid changes in your business, you should set aside time at least once a year to review the status of your business and the arrangements you have made. If the form of your business doesn't match the realities of your operation, you may be losing money or running unnecessary risks. An annual checkup will protect you.

Any change is possible, but you can't switch back and forth from year to year depending on your tax situation in any particular year. Engage the services of an attorney and/or an accountant to help you fully understand the implications of a proposed change.

Your Support System

In establishing and maintaining your business, you will require the help of competent professionals. Your lawyer, accountant, banker, and perhaps insurance agent make up your business support system. How do you find the professional help you need? One way is to ask for referrals from other consultants who are not your competitors. Alternatively, you can buy an hour of time with the senior partner of a leading law or accounting firm. You will get a referral to either a junior staff member who bills out at a lower rate or someone outside the firm. This approach works better for finding a lawyer than an accountant.

Make your selection of professionals with some deliberation. Some points to consider include the following:

- Does the professional have the expertise that suits your needs?
- Can you establish a harmonious working relationship with the professional?
- Are your personalities compatible? When you don't like dealing with a person, you cannot reap the full benefits of his or her assistance.
- Is an independent practitioner more or less appropriate for your practice than is a large firm? Larger firms often cost more, but one staff member is generally ready and willing to turn you over to another as necessary and appropriate. Even though solo practitioners tend to cost less, they might be hesitant about turning you over to another professional outside the firm.

Choosing a Lawyer

In addition to helping you select the form of business that best suits your needs, your attorney can advise you in several other areas that require legal expertise. Two of these are described below.

The unauthorized practice of law. The work of many consultants involves what amounts to practicing law. A financial planner, for example, may be asked about a point of tax law. If the question is simple and straightforward, the consultant can respond without being concerned about practicing law. But consider a more complex question, such as whether a client might be considered a tax evader because of a certain tactic. The planner who advises action of any kind in this example is likely practicing law without authorization, which is not to say that a consultant cannot perform any legal functions.

You may, for instance, act in behalf of others when you have a formal power of attorney. Or you may prepare a contract that you and your client both agree to sign.

Perhaps the best rule to follow is to consult your attorney when you find yourself performing services normally provided by an attorney. In this way you are protected at minimal cost to yourself and your client.

Malpractice. Theoretically, *malpractice* means neglect. Professional people cannot be held responsible for failing to cure patients, losing a legal case, or failing in a consultation if they did everything that could be reasonably expected. However, there is a fine line between what constitutes your best effort and what comprises neglect.

In general, consultants do not guarantee that their advice will solve the problems for which their services are retained. The law normally requires that they give the best advice possible under the *prudent man doctrine,* meaning that errors in decision making are not usually sufficient to constitute neglect. Only if your client can demonstrate that you have been fraudulent or grossly negligent could you be held liable for damages.

Some consultants face a greater liability because they work in a profession licensed or regulated by the state. This kind of liability, known as *professional* or *personal liability,* is similar to a medical doctor's liability. Those with professional liability are normally required to warrant their work in compliance with a set of standards established by law or their profession.

Malpractice or professional liability insurance is usually available for consultants with a professional liability requirement. If you feel that you may be professionally liable, you should check with a lawyer and the appropriate state or federal agency that regulates your profession. Contractual limitations of liability exist in all states covering the rights of individuals that may be removed by contract. For such limitations, as for all legal questions, competent legal advice is a good investment.

Choosing the Right Accountant

In selecting an accountant, consider retaining a certified public accountant (CPA). CPAs generally have a higher level of training and are considered to be better prepared than accountants without the CPA designation. Their analyses may, therefore, be considered of greater worth. In addition, under certain circumstances your books may have to be reviewed by a CPA anyway. Having one do the work originally saves you the time and expense of getting another accountant. Excellent non-CPAs are available, but this option should be approached with caution.

The working relationship you establish with your accountant is especially important during the beginning phase of your practice. To obtain guidance and information about financial matters, you should be comfortable talking with your accountant. If you feel intimidated about asking questions or don't understand what you are being told, the problem may be with your accountant.

When your practice is larger or you are working with several consultants, you may need the services of a larger accounting firm. Because you will have acquired knowledge of accounting practices, you can then afford to have a more distant relationship with your CPA.

Selecting a Banker

A bank is more than a place to keep your money and apply for loans—it is also a source of information and guidance. A good bank is interested in helping its business depositors and ensuring that any business to which it loans money succeeds. The traditional interpretation of a banker as a "partner" in a small business, however, is changing as banks centralize, downsize, computerize, and the like. A banking relationship is a business relationship, even if the banker is your brother-in-law or family friend.

Because the banking system in this country developed somewhat haphazardly, there are federal banks, state banks, commercial banks, savings banks, and savings and loan institutions. During the 1980s and 1990s, the banking system has been undergoing a transition toward a more unified system. One result is that banks are striving to be more competitive and are offering more services, particularly to business customers.

In most communities the commercial bank is still the primary institution for financing business. A large established bank often suggests to those you do business with that you are solid. On the other hand, many fine, but smaller, commercial banks specialize in different approaches to business financing. Feeling that such banks give better, more personalized service than the giants, many consultants choose one of these smaller banks.

A growing number of other lending options are available to businesses, including venture capitalists, state economic loan funds, and loans to targeted segments of the population or geographic locations. If you need a loan and your bank turns you down, don't give up until you investigate all your options.

Professional Associations

Professional associations related to consulting are worth consideration. At meetings you can mingle with prospective clients in an informal setting. Joining a local organization for consultants also offers you the opportunity to size up the competition as well as keep up with the latest developments.

The professional organizations to which you belong may impress prospective clients. Some organizations, such as certain national engineering societies, are open only to members who meet certain requirements. Others accept anyone who has the entry fee and can pay the dues. A few savvy clients know which organizations have stiff standards, but most simply glance at the list of societies to which you belong.

Joining civic organizations, such as a chamber of commerce, provides access to business people and presents you as a business owner in your own right. The benefits of joining other, more socially oriented organizations, such as country clubs, depend on the kind of clientele you will be working with and the cost of joining, which can be considerable.

Below is a list of some of the major societies and organizations for management consultants. These and other organizations for almost any specialty are listed in the

Encyclopedia of Associations or *National Trade and Professional Associations of the United States.* See the bibliography for more information about these sources.

> The Association of Management Consulting Firms (ACME)
> 521 Fifth Ave., 35th Fl.
> New York, NY 10175
> 212-697-9693

Founded in 1929, ACME is the grandfather of management consulting groups. Originally limited to larger firms, it is now more representative but still maintains strict entry requirements. ACME reaches beyond its membership, however, conducting surveys and maintaining an information center covering a wide segment of the profession. The 50 member firms, 15 percent of which are foreign based, have offices in 100 countries worldwide. ACME also maintains an office in Brussels for international representation. Member firms employ more than 45,000 management consultants, have annual billings in excess of $5 billion, and list more than 130 separate areas of practice.

Applicants must normally have been in business for approximately five years, have a permanent staff of at least five full-time consultants, and derive more than 50 percent of total revenue from management consulting services. Other considerations include experience, references, and evidence of professional and ethical conduct. All members adhere to a strict code of professional responsibility.

Dues are based on billings. The minimum is $4,950, and the maximum is $49,500. In addition to meetings, the association offers professional growth and development training sessions, representation in Washington, D.C., research reports, referral service, resume files, management surveys, library facilities, public relations, newsletters, and international representation.

In addition to its directory of members, the association also offers *How to Get the Best Results from Management Consultants.* A price list of other publications is available.

> Institute of Management Consultants (IMC)
> [Includes the former Association of Managing Consultants (AMC) and
>   Society of Professional Management Consultants (SPMC)]
> 521 Fifth Ave., 35th Fl.
> New York, NY 10175-3598
> 212-697-8262

A certifying body for individual management consultants, the IMC grants the designation Certified Management Consultant (CMC) to those who qualify. It was founded in 1968 and represents a major, well-regulated commitment to professionalism. Approximately one-third of the more than 2,200 members are consultants in the larger independent management consulting firms. Another one-third are Management Advisory Service (MAS) practitioners in the major CPA firms, and the rest are practitioners and consultants in smaller firms.

Membership is restricted to individuals who spend well over one-half of their working time in the public practice of management consulting (by serving a number of different clients on a fee basis). Candidates for certified membership must have at least five years of management consulting experience, including a year of project responsibility, with three of the five years immediately prior to application. A college degree or the equivalent is required. Applicants must fill out a detailed form ($100 fee) and pass a written examination and oral review. Candidates for membership must be practicing full-time in the management consulting field and be sponsored by a CMC.

Certified member dues are $300 per year with a one-time $150 entrance fee paid after election to certification. Member dues are $150 per year. The institute offers opportunities for professional development and networking via chapter, regional, and national activities. Other membership benefits include a monthly newsletter, a directory, and numerous discount programs and services. The directory is available to nonmembers for $50. The institute provides free membership information, including a copy of its *Code of Ethics.* Also available to members and nonmembers for $16 per year is *Update II,* a quarterly newsletter that offers practical advice for consultants by consultants.

Management Consulting Services (MCS) Division
American Institute of Certified Public Accountants (AICPA)
1211 Avenue of the Americas
New York, NY 10036
212-596-6200

The AICPA is the professional society for CPAs in public practice who provide accounting, audit, tax, and management consulting services for clients as well as being the society for CPAs in industry, government, and universities. The MCS Division of the AICPA focuses on consulting services provided by CPAs and issues practice standards for those services and practice aids, which may be purchased by nonmembers.

The MCS Division also administers the MCS Membership Section of the AICPA, which has more than 5,000 CPA members who pay an additional fee to receive the division's quarterly newsletter, *CPA Management Consultant,* and other MCS Section membership benefits. Institute members may join the MCS Section and qualified non-CPA consulting personnel in CPA firms may be sponsored as MCA Section associates.

More than 20,000 full-time consultants are in CPA firms, mainly in the six largest firms, but most of the more than 130,000 institute members in public practice provide some management consulting services to their clients.

American Consultants League (ACL)
1290 N. Palm Ave.
Sarasota, FL 34236
941-952-9290

Founded in 1983, the American Consultants League is an interdisciplinary national association embracing 220 disciplines with approximately 1,000 members. The league has two divisions—the Consultant's Library (the publishing arm) and the Consultants Institute (an educational division). A complete list of titles for the former is available. The latter offers individual consultant courses and a Certified Professional Consultant (CPC) certificate upon successful completion of six courses.

Membership dues in the organization are $96 per year and entitle members to a bimonthly newsletter, *Consulting Intelligence,* the *ACL Directory,* and other benefits. The ACL also offers its members a consultant's hot line with expert advice on consulting practice.

Many other professional and trade organizations might be beneficial for you to join. Two such groups are:

American Society for Training and Development (ASTD)
1640 King St.
P.O. Box 1443
Alexandria, VA 22313
703-683-8100
55,000 members

International Association of Business Communicators (IABC)
1 Hallidie Plaza, Ste. 600
San Francisco, CA 94102
415-433-3400
12,500 members

The ASTD is composed mainly of trainers and those engaged in organizational development. Many consultants and industry representatives are members. The IABC is for individuals engaged in organizational communication and information management either in-house or as consultants.

National Consultants Referrals Inc. (NCRI)
4918 North Harbor Drive, Ste. 103
San Diego, CA 92106
800-221-3104
http://referrals.com
Founded in 1979; 6000 members

The NCRI maintains an electronic database containing the full background material on each of its members whose credentials are matched against requests from clients worldwide. The NCRI advertises its toll-free number in directories and trade publications and has an active Web site with interactive request forms and a product catalog, *The Practical Tools of Consulting,* featuring educational publications and business aids. An e-mail forum and discussion group for consultants is provided through its mailing list, consulting-tools.

The NCRI has no membership dues except for an initial affiliation fee used for reference checking and administrative costs. The matching service is free to clients using the service and the marketing effort is financed through referral fees paid by consultants from revenue received from NCRI assignments. As an added benefit to members, the NCRI supplies their requests for additional expertise for proposal support or special projects.

These and similar organizations can provide contacts with potential clients and give an overview of what is happening in your area. The value of belonging to such organizations depends on your needs and whether the organization offers services to meet these needs. Membership composition and activities vary considerably from city to city, but attending one or two meetings will give you a good idea of whether association with a particular group is of potential value. The reference materials listed in the bibliography, such as the *Encyclopedia of Associations,* will guide you to several potentially useful societies in your field of specialization and geographic area.

Specialty Business Consulting Associations

The following specialty consulting associations related to business are listed in the *Encyclopedia of Associations* (see the bibliography). Consult this source for detailed information on each association and for specialty associations in other fields, such as health care, engineering, and education.

American Association of Dental Consultants (AADC)
P.O. Box 3345
Lawrence, KS 66046
913-749-2727
Founded in 1977; 350 members

American Association of Healthcare Consultants (AAHC)
11208 Waples Mill Road, Ste. 109
Fairfax, VA 22030
703-691-2242
Founded in 1949; 244 members

American Association of Insurance Management Consultants (AAIMCo)
c/o Oakin Corporation
P.O. Box 744
Oakville, Ontario L6J6G6
Canada
905-844-2911
Founded in 1978; 35 members

American Association of Legal Nurse Consultants (AALNC)
4700 West Lake Ave.
Glenview, IL 60025-1485
847-375-4713
Founded in 1989; 1,400 members

American Association of Political Consultants (AAPC)
900 2nd St., N.E., Ste. 217
Washington, DC 20002
202-371-9585
Founded in 1969; 650 members

American Association of Professional Consultants (AAPC)
[A regional division of the National Bureau of Professional
   Management Consultants]
9140 Ward Pkwy., Ste. 200
Kansas City, MO 64114
816-444-3500
Founded in 1983; 250 members

American Consulting Engineers Council (ACEC)
1015 15th St., N.W., Ste. 802
Washington, DC 20005
202-347-7474
Founded in 1973; 5,000 member firms

American Society of Agricultural Consultants (ASAC)
950 S. Cherry St., Ste. 508
Denver, CO 80222
303-759-5091
Founded in 1963; 260 members

American Society of Consultant Pharmacists (ASCP)
1321 Duke St.
Alexandria, VA 22314
703-739-1300
Founded in 1969; 6,500 individuals, 120 member firms

American Society of Consulting Arborists (ASCA)
15245 Shady Grove Road, Ste. 130
Rockville, MD 20850
301-947-0483
Founded in 1967; 200 members

American Society of Consulting Planners (ASCP)
1776 Massachusetts Ave., N.W., Ste. 400
Washington, DC 20036
202-872-1498
Founded in 1966; 50 firm members

American Society of Trial Consultants (ASTC)
Speech and Mass Communication
Towson State University
Towson, MD 21252
410-830-2448
Founded in 1982; 400 members

Association of Bridal Consultants (ABC)
200 Chestnutland Road
New Milford, CT 06776
860-355-0464
Founded in 1981; 1,550 members

Association of Consulting Chemists and Chemical Engineers (ACCCE)
40 W. 45th St.
New York, NY 10036
212-983-3160
Founded in 1928; 200 members

Association of Consulting Foresters of America, Inc. (ACF)
1403 King St.
Alexandria, VA 22314
703-548-0990
Founded in 1948; 510 members

Association of Executive Search Consultants (AESC)
500 Fifth Ave., Ste. 930
New York, NY 10110
212-398-9556
Founded in 1959; 123 member firms

Association of Outplacement Consulting Firms International (AOCFI)
1200 19th St., N.W., Ste. 300
Washington, DC 20036
202-857-1185
Founded in 1982; 120 member firms

Association of Professional Communications Consultants (APCC)
3924 S. Troost
Tulsa, OK 74105
918-743-4793
Founded in 1982; 200 members

Consultants' Network (CN)
[Market-support organization for a variety of independent consultants]
57 W. 89th St.
New York, NY 10024
212-799-5239
Founded in 1972

Foodservice Consultants Society International (FCSI)
304 W. Liberty St., Ste. 201
Louisville, KY 40202
502-583-3783
Founded in 1979; 700 members

Franchise Consultants International Association (FCIA)
5147 S. Angela Road
Memphis, TN 38117
901-368-3333
Founded in 1987; 300 members

Independent Computer Consultants Association (ICCA)
11131 S. Towne Square
St. Louis, MO 63123
314-892-1675, 800-774-4222
Founded in 1976; 2,000 members

Institute of Certified Professional Business Consultants (ICPBC)
330 S. Wells St., Ste. 1422
Chicago, IL 60606
312-360-0384
Founded in 1975; 295 members

Institute of Tax Consultants (ITC)
[Certifying board of the American Society of Tax Professionals]
7500 212th St., S.W., Ste. 205
Edmonds, WA 98026
206-774-3521
Founded in 1980

International Merger and Acquisition Professionals (IMAP)
60 Revere Dr., Ste. 500
Northbrook, IL 60062
847-480-9037
Founded in 1973; 45 members

International Association of Professional Security Consultants (IAPSC)
808 17th St., N.W., Ste. 200
Washington, DC 20006
202-466-7212
Founded in 1984; 77 members

International Society of Speakers, Authors and Consultants (SAC)
P.O. Box 6432
Kingwood, TX 77325-6432
713-354-4440
www.ISSAC.com\ISSAC

Investment Management Consultants Association (IMCA)
9101 E. Kenyon Ave., Ste. 3000
Denver, CO 80237
303-770-3377
Founded in 1985; 1,100 members

National Alliance of Independent Crop Consultants (NAICC)
752 E. Brookhaven Circle, Ste. 240
Memphis, TN 38117
901-683-9466
Founded in 1978; 277 members

National Association of Computer Consultant Businesses (NACCB)
1250 Connecticut Ave., N.W., Ste. 700
Washington, DC 20036
202-637-9134
Founded in 1987; 280 members

National Association of Management Consultants (NAMC)
4200 Wisconsin Ave., N.W., Ste. 106
Washington, DC 20016
202-466-1601
Founded in 1985; 50 members

National Association of Personal Financial Advisors (NAPFA)
355 W. Dundee Road, Ste. 107
Buffalo Grove, IL 60089
847-537-7722
Founded in 1983; 350 member firms

National Association of Personnel Services (NAPS)
3133 Mt. Vernon Ave.
Alexandria, VA 22305
703-684-0180
Founded in 1960; 1,300 member agencies

National Bureau of Professional Management Consultants (NBPMC)
Management Consulting Center
2728 Fifth Ave.
San Diego, CA 92103
619-297-2207
Founded in 1989

Professional and Technical Consultants Association (PATCA)
P.O. Box 4143
Mountain View, CA 94040
415-903-8305
Founded in 1975; 400 members

Project Management Institute (PMI)
130 S. State Road
Upper Darby, PA 19082
610-734-3330
Founded in 1969; 11,500 members

Public Relations Society of America (PRSA)
33 Irving Pl., 3rd Fl.
New York, NY 10003
212-995-2230
Founded in 1947; 17,000 members

Qualitative Research Consultants Association (QRCA)
P.O. Box 6767, FDR Station
New York, NY 10022
212-315-0632
Founded in 1983; 570 members

Society of Risk Management Consultants (SRMC)
300 Park Ave., 17th Fl.
New York, NY 10022
212-572-6246
Founded in 1984; 134 members

Naming Your Consulting Practice

What's in a name? Marketing experts take the naming of a product or service seriously. To make your company's name sell itself, consider the following:

1. Should the name of the practice contain your name?
2. Should the name of the practice communicate the services that you provide precisely and immediately?
3. Should the company name cause others to view your practice as being a public interest, nonprofit organization?

Using your name in your practice's name has a distinct advantage. Clients like the personal touch. If your practice consists of your individual services, your marketing efforts may well be helped by having clients and prospects identify you as an individual.

Some marketing authorities say that specifying your services in the name of your business or practice makes your marketing more efficient. The name helps sell the services. A few examples of such names are:

- Solar Energy Systems Advisory Group
- Telephone Marketing Consultants
- Medical Automation Services, Inc.

Naming your business so precisely has one disadvantage—it locks you into a predetermined market and service. If you later decide to expand your services, the name may be a hindrance. Some marketing authorities argue that for maximum impact the name of a consulting organization should imply a public service of a not-for-profit nature. If you accept this argument, then the name of your firm should make the company sound like a public interest organization instead of a commercial one. Public interest groups usually have names with such phrases as:

- The Center for _____
- The _____ Resources Center
- The Institute for the Study of _____
- The Alliance to _____

The marketing advantages of such names are worth considering. Most consultants using this approach believe that the advantages have to do with prestige. They feel that just being introduced as the director of an institute lends credibility to their image. The fact that their field is important enough to warrant the founding of an institute or center is also a plus.

One question that arises in connection with prestige is the use of titles after your name. If you have a Ph.D. or other prestigious title, using it will obviously have a favorable impact on some clients. Others, however, may feel that you are another impractical "egghead." Client attitude is the determining factor. In general, a Ph.D. is regarded as a significant achievement that demonstrates important, useful attributes. On balance, having one is still likely to be of benefit.

You may want to consider the use of a fictitious name other than your business name. This is also called an *assumed name* or *doing business as* (d/b/a). The advantage is that you keep your operating name distinct from the corporate name. If you want to retire or just withdraw from your business, you can sell your operating name but keep your corporation. Fictitious names are also useful for trial efforts. If a business flops, no harm is done. When it succeeds, you simply have your corporation take the credit.

Requirements for establishing a fictitious or d/b/a name vary from state to state and, in some cases, within states. In some cities you simply go to the office of any newspaper of general record, fill out a fictitious name statement, and submit it to the newspaper. The newspaper sends a copy to the county recorder and publishes the notice three times. The charge is usually nominal. In other states you fill out a form and submit it with a fee to a state agency. The rules vary from state to state and even from city to city. The advice of a lawyer and perhaps of an accountant is helpful.

Whatever name you choose for your business, it must contribute effectively to your marketing approach. At the very least it should not undermine your marketing. So consider your company's name long and wisely. It will affect you now and in the future.

Developing a Brochure

Most consultants include a brochure as part of their marketing plan. (See Figure 2.2.) A good brochure describes what you have accomplished and outlines what you can do for clients. But its main aim is to get a potential client interested in you. Some consultants find it appropriate to develop a video or a computer disk or CD-ROM instead of or in addition to a printed brochure. If you are a videographer or a computer consultant, perhaps one of these newer methods is right for you. If you seek clients from a broad geographic range, then perhaps a Web page is for you. Professionals can help you develop and maintain a Web page, thus allowing you to project a leading-edge image.

Generally, clients are more interested in what you have accomplished than in what you have learned. Concentrate on past successes, not on your education. Those successes don't even have to come from your consulting practice. They only need to stimulate the prospect's interest in buying your services.

FIGURE 2.2   Sample Brochure

Marketing Planning & Research

Marketing Plans for Strategic Direction and/or Outside Financing, Focus Group Research Studies for Consumer Testing, On-Line/Off-Line Market Information Searches, Market Feasibility Studies, Advertising Media Planning and Placement.

Promotional Writing & Project Planning

Consumer & Trade Publicity Planning, News Releases, Fact Sheets, Backgrounders, Full Media Kits, Freelance Writing/Feature Story Placement, Speechwriting/Slide & Overhead Presentations.

Marketing/Sales Literature Planning and Coordination

Catalogs/Brochures/Posters/Sales Kits, Direct Mail Programs, Point of Purchase Displays, Advertising Specialty/Premium Items.

Trade Show Planning & Coordination

Portable Trade Show Booth Rentals, Booth Signage and Layout Planning, Pre/Post Show Marketing Programs.

Professional Speaking, Training & On-Site Mentoring Specialty Presentations; Customized on Request!

- Sports Spark: *Sports Marketing Secrets for Success!*
- Don't Replace . . . Reposition! *Adding New Life to Mature Products*
- Show Stoppers: *Trade Show Tactics That Work!*
- 101 Ideas to "Spark" Your Marketing: *New Ways to Ignite Market Potential*
- Position Yourself As An Expert: *Successful Service-Based Marketing*

MarketSpark
P.O. Box 22794 • Portland, Oregon 97269-2794
(503) 222-6871 • FAX (503) 222-3872
e-mail: marketspark@marketspark.com
http://www.marketspark.com

Special thanks to our "sparky" suppliers!
*"Sparkler" photography courtesy of Photo-Art Commercial Studios, Inc.
Design by Daniel Underhill / Keyframe Multimedia Development
Portraits by Chris Anderson Photography • Printing provided by Premier Press*

A Marketing Ideas Company
Sports Marketing Our Game
http://www.marketspark.com

Source: © MarketSpark Sports Marketing. Used with permission.

FIGURE 2.2   Sample Brochure (Continued)

MarketSpark is a marketing ideas company *Your* dedicated to "igniting" the potential of client products and services. We *"One-Stop"* offer innovative marketing research, planning and promotions all targeted *Marketing* at *increasing client growth and profitability.* Our company provides the following *Resource* services on a contract or retainer basis to meet virtually every budget and deadline.

MarketSpark goes the extra mile for you. We're experts at identifying *Cost-Effective,* creative, cost-effective solutions *and* results for the most perplexing *Creative* marketing projects! Our experience and relationships with numerous *Solutions* suppliers allows us to tap a wide variety of resources to get the job *and Results!* done on time, on target, on budget and *on fire!*

Market Planning & Research

MarketSpark provides market research and planning to help clients target new products, reposition mature products, or tap new markets. Services include on-line computer searches, market analysis reports, strategic marketing plans for both internal planning and external financing, and moderating focus group studies for consumer testing.

Promotional Planning & Coordination

Trade or consumer publicity, sales brochures, spec sheets, point-of-purchase displays, repackaging . . . what are the best tactics to use for increased sales? MarketSpark works with clients to determine market objectives and implement options to *maximize the return on each dollar spent.*

Trade Show Coordination & Portable Booth Rental

MarketSpark helps boost trade show effectiveness through coordination of pre-show mailings, booth design/set-up and signage. We also offer different styles of 10' portable booths for rent on a daily or weekly basis.

Professional Speaking, Freelance Writing & In-House Training Seminars

Need an energetic speaker for your company meeting? An experienced "ghostwriter" for PR articles? A mentor to work with multi-function staff doing "marketing projects?" MarketSpark offers 20+ years corporate marketing/sales experience "on-call!"

Kellee K. Harris, M.B.A.
President, MarketSpark

FIGURE 2.2 Sample Brochure (Continued)

5 Reasons to call MarketSpark Today . . .

1 Staff Overload:

Too much work, too few people. Key employees carrying multiple responsibilities. *The Challenge:* Keeping top people on top priorities.

2 Slashed Budgets:

Doing more with less. Stretching fewer dollars further. *The Challenge:* Generating demand with cost-effective programs.

3 Lack of In-House Expertise:

Everyone is expected to be an expert on everything. Time and money lost searching for resources and learning new skills. *The Challenge:* Getting the job done when no one knows where to start.

4 Tight Deadlines:

Major opportunities, minimal timelines. There's no time for mistakes, and no second chances. *The Challenge:* Making it happen when the heat is on.

5 No Time To Plan:

Day-to-day operations take up every minute. The company needs new product concepts, competitive analysis, targeted research . . . components to help chart a path for future growth and increased profitability. *The Challenge:* Finding a resource to speed planning efforts.

MarketSpark *is the solution to these and many other marketing opportunities. Call, FAX or E-Mail MarketSpark today, and watch the "sparks" fly!*

FIGURE 2.2 Sample Brochure (Continued)

MarketSpark Clients Comment on Results!

"MarketSpark did a masterful job of researching the potential for our new product through focus group sessions, and followed with a comprehensive market analysis and strategic marketing plan to maximize our sales efforts."

Dr. Robert Cook, Chairman
BioArch[3] Foot Orthotics; and Former Team Physician, NBA Portland Trailblazers

"We have used Kellee Harris on several projects. She has never missed a date and the end results have always been excellent. We even worked one rush advertising project by fax with me in Hawaii, Kellee at a tradeshow in Atlanta and her graphic artist in Portland. It came off without a hitch! I've worked with bigger agencies and paid a lot more for less service and weaker results."

Mr. Paul Needham, President
Media Architects, Inc.

"Your professionalism makes it a pleasure to work with you. The attention to detail and your commitment to documentation is definitely appreciated. I feel so fortunate that we found you. I look forward to the next terrific project you complete for us."

Mr. Mike Beard, Vice President-Communications
Northwest Forestry Association

"Kellee's work is always of the highest quality. She is extremely organized and highly creative. We have been delighted with every project she has done for us. Give her a try, you will love the results."

Mr. Barry Garlick, Vice President
InSport Athletic Apparel

"Your expertise and creativity are superior, and I appreciate your skills. We have been exceedingly pleased with the continuity, quality of work, and professionalism exhibited by MarketSpark."

Mr. Phil Riley, President
Quest Industries, Inc.
Shockers Eyewear Retainers & Sports Accessories

"MarketSpark's work with one of our sports vendors was so impressive, we decided to hire them for our store! In addition, they connected us with some of their other clients in cross-promotions."

Noel Vest, President
Brace Yourself Sports Medicine Store

Don't let your ego dictate which accomplishments to include in the brochure. Make your selections based on what you think clients want to hear. One consulting firm included the following vignette in its brochure as an example of its past accomplishments as an incentive to buy their services:

> The management of a major trunk airline wanted to change its advertising campaign to reclaim its market share on its major (and highly competitive) routes. In the past they had changed advertising emphasis from personnel to timeliness to food service to quality of ground service, and so on. The philosophy had been to keep the name of the carrier in front of the public and to stimulate awareness by changing ad content.
>
> Unsatisfied with the modest results they were getting, the airline and its advertising agency retained the market division of our agency to find out what the ads should say. In less than 60 days, with an expenditure of less than one week's budget, we undertook a comprehensive consumer study to determine the factors that caused an air traveler to choose a given air carrier in those competitive markets.
>
> The results of this study were used by the carrier's agency to develop a totally revolutionary emphasis for the carrier's advertising program. Today, that airline is a leader in five of its seven competitive trunk lines.
>
> The techniques applied in this important consumer research are applicable to a number of industries. We think you, too, will be amazed by these findings and our agency will be pleased to share the findings with qualified inquirers.

In a few brief paragraphs, this vignette has explained a substantial success. It has also provided an opportunity for the reader to learn more.

Aside from vignettes, you may include such information as that listed below in your brochure.

A list of previous clients or references. In general, don't link names of clients with specific accomplishments described in your vignettes; clients may prefer to be treated with confidentiality. However, a list of references or clients served is acceptable. Many consultants feel that it is not appropriate to place the names of previous clients or references in the capabilities statement. You should be prepared, however, to supply a list of individuals who can attest to your credibility, competence, and character.

Client testimonials. No selling of your capability is more powerful than that rendered by those for whom you've worked. Have the quotes from clients speak of the results you produced for them—the more tangible and result oriented the better. As mentioned above, you may want or need to keep testimonials anonymous, which many consultants do by providing the initials or title of the quoted client. You can also keep the company name confidential by citing it in general, nonidentifiable terms (e.g., vice-president of marketing, mid-sized computer technology corporation).

Your credentials or capabilities. Only a select few interest your readers. Don't underestimate the importance of practical, hands-on, on-the-job experience. For many clients it is the determining buying factor.

A statement of your operating philosophy and practice. Describe how you run your practice, how fees are charged or determined, your ethics, and other important points. Ask yourself: Is this information critical to the reader's buying decision?

The obvious but sometimes forgotten. Remember to include your address, phone number, fax, e-mail address, Web site, and other obvious information that is sometimes left out.

Testing the Message

We are often our own poorest critics. Once you have drafted your message, ask a few uninvolved people to tell you what your message communicates to them. One way to get this feedback is to ask others to tell you what they understand your message to mean. This is a *test of face validity,* like the test undertaken by a questionnaire designer to make sure that the words communicate what the writer intended.

More important is the *test of image.* You want to find out what assumptions or feelings others have about you as a result of what you have said. One inexpensive and useful way to run such a test is to contact the marketing department chairperson at a local college or university. Explain that you would like to work with one of the upper-division or graduate marketing classes to conduct some marketing research.

You will probably be referred to a faculty member or to the student marketing association. Before long you will have a captive group to assist you. The group will review your message or a mock-up of your completed brochure and write a pencil-and-paper description of the consultant who would mail it out.

After obtaining these written reactions, which provide a kind of psychological profile, you can have a discussion with the group and learn more from group interaction. You'll probably be surprised by what you learn about yourself and your image. Use this information to modify your brochure and make it more effective. Your changes serve as a case study for the class and allow the teacher to explain the theory behind your research. It would be a nice touch to contribute to the scholarship fund or student marketing organization in exchange for the valuable input you have received.

Producing the Brochure

Now you have your words. What about the medium? If you opt for the written word, you should consider seeking professional help from a graphics consultant or graphics house. One good way to select a graphics consultant is to interview individuals whose brochures have struck you as particularly effective or attractive. The extra money you invest in graphic design, typesetting, quality paper (stock), and high-quality printing more than pays for itself.

Suppose you want 2,000 copies of a one-page, 8½ × 11, two-sided brochure. The cost differential between doing a so-so and a quality job may be only two or three cents per brochure. The small additional expenditure is well worth the payoff in results.

Technology now allows you, in a very cost-effective way, to create several brochures, each featuring a different aspect of your practice. By keeping several versions of the brochure on your computer, you can turn them out as needed and customize each according to the person receiving it. Technology has greatly increased a consultant's ability to seek clients in highly focused areas.

Distributing the Completed Brochures

You should plan how you will distribute your brochures long before they arrive from the printer. Generally, unsolicited mass mailing of a brochure does not work, even though it costs dearly. For the most part, your brochure is something you might leave with a prospective client after a face-to-face meeting. Or you might mail one after an initial written or phone communication when a prospective client has asked to know more about you.

Brochures are also useful for handing out after presentations to a civic or professional group. They may also be mailed to attendees the day after a presentation as a follow-up communication. Give thought to mailing a brochure along with a summary or transcription of your remarks about a week after your talk. An accompanying letter might indicate: There were so many requests for a text of the talk, we decided to send them to everyone.

Brochures can be mailed out in response to ads. When your market is broad and likely to fully understand the nature of your consulting services—bookkeeping, computer programming, interior design, advertising, market research—give thought to small space ads in professional or business publications. These ads should encourage readers to contact you to obtain a copy of your brochure.

Developing an Internet Presence

The Internet exploded as a promising marketing and information medium in the mid-1990s and is one that many consultants are using as an adjunct to their capabilities brochure and other marketing efforts. Figure 2.3 is an example of a good World Wide Web page developed by a consultant to promote her services on the Internet.

The elements of effective Web pages are much the same as those for brochures. The major difference is that literally thousands of prospects for your services can gain access to information about your practice without your initiating the contact or, for that matter, even knowing about it.

The strategic value of a presence on the Internet needs to be weighed carefully before deciding to pursue it. Although having a Web site developed for you and placed on the Internet need not be a huge capital investment, it is an investment nonetheless. And like all investments, you will want to assess what you want out of it by way of return before you forge ahead.

If your consulting practice, for example, is going to focus on serving clients located in just your local area, a Web site on the Internet may not be needed. The Internet is no substitute for personal contact with prospective clients—contact that

FIGURE 2.3 Sample Web Page (MarketSpark)

||| **Home Page** ||| <u>**Contact MarketSpark**</u> ||| <u>**Consulting**</u> | <u>**Speaking**</u> | <u>**Booth Rentals**</u> |

| *Spark of the Week* | *Sparklers* <u>Newsletter</u> | *Sparklers* <u>Audio Tapes</u> | <u>Kellee Harris, M.B.A.</u> |
- - - - - You can <u>sign</u> and <u>view</u> our Guest Book! - - - - -

MarketSpark - Portland, Oregon, USA

A Marketing Ideas Company - Sporting Goods Marketing Our Specialty! <u>**Kellee K. Harris, M.B.A., President**</u>

 MarketSpark is a marketing ideas company specializing in sports and fitness product marketing. We are dedicated to "igniting" the potential of client products and services through innovative market research, planning and promotions all targeted at increasing client growth and profitability.

We provide these services on a project contract or retainer basis:

> <u>**Marketing Consulting**</u>
> Marketing Plans, Research, Sales Literature, Public Relations
>
> <u>**Professional Speaking**</u>
> Keynotes, Seminars, Workshops
>
> <u>**Rentals of Portable Trade Show Booths**</u>
> 10' Backwalls & Tabletops -- Weekly Rates
>
> <u>***Sparklers* Newsletter**</u> **and** <u>**Audio Tapes**</u>
> Marketing newsletter, and cassette tapes of seminar presentations.

 While you're here, please <u>**sign our Guest Book**</u>.

> A *Sparklers* <u>audio tape</u> will be given at random each week to all who sign!

 Contact <u>**MarketSpark**</u> **for complete information.**

Source: © MarketSpark Sports Marketing. Used with permission.

FIGURE 2.3   Sample Web Page (MarketSpark) (Continued)

||| **Home Page** ||| **Contact MarketSpark** ||| **Consulting** | **Speaking** | **Booth Rentals** |

| *Spark of the Week* | *Sparklers* <u>Newsletter</u> | *Sparklers* <u>Audio Tapes</u> | <u>Kellee Harris, M.B.A.</u> |
- - - - - You can <u>sign</u> and <u>view</u> our Guest Book! - - - - -

MarketSpark Consulting

MarketSpark offers marketing consulting services on a project or retainer basis.

All programs are targeted at increasing client growth and profitability, *not* winning awards and gratifying our egos. Our areas of expertise include:

 Market Planning & Research

> **Marketing plans for strategic direction and/or outside financing**
> **Focus group moderating & research studies for consumer testing**
> **On-line/off-line market information searches**
> **Market feasibility studies**
> **Advertising media planning and placement**

"MarketSpark did a masterful job of researching the potential for our new product through focus group sessions, and followed with a comprehensive market analysis and strategic marketing plan to maximize our sales efforts."
　　Dr. Robert Cook, Chairman
　　BioArch Foot Orthotics and Past Team Physician, NBA Portland Trailblazers

 Promotional Planning & Coordination

> **Consumer and trade publicity programs**
> **News Releases/Fact Sheets/Backgrounders/Full Media Kits**
> **Freelance Writing/Feature Story Placement**
> **Speechwriting/Presentation Graphics**

"Kellee's work is always of the highest quality. She is extremely organized and highly creative. We have been delighted with every project she has done for us. Give her a try, you will love the results."
　　Mr. Barry Garlick, Vice President
　　InSport Athletic Apparel

Marketing/Sales Literature Planning & Coordination

FIGURE 2.3 Sample Web Page (MarketSpark) (Continued)

Catalogs/Brochures/Posters/Co-Op Advertising/Sales Kits
Direct Mail Programs
Point-Of-Purchase Displays/Retailer Kits
Advertising Specialty Items

"We have used Kellee Harris on several projects. She has never missed a date and the end results have always been excellent. We even worked one rush advertising project by fax with me in Hawaii, Kellee at a trade show in Atlanta and her graphic artist in Portland. It came off without a hitch! I've worked with bigger agencies and paid a lot more for less service and weaker results."
Mr. Paul Needham, President
<u>Media Architects, Inc.</u> Software Developers

<u>MarketSpark@marketspark.com</u>
Web Site Design: <u>Ecola</u>

should be easy to make if your practice is limited to your local area. On the other hand, if your prospects are national or international, an effective Web site may help prospective clients, who would not otherwise even know you and your services exist, find you.

In some circumstances, having a Web site may be necessary simply to demonstrate that you have the high-tech savvy and capability demanded by your target market. Many consultants operating in technology specialties, for example, have determined that they must have a Web site to be credible in the eyes of their clients and prospects even though they do not expect their Internet presence to directly generate new business.

In addition to creating your own site, there are a growing number of companies that are using the Internet as a connection point between consultants and those looking for outside expertise. National Consultant Referrals Inc. (NCRI), for example, has established a Web site and among the services it provides is the showcasing of its member consultants. The NCRI is the oldest and most prominent organization in the United States that makes consultant referrals. It maintains a database of consultants representing a multiplicity of specialties and makes referrals to clients according to clients' specified needs.

The NCRI has traditionally let prospective clients know about its consultants through advertising. Clients call to describe the particular type of consultant they are looking for. The NCRI searches its database for appropriate consultants and then makes referrals.

With the Internet, now the NCRI not only provides the service in its traditional mode but online as well. Someone from a prospective client organization browsing the World Wide Web can enter the NCRI's Web site, search for a certain consultant profile, and then immediately get information about those NCRI members who match the profile. Figure 2.4 is the opening page of the NCRI's Web site.

FIGURE 2.4   Sample Web Page (NCRI)

A Free Referral Service

Networking Clients with Consultants and Experts since 1979

Our offices overlook the
beautiful San Diego Harbor.

Do You Need a

- **Consultant?**

- **Expert Witness?**

- **Speaker, Seminar Leader, or Trainer?**

Other Information of Interest

- **Membership Information**

- **Practical Tools of Consulting**

- **Newsletter and Articles**

- **About National Consultant Referrals, Inc.**

- **Contact Us**

Home   Consultant?   Expert Witness?   Speaker/Trainer?   Membership   Catalog   Articles   About NCRI   Contact Us

National Consultant Referrals, Inc.

4918 North Harbor Drive, Suite 103
San Diego, California 92106, USA
(800) 221-3104 -- (619) 523-2188 -- Fax (619) 523-2184
http://www.referrals.com
kline@referrals.com

NCRI home page used with permission.

FIGURE 2.5   Sample Web Page (CMI)

CMI HOST Hub

The place to connect with professional Speakers, Authors, Trainers, Consultants, Seminar Leaders, and related companies/organizations

The
HUB
ONLINE
for
SPEAKING
and
TRAINING

The complete international online resource
for planners, presenters and organizations

http://www.cmihub.com
Castleman Motivational Institute, Inc.

Demonstrations | Registration | Information | New and News

The CMI HOST Hub is Netscape enhanced.

This site uses the TrueSpeech Audio Player to give real-time audio over the Internet.

Use the CMI HOST Hub, a SECURE , multi-media showcase, to quickly FIND professional:

Speakers
Authors
Trainers
Consultants
Seminar Leaders
Industry Related Companies

Quickly and easily SEARCH for presenters by:

Presenter Name
Topics and Categories
Regions or States
Industries Worked In
Participants Worked With
Full Text (keyword) SEARCH

CMI web page used with permission.

FIGURE 2.5   Sample Web Page (CMI) (Continued)

Demonstrations | Registration | Information | New and News

Click an area on the CMI HOST "HUB"
(User Name and Password registration required)

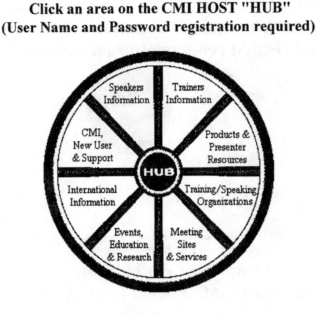

SpeakerS | TrainerS | Products | Orgs | Sites | Events | Intrnatl | UserInfo | Hub | News

Another variation of this Internet matching model is provided by the Castleman Motivational Institute (CMI) Host Hub (Figure 2.5). The CMI creates individual Web pages for speakers, trainers, and consultants who are accessible within its Web hub. Included for each entrant is a picture, audioclips, and videoclips so that prospective clients can get an even better feel for the appropriateness of the consultant.

The CMI's innovative variation is that their site is "locked" and only client organizations who pay a nominal fee may access information from the site. This limitation ensures that the only people accessing the site—and previewing the consultants in the system—are those who are indeed seriously looking for consultants.

To an individual consultant, the advantages of being part of a site like NCRI's or CMI's are twofold. First, someone else keeps the site maintained and up-to-date, in terms of both information and rapidly changing technology, thus saving the consultant time and money. Second, inclusion in the site of organizations like these serves implicitly as an endorsement for the consultant. Having one's own Web site is clearly self-promotion. However, being part of the site of a third-party organization whose mission is to connect clients with appropriate consultants is a more subtle promotion.

Beyond Web sites, e-mail on the Internet offers an effective and now nearly essential communication medium for consultants. Having an e-mail address and using e-mail as a business tool are probably as important as having and using a fax machine in today's consulting practice.

☞ Tips

Getting off to a solid businesslike start is one of the best ways of ensuring that you will be a success as a consultant. Struggling along in an unsatisfactory partnership instead of being in business for yourself or failing to keep proper financial records can sabotage your chances of success, even though you are writing and completing plenty of contracts. A strong beginning means selecting the right form for your business, having a solid support system, choosing a good name, and creating an effective brochure to distribute to prospective clients.

You may not need to have a lawyer on tap if your practice doesn't involve legal questions. You may be able to take care of your own financial records if you have an aptitude for it. You may not need a brochure if you can sell yourself effectively in other ways. (And a brochure alone is not a marketing strategy. You need to do a lot more than hand out a piece of paper to market your skills, as we will see in Chapters 6 and 7 on marketing and advertising.) But you do need to be able to take care of each of these areas—legal, financial, banking, selling, selecting a name—if you are going to succeed.

Over and above the demands of most businesses, consulting requires a special kind of self-confidence that you can develop by taking stock of what you can bring to the profession.

Taking stock begins with an inventory of your personal resources. In the next chapter we will guide you in reviewing what you can do as a business manager and as a consultant. You will discover some skills you may not have known you possess. This review can benefit those consultants who are just beginning a practice and those who are already well established.

The next step is learning how to turn your skills into business opportunities. We will explore how to find opportunities and how to turn them into money-making business enterprises. The extent to which you take your skills, apply them to opportunities, and manage your business determines your level of success.

CHAPTER 3

Developing Your Skills Inventory

You are a consultant, or wish to be one, because you have the self-confidence to explore new areas and to accept new challenges. As a consultant your stock-in-trade is the skills and talents you have to offer. In any given field many employees and researchers have expertise to spare. Yet they are not consultants because they do not feel sufficiently self-confident to promote their expertise and to carry it over into unfamiliar territory. While knowledge is a vital part of consulting, confidence in your ability to apply your knowledge to the problems of a client is more important.

This may sound like a pep talk, but *self-confidence is a key trait for consulting*. Your reputation as a consultant almost invariably arises from the confidence you demonstrate to others. Their trust then feeds your own self-confidence. Without confidence in yourself and your abilities, all your expertise won't help you a bit.

Most people—even some who wish to enter consulting—simply do not have a high enough opinion of themselves to merit a lot of self-confidence. They are too modest to recognize their special abilities and accomplishments. As a result, they do not know the value those abilities and accomplishments have in the marketplace. Some people have an imperfect recall of their past successes. Others function so effectively, yet so effortlessly, that they are unaware of their talents.

A review of the resources you bring to consulting will encourage that self-confidence. Nothing boosts your self-image more than remembering and recording past achievements and strengths.

There's no better way to boost your confidence as a consultant than to make up a comprehensive inventory of all the abilities you bring to your consulting specialty.

Even if you have been a consultant for years, you probably have many abilities and talents that you don't recognize. The old hand at consulting may benefit more from a skills inventory than a newcomer. With plenty of experience under your belt, you have more opportunity to discover your skills and talents. Our most valuable abilities are hidden, and they are discovered by looking at our experiences in a new light.

A quick rise to success in consulting springs from a grouping or pattern of abilities peculiar to an individual's background. In this search for skills, you'll look for unique combinations of strengths and abilities. However, to use these skills you must learn about them in detail.

Paradoxically, the skills and strengths that are likely to be of the greatest use are also likely to be invisible. If you do something a lot more easily than most people do, you probably have a special ability but don't realize it. Taking a systematic inventory of your skills will reveal those talents.

The Skills Inventory

This inventory emphasizes specific skills and accomplishments. Just listing some abstract words like *creative, energetic,* and *dependable* won't do much good. By listing specific accomplishments and examining them for the skills that you displayed, you will learn what you do. Then you can construct an action list of your skills.

The inventory is taken in three steps:

1. A comprehensive listing of all your past achievements
2. A search for skills by expanding and rephrasing the items in your listing
3. A search for talents by sifting through your skills

Use the worksheet in Figure 3.1 for your skills inventory . List your achievements in the left-hand column and the skills you used in the right-hand column.

Listing Your Past Achievements

Start by relaxing and just thinking about the challenges you have handled in the past. Simply let your mind wander and review some situations at work or in life where you succeeded. What are some of the problems at work that you solved? Did you work out a particularly tricky production schedule, make an important sale, or find a new application for an old technology? Use the lists that follow this section as a thought stimulator.

The focus of this skills inventory is best placed on problem solving. Normally, people are not highly paid for doing routine, predictable work. The people who are well paid are those who can deal with and prevent problems. This rule is especially applicable to consulting. As clients come to see you as a problem solver, they are more likely to pay for your services. However, first you must see yourself as someone who can tackle and solve difficult problems. And you need the self-confidence to present yourself that way.

For some people, listing accomplishments is difficult. They either feel uncomfortable tooting their own horn, or they just can't seem to remember anything. Don't let this initial difficulty put you off. If you skip this important step, you may cripple all your other efforts in consulting. A skills inventory is of paramount importance because you need a single unifying theme for your consulting practice. In addition,

FIGURE 3.1 Skills Inventory Worksheet

Activities/Achievements	Skills

you can never be comfortable with your role as a problem solver until you recast your past experience in terms of that role.

Don't give up on your list of personal accomplishments. After a while you will start seeing everything you've done as either a solution to a problem or a way of preventing one. Then you are forming the mind-set that is crucial to being a successful consultant.

Skills Inventory Aid

As you review your achievements, use the following lists to help compose your inventory of skills. Your abilities are demonstrated in five areas of achievement:

1. Past work positions
2. Previous projects
3. Education
4. Formal credentials
5. Free-time activities

Working backward in time, list your achievements in each of these five areas on the left side of the form; then ask the following questions:

1. What was the problem?
2. What was my diagnosis?
3. What skills did I use in my diagnosis?
4. How did I prevent or solve the problem?
5. What skills did I use in preventing or solving the problem?

As you think over your answers, keep the following points in mind:

- *Bizarre or dubious achievements are good.* The worksheets are designed to stimulate your memory, not inhibit it. Gems may be hidden among these unusual feats.
- *Minor achievements are good.* Don't ignore seemingly unimportant accomplishments, and don't be ashamed to list them. Special skills are often hiding here.
- *Dealing with human beings is good.* In consulting, human relations skills are both prized in their own right and useful adjuncts to technical skills.

In writing down your list, *avoid* the following:

- *Elegant phrasing*
  Your purpose is to open the floodgates of your memory and imagination. You'll have plenty of opportunity for polishing later, but at this stage you want only the rough, raw material. This is almost like brainstorming.
- *Professional jargon*
  You are looking for abilities that are transferable. Jargon tends to restrict your thinking to a situation in which you happened to demonstrate a skill.

After you've listed your accomplishments, write down on the right side of the form a second list of the skills you used in solving or preventing each problem. Suppose one of your problems was finding a new supervisor to replace one who was promoted. You solved the problem by realizing that one of your employees had leadership potential that others had failed to see. Your skill was recognizing another person's abilities. For each achievement write down one or more skills that you used, and underline the action word in that skill.

Evaluating Your Skills

Once you have drawn up your list, write down comments about the problem situations you solved, using the worksheet on evaluating skills in Figure 3.2. To help you evaluate your skills, ask these questions:

- How successful was I at solving or preventing the problem?
- How did human relations skills (or lack of them) affect me in—
  a. diagnosing the problem?
  b. devising a way to solve or prevent the problem?
  c. implementing the solution or prevention?
- Would I do anything differently if I confronted the same situation today?

One consultant selected three accomplishments from his list to concentrate on. In college his fraternity was close to dissolving; he was elected president and cleaned up the mess. On one job he solved a tricky problem with computer programming even though he was not trained as a programmer. He had also shown one of his coworkers, who was on the verge of being discharged, how to assess her likes and dislikes so she could find another, much more satisfying, job.

Each of these situations was seen as a problem that the consultant solved. Like him, you don't have to restrict your list to problems that you handled on the job. Any problem-solving ability can be applied in business.

Next, the consultant wrote down his skills. For the mess at the fraternity, he was able to analyze a complex problem and organize people. For the computer problem, he simplified it to find a solution. For his coworker, he elicited the reasons for her dissatisfaction.

The consultant applied the three evaluation questions to each situation, rating his level of success in solving each problem. Finding that each of the problems had been handled very successfully, he then applied the second test. His understanding of people helped him diagnose the problems at the fraternity and gave him insight into his coworker's job difficulties. The computer problem didn't require human relations skills to diagnose or solve.

In reviewing the outcome of his fraternity presidency, he realized that he had solved the problem, but the way he did it cost him the friendship of his fraternity brothers. He resolved to handle similar situations less autocratically, giving others more room to provide input. He had implemented the solution to his coworker's problem skillfully by leading her to find her own answers, and she was very grateful for his help.

FIGURE 3.2 Evaluating Skills Worksheet

1. Successful in solving problem?

2. Human relations skills involved?

3. Different approach to problem?

<table>
<tr><td></td></tr>
<tr><td></td></tr>
<tr><td></td></tr>
<tr><td></td></tr>
<tr><td></td></tr>
<tr><td></td></tr>
</table>

He came to realize that, although the computer-programming problem was solved without human relations skills, implementing the solution required tact in moving the technicians to try his approach. He came away from this exercise with an understanding of the importance of human relations skills in resolving any organizational problem.

In analyzing the situation at the fraternity, he realized that he may not have been a good president in all respects, but he had acted like a good consultant. A consultant comes in and takes charge of a problem without getting involved in the organization's politics. If there are bad feelings associated with changes, the consultant leaves and takes the feelings with him. As chapter president, our consultant wasn't able to leave gracefully when the job was done. This underscores the importance of taking a close look at seeming failures or dubious achievements because special skills that are important to a consultant may be hidden in them.

Go through your list with the same detail. Take a long, hard look at your accomplishments, aiming at a thorough understanding of your ability at problem solving.

Search for Skills

Skills are abilities that are acquired by experience. Very often we pick up skills without even knowing what we are doing. As a result, many skills may lie hidden among our achievements. To crystallize your skills, you must go back over your inventory, expanding and rephrasing each item. Use the expanded skills inventory worksheet in Figure 3.3 to do this.

You expand an item by breaking it down into the skills that you used in solving it. Let's say you listed handling a labor-management dispute as one of your solved problems and an ability to find the real cause of the conflict as your skill. Based on the steps you actually took to solve the problem, this skill might be expanded to several steps as follows:

1. *Suspected* that neither side was voicing its real concerns
2. *Won* confidence of each side's leader
3. *Listened* to leaders' recitals of demands
4. *Elicited* reasons behind demands
5. *Analyzed* motivations behind demands
6. *Inferred* plausible hidden causes for dispute

Your objective is to isolate a matrix of unique skills that will enable you to establish a working "patent" on your business. Your original skill may be too broad to protect your "turf"—your particular consulting area—from infringement by other consultants, but one or more of the subskills you discovered by analyzing the original skill might be "patentable."

One more step is required to ensure that your skills are listed in a form that reveals your unique abilities: You need to rephrase your skills to make their description as independent as possible from the particular environment in which you used them. Look at each skill description and ask yourself: Could this ability be useful in other environments and, if so, what is the general description of the ability involved?

FIGURE 3.3 Expanded Skills Inventory Worksheet

Skills	Subskills

As an illustration, let's take the six subskills in the previous example and re-phrase them so that their general usefulness is more obvious.

1. *Suspected* could be rephrased as an ability to recognize when communications are confused by hidden factors.
2. *Won confidence/listened/elicited* can be combined as interviewing leaders for sensitive information in stressful situations.
3. *Analyzed/inferred* can be combined as discerning hidden motives in conflict situations.

These skills are now beginning to form a cluster related to handling difficult situations involving negotiations. If you look at the situation only as a problem in labor negotiations, you might be limited to that kind of negotiating. But negotiations take place in a great many situations, and many organizations experience political conflicts.

Given this skills matrix, you might be very good at consulting with organizations that are experiencing difficulties related to internal politics. Figure 3.4 is a list of consulting-related skills—activities consultants engage in—to help in analyzing your list of subskills. This is only a fragment of what consultants do, so don't feel limited by it.

Search for Talent

Talents, unlike skills, are not acquired. Instead, they seem to be with a person from birth. *Talents* are natural endowments and involve special abilities or creativity.

If you emphasize your talents, your chances for achieving a great advantage in the consulting marketplace are far greater than they would be if you relied on skills alone. Others can learn your skills and can acquire your knowledge, but unless they also have your talents, they cannot compete with you effectively in the marketplace. Recognizing and exploiting your talents can be an extremely profitable exercise.

Ironically, talents are likely to be even more invisible than your skills. They are far more natural for you than your skills, and you exercise them less consciously. Therefore, you should be especially thorough with this step of the exercise. By failing to detect a talent, you could be giving up a gold mine of consulting advantage. Figure 3.4 shows a good way to proceed.

- Examine your list of achievements, and note any that came easily.
- Look over your problem-solving history, and note where you exhibited the special vision needed to prevent problems.
- Evaluate your skills as listed. Talents will reveal themselves if you ask yourself these questions:
  a. Are there any groups of skills that have something in common?
  b. Which skills did people especially value?
  c. Where was I the obvious choice?
  d. Which skills did I particularly enjoy using?

FIGURE 3.4 Consultant's Activities

Research
    Identify suppliers.
    Identify target markets for ideas or products.
    Identify talent.
    Identify experts.
    Identify commercial possibilities for ideas or concepts.
    Assess the public mood.
    Examine political realities.
    Trace problems, ideas, etc., to their source.

Invent
    Create commercial possibilities for abstract ideas or concepts.
    Design events.
    Improve on others' ideas.
    Update others' ideas.
    Adapt others' ideas.

Communicate
    Arbitrate disputes.
    Negotiate agreements.
    Terminate people/projects/processes.
    Translate jargon.
    Help others express views.
    Help others clarify goals and values.
    Handle difficult people.
    Interview.

Motivate
    Sell an idea, program, or course of action to decision makers.
    Raise capital for nonprofit institutions.
    Raise capital for business ventures.
    Recruit leadership.
    Direct creative talent.

Analyze
    Classify date.
    Perceive and define cause-and-effect relationships.

Synthesize
    Summarize.
    Assess people's needs.
    Extract the essence from large quantities of data.

Evaluate
    Assess monetary value.
    Judge people's effectiveness.
    Identify and assess others' potential.
    Analyze communication situations.

Recommend
    Suggest experts.
    Suggest suppliers.
    Allocate scarce resources.

Forecast
    Plan financial matters.
    Predict obsolescence.

Adapted from *What Color Is Your Parachute?* Richard N. Bolles (Ten Speed Press)

Talents that are not revealed through self-examination may turn up in other people's comments about you. Don't hesitate to solicit these comments for this step. You may also recall people's comments from formal or informal work evaluations or from other situations. You can get an idea of the kinds of talents that are important in consulting from Figure 3.5.

Having completed this self-assessment, you have done something that most people never do. You have methodically produced a thorough, exhaustive listing of what you have to offer. Your special skills and unique talents provide a basis for entering the consulting profession or rejuvenating your existing practice. Periodic changes in the scope and thrust of your consulting services in response to changing market conditions are part of the normal cycle of practice development. But even more important is a regular reassessment of your skills and talents. This reevaluation, reflecting an increased awareness of the full breadth and applicability of your talents, may suggest changes in direction or emphasis that will make you more effective and efficient in providing your services.

☞ Tips

The list of consulting services that you offer is your inventory. Your services are analogous to products in that they require strong management and selling skills. In developing your inventory of consulting services, you will be looking for creative ways of applying your skills and talents to specific situations.

Figure 3.6 covers some of the many services consultants offer. Use the consulting inventory worksheet in Figure 3.7 to list your skills and talents in the left-hand column and potential consulting offerings in the right-hand column.

Suppose you work in security. You can give management seminars on security. You can offer consulting on such topics as employee theft prevention, shoplifting, industrial espionage, and computer security. You might further specialize in certain industries, such as construction or retail clothing outlets.

Even in a fairly limited area, you can produce an extensive list of consulting services. But a big inventory isn't necessarily good. By offering too many services, you may be spread too thin, and you'll have trouble targeting markets. You may be able to do all those things on your list, but can you sell them all at once?

On the other hand, you want to be able to provide enough services so that you have the flexibility to respond to changes in the marketplace. In other words, you want to be process oriented rather than task oriented. Of course, if you do one thing well and there is a steady demand for it, you can be quite successful. However, if the market changes, you need to be prepared to change, too.

In drawing up a potential inventory, go over your list of skills and talents. How can they be exercised in your chosen area to produce particular offerings? Suppose you have a talent for anticipating future trends and you specialize in inventory. You may want to offer warehouse-space planning or

FIGURE 3.5 Talents in Consulting

General
  Separating the "wheat from the chaff"
  Perceiving and defining cause-and-effect relationships
  Creating order out of masses of information

Data Handling
  Ordered, systematic manipulation of data
  Classification of data
  Mathematical ability
  Building systems for efficient storage and access of data

Management
  Attracting talent or leadership to yourself
  Getting diverse groups to work together
  Directing creative talent
  Building teams

Human Relations
  Alertness in observing human behavior
  Developing rapport/trust
  Bargaining
  Diplomacy
  Confronting others with touchy or difficult personal matters
  Judging people's effectiveness and/or potential
  Bringing out the creativity in others

Communication
  Public speaking
  Writing ability
  Thinking quickly on your feet
  Explaining and teaching difficult concepts
  Inventing illustrations for principles or ideas
  Hearing and answering questions perceptively

---

setting up inventory procedures for new plants. Or you may decide to apply your talent in other areas, such as market analysis. Based on your skills and talents, draw up a list of four or five potential consulting offerings.

In the next two chapters, we'll learn how to find and exploit opportunities. The work you have done in this chapter will enable you to match your skills and talents with opportunities to produce an inventory of consulting offerings. If you are clear about what you are marketing, you have a better chance to make a sale—and that leads to success.

FIGURE 3.6 Some Consulting Specialties

Management
Planning
Organizational structure
Strategic business planning
Feasibility studies
Management audits
Public relations
Business surveys
Customer satisfaction improvement
Business process improvement

Administration
Office design and planning
Office management
Office procedures
Scheduling
Data management

Marketing
Market strategy
Product research
Sales forecasting
Sales training
Direct mail
Advertising
Marketing audits
Pricing
Consumer survey
Product design and packaging
Competitive analysis

Human Relations
Labor relations
Wage and salary structure
Management development
Personnel
Attitude surveys
Training programs
Company communications
Health, safety, and security
Compliance
Employee incentive
Employee assistance programs

Plant Operation
Plant management
Plant location
Plant design
Warehouse utilization
Inventory management
Production planning
Quality control
Shipping and distribution
Automation and robotics

FIGURE 3.6 Some Consulting Specialties (Continued)

Finance and Purchasing
    Accounting
    Cost control
    Financial planning
    Capital investment
    Taxes
    Collection
    Purchasing
    Capital expenditures
    Cost accounting

Technology
    Computer system installation and maintenance
    Software development and maintenance
    Telecommunications system development and maintenance
    Desktop publishing
    Point-of-purchase system installation
    Product packaging and design
    Systems testing
    Internet service design and maintenance

FIGURE 3.7 Consulting Inventory Worksheet

Skills and Talents	Consulting Application

CHAPTER 4

Finding Consulting Opportunities

Identifying consulting opportunities is largely an intuitive process that cannot be taught and should not be thought of as scientific. Experienced consultants usually develop a sensitivity to promising new areas for the application of their skills. This chapter shows how to uncover new sources of consulting opportunity by applying your experience and intuition to an organized review of possibilities. You may end up with more ways of increasing consulting opportunities than you even wished for.

Even in as nebulous an area as matching opportunities to your talents, you needn't resign yourself to good luck. You can actively seek out opportunities and evaluate their suitability to your goals as a consultant. Most opportunities don't come to you. You have to find them and, in some cases, help to produce them. The secret is learning to orient yourself toward filling the needs of clients as opposed to looking for clients who meet your requirements. And you can actively pursue "add-on" opportunities with current clients in addition to taking on new accounts.

Many consultants limit their search for opportunities to a specific industry or organization. Although you want to be seen as standing for something, neither do you want to focus your practice so narrowly that you severely limit your opportunities. You'll want to have target markets—types of organizations or market segments—on which you can focus your marketing energies, but you don't want to "niche" your practice so tightly that it can't be successful.

A new consultant with a marketing and merchandising background in retail, for example, has decided to focus his practice on museum gift stores. The reason? He was enamored with museums, felt he could really help their stores, and wanted to build his practice around working with those for whom he felt an affinity. The problem, of course, is that the sheer number of museums is limited and even fewer have the money and/or the interest to invest in upgrading their stores. This consultant reached his earning potential very early in his consulting practice. Faced with no other choice, he broadened his target market to include gift stores in general and has gone on to develop a workable and profitable practice.

If focusing on a single, narrow market niche can be productive in some specialties, for most it significantly limits a consultant's eligibility for greater success. Why limit yourself to one industry or business? Consulting opportunities arise in all industries and organizations. If you know the earmarks of a consulting opportunity, you can recognize it in any situation. By not limiting your consulting specialty, you can take advantage of an opportunity wherever you find it.

To ensure that you seek out a broad spectrum of opportunities, it is useful to approach the market with an understanding of the eleven situations or circumstances that give rise to the use of a consultant.

Eleven Situations That Create a Need for Consulting Services

1. Shifting business strategies
2. The need for technical assistance
3. The need for specialized skills
4. Cash flow and business problems
5. The need for capital
6. Resource acquisition
7. Compliance legislation
8. Political situations
9. The "hotfoot" situation
10. Training
11. Need for an unbiased opinion, evaluation, or critique

Shifting Business Strategies

Today's business climate favors downsizing, job buyouts, outsourcing, and similar devices to reduce the workforce of a company or replace some of the workforce with technology. Payroll and legally required and company-offered benefits are often the biggest line items in a company's budget. Reducing the workforce, from top management on down, is seen as a way for companies to save money. This trend, while not favoring employees, offers many opportunities for consultants.

You may even have decided to develop your consulting practice after experiencing downsizing, being offered a job buyout, or taking early retirement. If so, you are intimately aware that a shift in business strategy promotes consulting opportunity: The people may go away but the need for certain skills, talents, and performance does not.

Most companies have learned that lesson well and plan and budget for the increased use of consultants and other outside contractors when they reengineer, downsize, or otherwise change business strategies. Although consultants charge more per day or hour than staff members receive in wages, consultants don't get expense accounts, company cars, health insurance, vacation time, sick leave, and other fringe benefits that create additional expense. Most consultants work on a project on an as-needed basis and thus, in the long run, typically cost far less than a regular staff member.

Consider, for example, the firm that eliminates its human resources department and then contracts with a consulting firm specializing in employee benefits, self-insured health policies, and/or hiring and firing. Another company might want robotics to replace people doing certain routine production work. Where will they turn for help? The company could turn to you if robotics is your area of specialty.

The Need for Technical Assistance

In the United States the single largest market for consulting work arises from the need for temporary technical assistance. This opportunity occurs in both the public and private sectors whenever an organization must increase its capacity and personnel, including as the result of downsizing and/or restructuring. Rather than searching for new or unusual skills, clients merely seek more of the skills they already have.

Many large firms regularly fill a significant percentage of their positions with temporary technical assistance consultants. Firms in the high-technology industries—aerospace, electronics, computers, education, health care—are particularly likely to follow this practice. Still other firms are now turning over significant portions of their information systems management and maintenance to technical assistance consultants. They may have a handful of software developers, programmers, analysts, and systems managers on staff but rely heavily on outside consultants to augment and keep information systems up and running.

Despite the fact that temporary technical assistance consulting is widespread and pervasive, it is not very romantic. You don't ride in on a white horse, do mysterious things with spectacular results, and then gallop off into the sunset with a big check in hand. Instead, you often find yourself commuting to a place of business and putting in a workday with fellow consultants and employees. Technically, you are a consultant. But on a day-to-day basis, you may find that you function more like an employee. The crucial distinction between temporary technical assistance consulting and the other ten opportunities is who is responsible for supervision.

In most consulting situations, you are viewed as the authority or expert. You may be managed, but you are unlikely to be supervised. In providing temporary technical assistance, however, you are viewed, not as the sole expert, but as a temporary employee—much like clerical help from an agency. These consultants often find their work less rewarding psychologically (and financially) than those in other fields of consulting, where fees are higher and responsibility broader. The advantages of temporary technical assistance consulting include the following: There are plenty of opportunities, and the job frequently produces other more rewarding consulting possibilities.

An organization has two basic reasons to seek out temporary technical assistance consultants: (1) Such assistance is often more economical than hiring permanent personnel, and (2) by using consultants, the organization remains more flexible than it could with permanent help.

Hiring costs an organization a lot of money. Firing can cost even more. Much of this expense is the result of complex government regulations and the need to train new employees in specific job duties. A team of well-paid personnel officers may be needed to interview and evaluate potential employees to make sure federal and state regulations are followed. Reliable statistics indicate that a large organization typically takes between five and seven months to locate, hire, train, and orient employees for managerial, technical, or professional positions. That estimate may sound high, but consider the severe shortages in this country of personnel who are available and trained to be installed in the right position. Consider also the complexity of the personnel process: advertising, prescreening, resume reviews, interviews, testing, follow-up interviews, medical examinations, orientation, break-in periods, and so on.

By the time a person is hired, trained, and oriented, most large employers can expect to expend from 70 to 90 percent of an employee's first-year salary. For someone hired at, say, $50,000 a year, that dollar amount would be $35,000 to $45,000! And during the hiring process, technology may leap forward, making the job description just created five months ago obsolete. For an organization to hire someone on a permanent basis, it must be very certain not only that the individual can and will do the job but also that the employee's talents will be needed for as long as he or she is with the company.

The organization's expense doesn't end when an employee is hired. Besides salary and benefits, an employer has overhead expenses with each employee, such as providing a place to work and support personnel. Changes in circumstances can cost money. Perhaps technology passes the company by, or a large government contract expires. In that case the organization must either arrive at a termination settlement with the affected employees, find other jobs for them to do, or simply "carry" them.

In the worst case, if an employee does not work out, an employing company may encounter further difficulties. In many states or in companies with strong union representation, a company cannot arbitrarily let an employee go. It must show just cause, such as inability to perform the work, unwillingness to do so, criminal activity, or some other good reason. Employees who respond with legal action can cost a company for an incalculably long time after they no longer produce any benefit for the company.

An organization does not incur the same cost or liability when it takes on a temporary technical consultant. Consultants pay part or most of their own hiring expenses. They often make themselves known and available through their promotional and advertising efforts, thus reducing the organization's cost of searching for them. Once on the job, they normally do not participate in the benefits enjoyed by permanent personnel. And management knows that if a consultant does not become a contributing member of the team within a reasonable period, the most the organization is liable for is payment over the short-term contract.

Because they are easy to discharge, consultants are obliged to become effective contributors sooner than employees. The role expectations for consultants are different from those for employees. Permanent personnel are expected to take a long time to become oriented and adjusted, whereas consultants are expected to start contributing on short notice. A temporary technical consultant must be noticeably effective almost from the start, contributing at least as much as a permanent employee.

The Need for Specialized Skills

In rare instances a person has a skill or expertise that few others have. Even more rare, an individual can offer a service that no one else offers. That person has something unique to sell. Classically, consultants are considered to possess specialized expertise—the command of special or unique talents, skills, and capabilities that make a person rare or unique in the marketplace. However, the success of such specialists arises from our perception of their uniqueness rather than its reality. In most cases specialists are not unique; they have merely found a niche in the marketplace in which the application of their skills creates the appearance of uniqueness.

One direct-response specialist has skills that are commonly available and uses techniques that are not unique. Yet this person is perceived as an accomplished specialist because he has taken general knowledge and applied it in a unique fashion to a specialized industry.

True uniqueness, then, is not a requirement. Fewer than 5 percent of all consultants have a truly unique set of skills, but many have found a way of being seen as special and different in their clients' eyes.

Cash Flow and Business Problems

Many opportunities exist in both the private and public sectors for consultants who wish to serve organizations that are experiencing business or cash flow problems. Previously confined to the private sector, these problems now extend to the once cash-flush public sector, which at one time could raise funds by going to voters or donors but now finds itself on hard times. In recent years, the use of consultants to assist public organizations has increased fivefold.

Consulting opportunities also arise when an organization runs into a cash shortage. A company experiencing a cash flow crisis typically reduces its expenses by laying off personnel and curtailing other costs. This situation gives rise to two types of consulting opportunities. The first is for temporary technical assistance to help the firm avoid the cost of hiring and maintaining permanent personnel. Temporary technical assistance consultants can come into the organization and perform the work, then cease being a financial obligation to the organization.

The second opportunity is the greater of the two. Whenever you see a firm trying to solve its cash flow problem by cutting costs, it probably has a deeper, more pervasive problem and the cash flow crisis is merely a symptom. Management soon realizes that reducing expenses is not enough to solve the larger problem.

With the realization that more than reducing expenses is needed, management usually recognizes the need for turnaround consultants. Two types are generally needed. The first specializes in creativity. Perhaps the firm needs more adaptive marketing, more ingenious engineering talent, more flexible personnel management, and the like. The creative consultant, in solving one part of the problem, typically becomes preoccupied with day-to-day matters. The other type of consultant is concerned with control and management. This is the hard-nosed, commonsense, bean-counter manager who ensures that the firm's creative energies are focused on turning a profit. Finding opportunity of this sort depends largely on keeping your ear to the ground. By the time a firm's problems become news in the trade, industrial, or professional publications, the time has come for the embalming committee, and the need for a turnaround consultant has long since passed.

For much more reliable referrals to dying-but-not-dead businesses, you can turn to local bankers, accountants, and attorneys, who are intimate with the financial standing of the community's businesses. Although you should not expect bank officers and professionals to give you any information about their customers and clients, you can make your services known to them. In turn, they may refer their clientele to you at their discretion.

You'll find that referrals do not come just from the goodness of bank officers' hearts. If a bank customer is in trouble, a bankruptcy could mean a loan gone sour. You can actually help the bank by saving the business. Everyone is happy—the business is saved, the bank's loan is repaid, and you earn your fee.

A number of consulting firms specialize in wresting businesses from the brink. One relies on only two banks for referrals of terminal businesses. With an hourly rate often exceeding $250 and more than 80 percent of its business from bank referrals, this firm has enjoyed a growth rate of more than 30 percent a year for the past five years.

The Need for Capital

Needing capital is different from needing cash. Even organizations that are cash flush have to go into the money market to raise long-term and short-term capital. Large organizations have people on staff to meet their capital needs, which means that few consulting opportunities are available there. But smaller firms, which don't need to raise capital as often as larger companies do, don't usually need to keep such talent around on the payroll full-time. When a smaller firm needs to raise capital, a consulting opportunity for you is created.

You should have many more such opportunities in the future. Economists predict capital shortages in this country at least until the year 2010 and perhaps beyond. Because of the present shortage of capital, the capital acquisition area is the fastest growing submarket of consulting opportunity in the United States.

A major factor in the growth of this submarket is the competition for funds from the public sector, which must now vie for the same capital that once flowed only into the private sector. The need for capital naturally affects public as well as private organizations. With their growing resistance to bonded indebtedness, increasing taxes, and tax overrides, taxpayers are forcing public agencies to turn to what was once the sole preserve of private firms to raise capital—institutional lenders. As public agencies draw upon funds normally reserved for the private sector, the capital shortage grows more acute, increasing opportunities for consultants.

Surprisingly, you don't have to be a financial specialist to benefit from this abundant opportunity. Much more is involved in raising capital than running down to the corner bank with a fistful of financial statements. Today, the process of obtaining capital requires the client to be packaged carefully for the close scrutiny that accompanies applications for capital. They must often demonstrate that

- they are in compliance with federal and state laws, such as those regulating equal employment opportunity, occupational safety and health, and citizens with disabilities;
- their personnel policies and practices will produce a steady stream of qualified, capable personnel into the organization in the future;
- their marketing is sufficiently large and well developed to ensure long-term sales;
- their production capability is appropriate and suitable to the market demand they are likely to encounter;
- their depth of management is sufficient to allow the company to continue even if key personnel should die or leave; and
- they can service the debt.

You may well possess nonfinancial skills that are valued in the capital acquisition area, provided you take the time to market them effectively.

Firms needing capital also have to spruce up their images, so if your specialty is in public relations, marketing, forecasting, product development, or any other field that can help a firm look its best, you may have a consulting opportunity.

Not only are the opportunities for consulting great in the capital acquisitions area, but the fees earned are among the highest. Capital-seeking organizations are quite willing to pay a substantial amount to raise capital. Because they operate on the assumption that a consultant's fee (cost of capital acquisition) will be repaid from the proceeds, they tend not to scrutinize the size or reasonableness of the fee quite as closely as they would in other kinds of consulting. If a firm is trying to raise $600,000 in capital, it usually won't mind investing $40,000 to $50,000 to get it.

Even if you can't get the primary contract for this type of work, you may be able to market your services to other consultants. Perhaps a team of consultants has to be formed to meet the needs of a client. Or maybe the firm's financial consultant identifies a number of areas that need attention—personnel, marketing, production. Because the first consultant is unlikely to be expert in all fields, the services of other consultants will be required.

If you have the appropriate skills, look for firms that are about to raise capital. Follow the business press for trends. See which industries are developing and which are getting a lot of business—these organizations will need capital. Look also for which public agencies are raising capital, reported in newspapers all the time, and follow their budgetary procedures.

Resource Acquisition

Resources can take the form of the physical plant, equipment, inventory, and personnel. Specialized consultants can make a good income by finding the resources a company needs. It is often much cheaper for a company to buy a factory and refurbish it than to invest in new facilities. Consultants with knowledge of who needs what and where to find it can charge hefty fees for overseeing a physical transfer.

FIGURE 4.1 Impact of Compliance Requirements on Consulting Opportunities

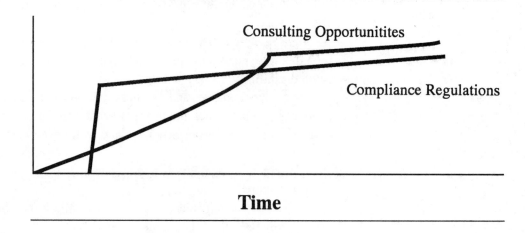

Consulting Opportunitites

Compliance Regulations

Time

Part of the job is finding what is needed; part is consummating the transfer. Some plant brokers also oversee the remaking of old facilities and even installing the workforce. However, significant parts of such a project are often handled by sub-contracting. Companies ready to make major equipment purchases may gladly seek help in researching technology and the marketplace.

Scarcity of resources creates special opportunities. Although the spot oil market was the hottest thing going for a while, shortages in any area can create opportunities. If you know how to find what is in demand, you can get contracts as a consultant.

Professional headhunters are also looking for a scarce resource. As a consultant your opportunity comes from your broad contacts in management. You may work at finding particular executives or employees, or you may specialize in putting teams of consultants together for demanding contracts. Even as companies provide executive searches as part of their services, many executive search consultants offer related services in response to market needs. Resource acquisition, one of the fastest-growing areas of consulting, is wide open to the freewheeling entrepreneur who knows how to find and exploit opportunities.

Compliance Legislation

Every time Congress convenes, every time a state legislature meets, and every time the county supervisors or city councils gather, legislators pass laws to make someone comply with something. Compliance legislation leads to the sudden availability of funds. Because of new laws, organizations have to respond rapidly and effectively to avoid sanctions and injunctions.

Consider environmental impact legislation. When this legislation became effective, compliance requirements jumped dramatically, pulling consulting opportunities along in a more gradual curve, as seen in Figure 4.1. Right after the effective date, the compliance requirements were minimal. But no one had much experience in writing required reports, so many firms turned to consultants. At that time you didn't need a technical doctorate to write an environmental impact report—all you needed were an understanding of the process and good writing skills. For a while the demand for good report writers was great. Consultants in this field were enjoying top fees, plenty of work, and a lot of independence.

Compliance issues affect the hiring process, building construction, pregnant workers, and plant locations, to name a few areas businesses must consider. As a consultant you can help, particularly in businesses not large enough to have a compliance officer. Eventually, however, demand is bound to taper off for a number of reasons, including the following:

1. People who are smart about procuring consulting services often use consultants as trainers rather than as consultants. In this way they get their own staffs trained and don't need consultants any more.
2. Many consultants are wooed away to become captives of client corporations at high salaries, thus taking over a part of the market that would ordinarily go to consultants.
3. Eventually universities and business school programs see the need for consulting specialists and begin offering suitable courses. Some years later those schools are turning out people who will be full-time personnel, trained in areas that used to belong solely to consultants.

Where do you find out about new compliance requirements? Browse through the *Congressional Record* on a regular basis. Don't read all of it—just by scanning, you can identify important legislative trends. If you read major metropolitan or trade newspapers, such as *The New York Times* or *The Wall Street Journal,* you will keep abreast of new legislation. On your local level, watch what is going on at supervisors meetings or at any meeting of local government agencies. When you see compliance requirements coming up, be ready. Find out the nature of the legislation. Determine what compliance is required. Keeping your eye on compliance legislation may lead to a number of business opportunities.

Political Situations

Both private and public organizations frequently engage in activities they deem essential for their survival but that are likely to provoke attacks from others. The news is peppered with stories about actions taken against organizations by activist groups, the general public, the government, competitors, and even an organization's own employees. A company or government agency under fire of this sort has, in other words, a political problem.

The company needs to shield or buffer itself from the adverse or unpleasant efforts of its opponents. In such situations the company often retains the services of a consultant to become the fall guy, to take the rap. Obviously, this type of consulting calls for a very thick skin.

The nature of this work is perhaps best demonstrated by a case example. The office of education in a major metropolitan county was supposed to start a regional high school and post-high school vocational training program. The office's management decided that such a program would be financially advantageous for the county as well as educationally desirable for students.

But the plan met some opposition. Most of the dozens of operating school districts in the county felt that the county office of education should not operate school programs, especially in competition with them. Moreover, the state, which paid out a sizable dollar amount for every hour of student instruction, feared that the anticipated program was large enough to bankrupt the state. The issue became very hot politically. With all this opposition, the county office was expected to drop the program because it had deferred to local pressure in the past. But this time the county office decided to press for its planned program despite the possible loss of voter support.

Rather than take the brunt of possible negative publicity and face the anger of local school districts, the county office decided to retain a consultant. As project director of a feasibility study, the consultant was highly visible and the target of much acrimonious criticism. The county office hid behind its hired gun, smiling benignly and protesting its innocence.

The county office didn't have to itself oppose local school districts or the state board of education. It buffered itself so that it could redirect any attack on the program or its feasibility to the consultant. If the feasibility study had gone against the program, the consultant would have made a very convenient scapegoat. Fortunately for the consultant, the regional occupational program was found to be feasible in every way—educationally, politically, and economically. With the approval of the state board of education, the program became a reality. In fact, it is operating now.

In the case of a political problem, consulting work is always booby trapped with the possibility of an ethical or moral dilemma. From the outset of the vocational program case, the unspoken dictum was that the study must prove the program feasible. The consultant was not really supposed to be concerned about what the data actually showed. In this case the study did show what the client wanted it to show. The consultant did not have to face the moral issue of having to tell the county office management that they were wrong about the program. But what would have happened if the study had indicated that the program was not feasible?

Sooner or later every consultant must face the problem of presenting clients with results they don't want to hear. This is particularly true for political situations. As a consultant, what do you do? Do you hide behind your professional standards? Do you shade your results toward your client's desires? In most cases the answers are not simple, not clear-cut.

Perhaps the best protection against this type of moral dilemma is to obtain a clear understanding from the start with your client about your ethical responsibilities. If circumstances seem to warrant bluntness, tell the client that your work must remain unbiased and that you cannot allow it to be influenced by any outside political factors. You should have the contract structured to ensure that you are compensated for your services even if the results are not what the client wants. By keeping the understanding clear from the start, verbally and in writing, you can avoid the dilemma that sometimes crops up in a political situation.

The "Hotfoot" Situation

Occasionally, a valuable and highly placed employee encounters a particularly troublesome problem. As the employee struggles to get out of the trap, he or she becomes merely more entangled. Although such an employee is an otherwise valued contributor to the company, someone higher up wants to dump the problem onto the employee. Perhaps the corporate officers are also looking for cuts in division management, or maybe a parent company wants to replace the subsidiary company's leadership little by little. In effect, the employee's feet are put in the fire and held there until the situation changes or the employee quits.

Consultants are often contracted in a situation like this to put out the fire or at least save the victim. This kind of consulting is becoming more popular as employees realize their employment is their principal economic asset. To an employee the job is what tools were to a tenant farmer. When the job and the employee's professional stature are threatened, steps have to be taken to ensure protection.

A case in point involved a company that had its regional headquarters in northern California and its national headquarters in New York. During a product development market test, the assistant branch manager in California was reporting to corporate headquarters in New York. The three-year program was in serious trouble. Running a year and a half behind schedule, it could not be regarded as working out well, even in the most optimistic opinion. A consultant was brought in, not by the New York office or the assistant branch manager, but by the branch manager in California. He knew that his assistant, while not performing adequately in the eyes of the New York office, was otherwise important to the operation of the branch. But New York was holding the poor man's feet to the fire.

The branch manager, aware there would be no opportunity for the assistant to grow with the company if he failed on this job, called in a consultant to help with the marketing study. The assistant branch manager's job was saved, though the product's fate was less certain. Even that limited success was helpful to the assistant branch manager and obviously useful to the consultant.

In another case a major bank in a California county went through an extensive personnel shake-up. The changes were so unusual for the banking industry that many observers wondered how the bank got away with them. Although the bank's managers made the decision internally, they knew they would be in for a scorching. Their solution was to have a consulting firm justify the decision, announce it, and take the heat.

Obviously, you don't market this kind of consulting work as such. No organization runs an ad saying: "The division manager is in big trouble at XYZ Co. Consultants, please apply at side door." In the course of marketing your services as a managerial or technical consultant, communicate to prospective clients your availability for other assignments. You might express that you have the sensitivity, discretion, and judgment to successfully negotiate in difficult circumstances.

In the course of your consulting activities, be alert to the following circumstances that might lead to consulting work of this nature:

- People in high enough positions in an organization can bring in their own consultants when they get into trouble.
- Supervisors sometimes retain consultants to help their subordinates. In this way the subordinates can't blame their poor performance on their superior's lack of ability in delegating tasks. Consultants act as third-party arbitrators in such situations.

- In a few rare instances, subordinates get together to retain a consultant for their superior.
- Consultants most commonly enter into hotfoot contracts laterally at the request of a peer of a person in trouble. For example, the manager of Division X will retain a consultant on behalf of the manager of Division Y.

A hotfoot situation calls for sensitivity and tact. You need a real understanding of the realities of corporate politics and management strategies to pull this one off. Besides earning your fee, you have the satisfaction of knowing that you have kept a good employee working for a company and may have saved the employee's career.

Training

We pointed out previously that some companies have consultants train employees as part of their contract, eliminating the need to periodically recontract for the same services. Some consultants use the fulfillment of training needs as the main source of their practices.

Training is a major growth area for consultants. Not only is it in demand in virtually every market sector, but internal training departments of many companies have been shrunk as part of the organizational restructuring and downsizing of the 1990s. For most organizations, shrinking training departments does not mean that training is any less of a priority. Rather, it means that they intend to rely more heavily on consultants to provide the training they need when they need it.

Ever changing technology in almost every field presents great opportunities for consultants who stay ahead of those changes to offer their services, not only to firms that want to upgrade their systems and need help in learning how to operate new equipment, but also to manufacturers and retailers of new equipment who find it in their best interest to help people understand how to use new technology systems.

One computer hardware and software consultant, for example, discovered that few of those in his target market were willing to engage him for selecting appropriate computer hardware and software programs but were very interested in his training capability once their new equipment was installed. As a result, he reorganized his practice and approach to become a training provider exclusively and one in very specific, highly technical computer programming languages. He has built a very successful practice as a result.

New legislation can also create a training opportunity. For example, a western city recently experienced an outbreak of hepatitis stemming from the poor hygiene of restaurant employees. The city council passed a law requiring training for these employees. Two consultants, recognizing that restaurants were not prepared to give such training, put together a program that met the city's requirements and was within the restaurants' budgets. For several months after the legislation went into effect, they were in high demand. There has also been a slower but consistent demand for their services after the original rush.

Training seminars are a special area of consulting in which the specific demands are constantly changing. New technologies, new applications of technologies, new legislation, and changes in the way organizations want to operate all present training opportunities. Whether training is the sole service you provide in your practice or only one of many, excellent opportunity exists for the consultant who can put a good program together and market it.

Need for an Unbiased Opinion, Evaluation, or Critique

Many executives realize that management has a tendency to tunnel vision. The company creates a corporate culture that encourages every employee to look at problems and business in the same way. A consultant can bring in fresh, new perspectives and opinions.

Trouble that company members don't see or are afraid to discuss may hover on the horizon. A consultant is under no compulsion to make the boss happy. Employees can confide in consultants and share concerns and perceptions that they usually hide—if, that is, the consultant communicates a sense of reliability and confidentiality.

Companies often fail to see opportunities that a consultant, as a result of wide experience in several different areas of free enterprise, is able to see. Working with several different firms in one year can give a consultant a special perspective and understanding of the direction an industry is taking. This knowledge is worth money to executives who recognize its value.

These eleven sources of consulting opportunity work because of the immediacy of need or benefits. Pressure in the form of cash shortage, legislation, deadlines, or a hotfoot situation creates an awareness of need, even a sense of urgency. As a consultant, you are able to step in and save the day. As a temporary technical consultant or an expert with a special skill, you can generate income for or stop the flow of money from a business. If you can make the advantages of retaining you apparent to businesses, these opportunities will turn into contracts and profits for you.

Opportunities with the Government

Because of the special conditions surrounding government contracts, consulting work with the government deserves its own section. The federal bureaucracy is vast and extremely complex, and it generates a multitude of consulting opportunities.

Measured in terms of the dollars it spends, the federal government is the free world's largest consumer. When its spending is combined with that of state and local governments, the total 1996 estimated budget of the U.S. government is $1.5 trillion. Even with cutbacks in spending, the government in Washington represents one of the largest markets in the world for consultants. As one area is cut back, another opens to create even more opportunities.

This market is especially suitable for temporary technical consulting. Because of bureaucratic timetables and delays, a contract recipient usually has to do a lot of work in a short period. Because a contractor doesn't have time for normal employment procedures, he or she needs effective assistance fast.

Most government contracts run for one year even though they often involve work that requires 13 or 14 months to complete. In addition, the government bureaucracy being what it is, a contract might not be signed for two, three, or more months after the start of the fiscal year. Contractors therefore typically have only nine or ten months for doing more than a year's worth of work.

In the past, when government contracts were relatively predictable, recipients of these contracts, aware of the time constraints, started work before the contract was signed and physically delivered. The awarding of government contracts is now less automatic. Funds might be impounded or the need for outside services eliminated by changes in legislation, congressional budget reductions in midyear, or changes in administrative policy.

With such changes, contractors who traditionally hired personnel, paid salaries, and incurred other expenses were occasionally notified that they had no contract. Left holding a bag of expenses and liabilities, they naturally became reluctant to pay high-level technical people to sit around waiting for a signed contract to come in the mail. Then, too, an increasingly budget-conscious government is unwilling to accept the additional high overhead that results from keeping a full-time staff waiting around for the next round of government largess.

By the time signed agreements are executed, contractors can't afford to waste five to seven months finding and breaking in the necessary personnel. They need expert help right away—and those with larger contracts need a lot of it right away—and hence the need for a temporary technical consultant.

Information on Government Contracts

Information about the contracts awarded in the public sector is plentiful and accessible. All government agencies are required to make public

- the names of available contracts;
- the dollar amounts they involve; and
- the nature of the contracted work.

The federal government publishes this information in a regular format that is readily available to the public. You may also request it from government procurement agencies at the state and local levels.

Relevant information about federal contracts of significant size is listed in the *Commerce Business Daily,* the federal government's procurement or purchasing newspaper. Published every business day, it is available in all major libraries or you can purchase a subscription from the Department of Commerce. This newspaper contains the contracts awarded by the federal government to both private firms and public agencies, naming the awarding agencies and the contract recipients. It also contains notices of the government's intent to contract, requests for proposals (RFPs), and requests for quotations (RFQs). You may not necessarily land a contract from the information in this publication, but you can always contact contract recipients to advise them of your availability, capability, and interest in working with them as a consultant. You should be able to find a great many opportunities because you're likely to be precisely the kind of talent needed.

Government and Foundation Grants

Billions of dollars are given out every year in this country in the form of grants, the bulk of it by the federal government, although sometimes through local and state agencies. In addition, many foundations dispense money. Where then do you find those billions of dollars?

Sources of Information

You can use the two main sources of information on grants—one for government funding and the other for foundations.

Government-issued grants are listed in the *Catalog of Federal Domestic Assistance,* which is published and sold by the Government Printing Office (see the bibliography). Information in this publication includes the following:

- Federal domestic aid programs that the federal government supports (the bulk of those programs release their funds through grants)
- The name of the funding program
- The enabling legislation
- The agency that administers the program
- How much money the agency gave away last year, is giving this year, and expects to give next year
- Eligibility requirements
- Examples of funded projects
- The official to contact to apply for a specific grant
- The criteria for selecting proposals

This catalog, which can be ordered from a federal government bookstore, is a subscription service that is updated quarterly. It is also available in any federal depository library or in any library with a significant research collection.

In the private sector the *Foundation Directory* lists the largest foundations in this country (see the bibliography). This directory, published by the Foundation Center, is available in almost every library with a research collection, and it contains the following information:

- A foundation's officers and directors
- The purpose and activities of the foundation
- Types of support offered
- How much money the foundation awarded the previous year (total dollars and number of grants)
- Total assets
- Application information
- Number of staff members

This book lists only the largest foundations. Other books, such as the *Directory of Research Grants* and the *Annual Register of Grant Support,* list some of the smaller foundations (see the bibliography). Interested readers should consult a major research library for additional information on government and foundation grants.

The Grant Process

As a consultant your role consists essentially of putting two parties together. One party is the funding source, which is either a government agency or a foundation. The other is the fiscal agent, sometimes endearingly called the *money drop*. As an independent consultant, you find the funding source, develop the grant application, bring the money into the fiscal agent's organization, and receive a subcontract back to do the work.

Many fiscal agents—public agencies or private nonprofit organizations—receive grant funds on behalf of a private individual or a consultant, who then enters into a contract with the recipient agency. For example, suppose that you are a consultant in the health care field and want to provide training to paramedics within hospitals. First, you find a grant to provide the funds to do such training. Then you find a fiscal agent that can be authorized as a recipient, such as a private, nonprofit hospital. When the grant funds arrive, you and the hospital work out a contract by which you design and deliver the training. You get the work you want, at the fee you want. What does the hospital get out of the contract? Obviously, it gets the training—but it also gets more.

Typically, fiscal agents skim the top of the grant. They take 10 to 12 percent of the grant for overhead expenses or grant administration expenses. That percentage can represent a substantial figure if a major university or hospital is involved. If a large university can land, say, $10 million worth of grants, the university will receive a million dollars or more just for administration expenses. Writing grants entails great economies of scale, because a grant that is ten times as large as another rarely entails ten times as much work.

Time is a key factor in obtaining grants. If the password is patience, then the countersign is perseverance. The federal government, for example, typically takes at least three months—and often five to six months—to give you the money after you identify the available funds. The largest foundations, such as the Rockefeller or Ford—are even slower in most cases than the federal government. Smaller foundations respond more quickly, typically in three weeks to two months.

Remember that funds are available. You need only time and patience to find a funding source and then wait for the money, assuming you have a viable use for it that meets the objectives and purposes of the granting organization.

Successful grantsmanship requires political awareness and skill at proposal writing. Ironically, proposal writing, which some often view as expensive and time-consuming, is not the most important factor in getting a grant. A good proposal is vital, of course, but not enough.

The actual writing of a proposal is only a nominal part of the grant process. Yet many grant writers spend a lot of time on their proposals, perhaps a great deal more than is warranted. The average amount of time spent by many review committees on a proposal is about 25 minutes. In less than half an hour, a decision is made on a piece of work that cost you three weeks of hard labor. Stacked in a pile of other proposals, your best effort becomes just one of many. About all a proposal team member might remember is that the proposal with the orange cover was a good one. Although you have spent weeks dotting the *i*s and crossing the *t*s, the committee rarely, if ever, gets to that level of detail. The lesson: Learn how to make a proposal look good without spending an inordinate amount of time writing it.

Information in the Private Sector

Thousands of technical and business publications are produced every year in the United States. You will undoubtedly find dozens of them that pertain to your field of interest. As you follow the business news in your specialty, you should ask: What information in this article suggests a demand for my consulting services? You can unearth scores of opportunities just by keeping abreast of events in your field. As you see opportunities develop, contact firms that need your services and let them know about you. You have every reason to expect to sign a consulting contract.

Consortiums

There is a vast market of clients who need more information for decision making in an increasingly competitive economy but don't have the dollars to spend on getting that information. A consortium research project enables you to serve this market. In consortium research a consultant combines the research and information requirements of several clients into one project. The fee for the project is then paid collectively by the clients served.

Suppose that all the hospitals in a given market area think they could benefit by hiring people who haven't had formal education or training for a variety of health care support positions, such as X-ray, autoclave, and medical records technicians. The hospitals might want to save money or make up for a shortage of trained labor. A research project can be designed to find out whether high school graduates would be suitable for designated health care support positions. The project would determine whether limited on-the-job training and instructions on hospital procedures would provide sufficient training for high school graduates to fill specified vacant positions. Let's say the study costs $75,000—more than any single hospital is able to pay. However, seven hospitals might find the study a reasonable and prudent investment on a collective basis, each contributing according to its number of beds.

The opportunities for consortium research are common and frequent. Usually a consultant needs to identify a specific research activity that would be of interest to a group of clients. At times an opportunity presents itself when a client expresses a need for work but doesn't have the money to fund it. In such situations look around for potential cosponsors.

A good consortium research idea has two main characteristics. First, the topic to be researched does not touch upon the business strategy or the proprietary interests of your clients. Not only are such areas confidential, but consortium research on them may be precluded by federal legislation. The second characteristic is that the idea contains the germ for an ongoing product or service. For example, a one-time report on consumer-buying intentions might be extended into a quarterly update. The circulation of the service might even be expanded beyond the original sponsors. To safeguard the subscriber-sponsors' proprietary interests, you might publish generic data, keeping more specific information confidential.

One university-based, part-time consultant developed the proprietary idea of a citywide bimonthly study of consumer buying and saving expectations. A sharp marketer, he signed up 35 mercantile, service, and financial institutions (at monthly fees from $800 to $1,400) within 17 months. These corporate clients received the bimonthly report and the opportunity to ask confidential and proprietary questions pertaining to their respective business planning.

One human resources consultant put together a consortium of small city governments that could not individually afford to retain a personnel director. He convinced the managers and councils of these cities that they would each receive a full range of personnel services by sharing the cost of retaining him as their manager. Each city paid a monthly fee based on the number of its employees. Each received in return a set of defined personnel services. The consultant created a workable and desirable situation for the cities while providing a good income for himself.

In addition, he positioned himself to be the consultant of choice for the cities if they needed assistance in areas beyond those prescribed in the consortium contract.

Formal consortiums, formed for a specific, even one-time activity, might become the grant development arm for a number of organizations, such as small colleges. Small public and government agencies frequently lack the financial ability to hire grant development personnel. By acting on behalf of a group, you can apply the consortium research idea to grants.

Professional Associations

Your creativity in discovering consulting opportunities is the only limit you have in finding new markets. For example, starting and administering a professional association is not such a wild idea as you might think. The feasibility of the project is demonstrated by the following true story.

A successful administrator of a national professional association gave up his position to move to a new city because of an excellent career opportunity for his wife. After discovering that the positions in his new locale did not offer the income that he was used to earning, he struck upon the idea of organizing his own professional association.

For the market test he selected a field that was not represented by an association—students attending law schools in the greater New York area, including neighboring states. Out of 700 students solicited, 43 mailed in checks for the membership fee of $45, a healthy 6 percent return. With 11,000 such students in the target market, the assumption was that the capture (response) rate would be 9 percent on the first promotional round with a follow-up campaign. A total number of 990 memberships could be expected at $45, producing total revenue of some $44,550 per year. After the cost of operating the association was subtracted, the sum of $27,000 would be available for the director's salary.

The funds collected from the test were returned to the 43 student participants. Another group that could afford higher dues was selected for the actual market. After one year, 1,301 members were each paying annual dues of $75 for a total revenue of $97,575. The dollars available for the director's salary and unrestricted reserves exceeded $70,000.

The professional association was operated as a not-for-profit organization, but others have been set up as profit-making companies. A professional association offers many other ways to obtain income: outside consulting by the director, rental of exhibitor space at the annual meeting, sale of the tape-recorded presentations at the annual meeting, library subscriptions to the journal or newsletter, charges for participation in the annual meeting, and so on. If you wish to represent the interests of a group in this society, no law says that the group must be formed prior to your taking an interest in it.

☞ Tips

Imagination and the willingness to look at a situation from a new point of view are your best assets in uncovering new consulting opportunities. Successful consultants view watching for new opportunities as being part of their work responsibility. They read newspapers, journals, and trade and general magazines with an eye for changes, problems, and situations that indicate the need for the kind of assistance they can render. And then they find ways to approach prospective clients who are facing the identified dilemma. The next chapter will show you how to sort out profitable opportunities so that you can use your talents to the fullest.

CHAPTER 5

Turning Opportunities into Profits

Selecting the best consulting opportunities for yourself is a matter of intuition. However, you can take certain measures and use specific guidelines to make the most advantageous choices. If you're planning for long-term success, you're looking for the consulting opportunity that gives you the edge over most or all other consultants.

Process Orientation

As we discussed in Chapter 1, consultants may be generally and broadly divided into two groups—those who are process oriented and those who are task oriented. Process-oriented consultants take a skills approach toward the market. Based on their broad skills and talents, they seek opportunities for consulting in different types of organizations, situations, and environments. They target prospective clients where they believe their talents can be usefully applied.

It is important to target prospective clients—to identify market segments, for example, where there is likely to be some common need for the skill sets you are marketing. But the organizations in your target market will probably extend beyond those with which you have had direct previous experience.

A successful security consultant who came out of the banking industry, for example, has not limited his market to the banking industry. His skills in planning, implementing, and fine-tuning procedures and systems that increase security for buildings, people, and information apply to many other industries. Yet he does not attempt to market his services to every organization in the United States—let alone the world. To do so would dilute his message—the ability to portray for prospective clients what he can do for their organizations. Instead, he has focused on five banking industry segments that include many more organizations than he could ever possibly serve in a lifetime. His potential market, therefore, is large enough for him to create and sustain a successful consulting practice. As important, the industries have sufficiently common security needs to allow him to get his same message across to all of them.

In contrast, task-oriented consultants see themselves more narrowly focused, seeking consulting opportunities in organizations similar to those where they have used their know-how in the past. If your approach is task oriented, you're looking for the type of assignment you had before, usually when you worked for someone else. That means you must wait for an opportunity that requires your proven abilities and past experiences. That opportunity may arise often or only rarely. In any case, the amount of work you get is too often beyond your control.

Uncovering consulting opportunities requires broadening the range of your services. A process-oriented approach enables you to offer your consulting skills in many environments, not just one or a few. You can actively seek out and service markets that are less crowded and competitive. You can go to markets rather than wait for markets to come to you.

Another distinct advantage of process orientation is its diversity. When you are narrowly task oriented, all of your potential clients tend to be more or less competitive with one another. Some clients may want to tie you up, withhold you from the market. At the least, they will probably require you to complete nondisclosure and noncompete agreements that bar you from performing the same tasks for someone else and make building a practice more difficult. A process-oriented consultant normally has clients from several different industries and/or geographic areas. A client's desire to prevent the consultant from serving direct competitors has much less effect if the practice is process oriented.

Some consultants have reservations about being process oriented. They feel they might be seen as false prophets who may be unmasked by potential clients. Perhaps *you* feel this way. You should have no qualms of conscience so long as you observe the following two policies:

1. Understand completely what clients are buying from you, the consultant.
2. Represent yourself to prospective clients correctly and ethically.

What the Client Buys

Clients are not so concerned with the theoretical comprehensiveness of your skills as they are with your practical experience and your ability to get the job done—and done well. You may have a string of degrees after your name, all notable accomplishments. But if you can't satisfy the needs of your clients, you haven't done what a consultant is supposed to do. In the simplest of terms, clients usually seek out a consultant who can solve a problem, prevent a problem, or help attain some gain they don't believe they can achieve without outside help.

In short, clients seek results. They may have only a general sense of what a desired result should look like when they first retain you. Part of your job then is to help describe more specifically an acceptable result. Nonetheless, what the client is paying for is results, not academic achievement. If, in a given field, you can accomplish what needs doing, you should not hesitate to hold yourself out as an authority.

A practical result, not an academically perfect or theoretically correct solution to a problem, is what you must be concerned about. The optimal solution may exist, but it almost always costs too much in terms of money or time to be practical. A business can go bankrupt trying to be perfect. Consultants work in the real world, which involves looking for the best solution that can be produced within the budgeted time and money. That solution is usually suboptimal and yet satisfactory.

Ethical Representation

Just because you are bringing your talent into a new field, you shouldn't hesitate to represent yourself as an authority. As a process-oriented consultant, you are applying your particular expertise to new problem areas that often call for the application of new technologies or techniques that may be foreign to the client. Indeed, the application of technology or knowledge to a new situation is a strong and highly respected talent. Just as engineers applied the aerospace technology of the 1950s and 1960s to education and health care in the 1970s, industry needs consultants who can apply the latest technologies to problems and needs as we move into a new millennium.

You may represent yourself as a problem solver—that is, someone who produces results or accomplishments. You are bringing two factors to bear on a client's need: a body of knowledge and your individual ability to apply that knowledge in the client's setting. The client has neither that knowledge nor that talent, at least not enough to achieve the desired result. Thus, the knowledge you apply is gratefully and usually uncritically received. You are rendering your clients a valuable service, and you have every right to call yourself an authority.

The first step is matching your skills with an area—or areas—of need that can benefit from them. Your knowledge and skill will likely come from a combination of sources—formal education, on-the-job training, practical experience, field research, interviews, and self-study. The source doesn't matter as much as the necessary information and skills you have to meet a client's need.

Much of the knowledge you bring to a client is available from a variety of sources—books, training programs, articles, and perhaps even employees in the client's organization. You may think: If an area is well documented, the information is as available to my potential clients as it is to me. Why do they need me?

Sources of Need

Clients need you for two reasons. First, in practice people are too busy, too lazy, or too resource-stretched to become self-sufficient. They either can't or won't invest the time or resources to address a given need. They find it easier, more timely, less costly, more politically prudent, or otherwise more advantageous to have a consultant address a need than to do it themselves.

A book on raising the level of giving in a church may be available, for example, but not many church leaders are going to read it even if the topic is important to them. To convince yourself of this fact, consider that there are over 350,000 churches, synagogues, and temples in the United States, according to the *Yearbook of American and Canadian Churches, 1991*. A book on fundraising normally doesn't sell more than a few thousand copies. Even if a church leader happens to read the book, the leader may still value your services highly because you have the ability to apply it. Besides, the church leader usually hasn't the time or inclination to master the information and implement it. In addition, the client may lack the energy and discipline you have to tackle the problems at hand.

Another, common illustration of clients' unwillingness to be self-sufficient is when a client organization's in-house staff could meet a particular need but the client opts for a consultant instead. Sometimes the reason is political, sometimes timing. Whatever the case, a client's ability to obtain information in-house doesn't necessarily foreclose opportunity for a consultant.

The second reason clients need you is an offshoot of the first. An organization's having extensive information about a subject does not guarantee its ability to achieve results or solve problems. It is your talent that produces results. This talent, coupled with hard data, is the marketable service. Your clients want to buy your result-producing capability.

Educating the Client

An unrecognized need is the same as no need. Some consultant services are needed, demanded, and understood even before consultants are available in the market to deliver such services. It is far easier to sell your services when a prospective client recognizes the need for them and values them. Such is the case for a consultant who knows how to raise venture capital. At the other extreme, some services that a consultant might provide have no such obvious need and hence demand. A potential client doesn't realize that a need exists for these services or recognize the benefits of the consultant's efforts. In such cases you must educate the client about the desirability of the services.

Educating the market, historically performed by large firms only, costs time and money. IBM created a huge market for itself by educating its markets during the early years of the computer industry. Microsoft has used the same costly, yet effective, strategy to educate the market about the advantages of each of its new software releases.

A large firm can afford to make that sort of expenditure. As a small business, however, you may not be able to. In fact, you could go broke trying to convince clients of their needs. If your clients don't see why they need you, you can get shuffled from one unaware decision maker to another and never close a business deal. Or you can advertise your services all over town, and the response might not cover the cost of the advertising.

A small consulting practice faces pitfalls in trying to educate clients. Uneducated clients can drain your time and money, causing you to spend your resources inefficiently and creating a market for other consultants. Once you awaken prospects to the need for your consulting assistance, you've created a market for any consultant who can win over the prospects. Even if you do convince potential clients of their needs, you still run the risk of losing some or all of your opportunity to other consultants who decide to cash in on your efforts. By that time you might not have any budget left to survive the ensuing competition for the actual contracts.

Some consultants, however, have succeeded in creating a market by educating clients. This strategy works when consultants offer services based on unique talents—talents that can't be copied by competing consultants—or when consultants do a good job of protecting their turf. If you have a promising approach to a problem that requires investment in client education, be sure you can put a working copyright on your ideas to keep others from poaching on your territory.

On the other hand, when a group of potential clients is already aware of its need, you can devote your time and money to persuading it to choose you over other consultants.

If your clients have been suddenly awakened to their needs by a dramatic, newsworthy event, much of the education process is done by the media. In effect, other people are spending their money to create your market. For example, around the time that the U.S. Supreme Court freed lawyers from bar association restrictions on advertising, lawyers' trade journals wrote about legal advertising in almost every issue. The press invariably tends to devote its greatest attention to simple, dramatic events, which in this case was the Supreme Court decision. The professional publications made the topic more than important; they made it hot!

Given an event like the Court's decision, you can use the media not only to promote your specialty but also to make the market aware of you. If you announce your specialty just as media interest is rising, the media will give you enough coverage to build a reputation for free. You don't have to spend a cent or talk to one prospect. Of course, you have to spend some money on promotion, but the money will be well spent. In addition, you can take advantage of the low-cost/no-cost methods for self-marketing discussed in Chapter 6.

Despite the fact that some consultants know full well that having an informed, interested client makes their marketing task much easier, they are intrigued by the challenge of creating demand or building a market where none exists.

You must pay special attention to the efficiency of your promotion. How much response do you get for each dollar or hour you spend building your consulting practice? A promotion aimed at a narrow group with highly focused interests is usually more efficient than one aimed at a larger group. By using subsets of mailing lists and even small advertisements in specialized publications, you can get a much better return on your dollar than you can with a wider promotion. When you have a narrow focus, you'll find it easier to get profitable speaking engagements at gatherings of potential clients. The same rule holds true for articles you write for publications read by potential clients.

The Internet, of course, has opened the possibility of reaching large numbers of people from a very wide geographic area. But for every story of how this opportunity has paid off for consultants, there are three horror stories. One training specialist, for example, built a World Wide Web page touting her training abilities and services. The first week, she received over 100 inquiries about her services. On the surface, the response was remarkable and more than promising. What she soon learned, however, is that none of the inquiries came from prospective clients. Rather, students writing papers on the training profession, job seekers looking for opportunities, and her competitors comprised the total group of inquiries.

Efficiency in your promotional efforts remains the key. Sometimes one or two serious responses to an effort can be worth more than hundreds of inquiries of mixed value.

Still, as an independent entrepreneurial consultant, you have an advantage over large consulting firms in the ability to enter new markets. You can establish your authority within months of developments that make clients aware of the need for your type of consulting. Six months after the Supreme Court decision that opened up advertising to lawyers, one consultant had absorbed all the printed material available on marketing professional services and was already consulting with lawyers on marketing their services. A larger organization would never have acted this fast. Typically, a large firm must have major new ventures approved at several levels of decision making, and all the decision makers seek to protect themselves from later recrimination if the venture goes bad. A large organization normally takes twice as long to decide to enter a new market as it takes you to actually do it.

When you're beginning to work with a market that has been suddenly and dramatically educated, you are often giving advice in an atmosphere of controversy. You can actually turn your small size and previous lack of connection with your potential client group into evidence of your credibility. In effect you're saying to the client: "This is my only business; I have no other interests to serve here apart from giving you the benefit of this field of knowledge." No large organization can possibly make this claim, and even solo consultants who have had previous contacts with the client group can't claim the extreme degree of specialization and credibility that you can.

You can cultivate the image of a lone, pioneering researcher in an uncharted area, seeking the best advice for your client group. This approach, with its public-spirited tone, improves the power of your promotion, enabling you to get information from live sources more easily.

Identifying Opportunities in a Newly Educated Market

Opportunities in a newly educated market are generally found through publications in both the private and public sectors. A wealth of information is available at low cost or no cost about changes in many areas. In just a few hours of reading a week, you can generally be well informed and specifically knowledgeable about events that affect your potential clients. Figure 5.1 contains a sample of the opportunities culled from reading a few months' worth of *The Wall Street Journal, Business Week,* and the *Harvard Business Review.* A description of the group that could benefit from consulting is listed in the left-hand column, with the affected fields of consulting specialization listed in the right-hand column. As you see from Figure 5.1, you may discover several promising opportunities for every hour you spend reading current business and professional publications. Your problem is having too many opportunities from which to choose.

FIGURE 5.1 Some Opportunities in Newly Educated Markets

Issue That Creates the Opportunity	Group That Is Affected
Blocking cuts in federal spending	Lobbyists
Increasing burden of government paperwork requirements	Small businesses
Dissatisfaction with schools leading to home teaching of children	Parents
Federal budget cuts creating need for fundraising and organizational change	Not-for-profits
Need to increase motivation and productivity of sales staffs	Companies facing increased competition
Job stress related to air traffic control	Air traffic controllers
Problems with productivity of high-level employees and professionals	Organizations having upper-level productivity problems
Lawsuits related to personnel files	Firms needing better security
Federal tight credit policy creating need for cash management	Small firms
Firms paying more attention to their quarterly reports and needing help with graphics, print production, and public relations	Companies concerned with public image and financial community
Interest in buying condominiums for office space	Professionals and small businesses
Corporations seeking to dispose of surplus real estate	Real estate brokers
Mergers and buyouts creating needs for legal advice and intercorporate gamesmanship	Corporations vulnerable to takeover
Need for organizational development consulting in firms with a predominance of mainly members at the top	Family-owned businesses
Estate planning to pass control of businesses to family	Founders of businesses
Security and protection against computer information theft	Organizations with proprietary information on computers
Need to increase meeting productivity	Managers
Need for understanding Japanese culture and business practices (or other countries where American companies are doing business)	Firms doing business in Japan or with Japanese businesses in the United States
Desire to involve workers in management functions to increase productivity	Factories and companies that have or want to remove midmanagement personnel
Need for international geographical, political, and economic knowledge	Companies interested in locating abroad
Shift to outsourcing data processing	Companies desiring to save money on that share of their budget
Legislative efforts to control health care costs	Companies confronted with rapidly increasing health benefit costs
Defending or improving children's TV programs	Corporations sponsoring children's TV programs
Need for general institutional management skills for hospitals that are failing from lack of management sophistication	Hospital managers
Chemical spill at manufacturing plant	Others using the given chemical
Irate employee goes on shooting spree	Security managers
Increases in consumer debt	Banks, finance companies

Generally, there is a time lag between the dramatic appearance of new conditions and an awareness by potential clients that the changes apply to them and that they need your services. This is true even if the need existed before events emphasized its existence. You can use this lead time to find the information and develop the skills you need. For example, lawyers needed marketing advice long before they were widely aware of this need. The few who took marketing seriously enough to seek expert advice benefited handsomely. The importance of the Supreme Court's advertising decision is not that it created a need among lawyers for marketing advice, but that it created an *awareness* of the need for marketing advice.

More than three years after this Supreme Court decision, less than 5 percent of all lawyers actually used advertising. Remember this example to avoid choosing a consulting specialty that you value but that your potential clients have yet to appreciate. Look instead for events and/or media coverage that focus the attention of potential clients on their need for a certain kind of service. In other words, look for the development of a new solution to a possibly long-standing problem among a class of potential clients.

Because of the lead time involved, you don't have to be able to deliver needed services now. You do, however, have to be able to combine your problem-solving and results-producing abilities with a relevant area of technology. The only requirement is that you quickly master the solution given your problem-solving abilities.

Danger Signals

Even when an opportunity meets all your requirements, you may have to walk away from a client if you detect one or more danger signals. These signals, listed below, indicate that for one reason or another the opportunity is not turning out as expected:

1. The presence of meaningful, market-saturating direct competition
2. Doubts about a potential client's ability to pay for your services
3. Doubts about a potential client's awareness of the need for your specialty area
4. Doubts about the value of your consulting to a potential client
5. The unsuitability of your talents or temperament to a client
6. Inefficient promotional channels

These danger signals also have another side. If an opportunity avoids all of these signals, you have a good chance to develop a new market for your consulting talents. If there is no direct meaningful competition and potential clients are able to pay for your services, if they are aware of the need for them and see them as valuable, and if they get along with you well and are easy to reach, how can you lose?

Direct Competition

All but the most "late-breaking" consulting opportunities probably include a few consultants. The question is usually not whether you have competition but who it is and how much is it. Your investigation of the competition, therefore, must be done in two stages.

Stage 1: *Make a list of all your possible competitors.* Sources for finding competitors include the following:

- Trade publications directed to your prospective client group—You'll find possible competitors among the advertisers and writers in these publications. Look especially for those listed as sources of advice or of support services especially designed for your potential client group. Concentrate on those who are making their services available in the geographic areas you expect to serve.
- *Consultants and Consulting Organizations Directory, Directory of Management Consultants,* and *Dun's Consultant Directory*—See also the "Consulting Directories and Reference Works" section of our bibliography for details on these and other references.
- Yellow pages of telephone books—Check under the appropriate listings: management/business consultants, training consultants, and the like.
- *Newsletters in Print, Oxbridge Directory of Newsletters,* and *Encyclopedia of Association Periodicals* (see the bibliography)—These references list newsletters and other publications for your potential clients. Their publishers and editors may be competitors themselves. If they aren't, they would certainly know who the competitors are!
- Other consultants and those who use consultants—Ask those you know who they know that are or may be offering the same kind of services you expect to provide.

Stage 2: *Determine how involved these competitors are in the field you are considering and in the geographic areas you expect to serve.* In addition, ascertain their plans for involvement. This research entails telephone interviews with your possible competitors, those who know about them, your potential clients, and newsletter editors in the field. Potential competitors may be reluctant to talk with you about their activities or plans in the area of your specialty because they consider you their competition. Perhaps they are interested in expanding into the specialty you are discussing. (And perhaps they are not making any plans, especially if they are unresponsive to all the topics you bring up.)

If you find direct competitors but the opportunity is otherwise a very attractive one, you must compare the significance of the competition to the size of the market. Maybe the market is big enough or complex enough to support many consultants. Or there may be a different subspecialty—or subspecialties—where you can create room for yourself. Limited competition may be healthy, particularly if you can identify certain weaknesses in competitors. Another alternative is to join forces with a competitor! After all, if joining forces to dominate a market were not often more advantageous for the parties than competing, the antitrust laws would be unnecessary.

Client's Ability to Pay

Regrettably, some clients in an otherwise viable market simply cannot pay for consulting services. Consider recent college graduates looking for jobs, who constitute an ideal client group in almost all respects. They know they need advice on marketing themselves to American industry. A large and easily accessible literature covers the kind of knowledge they need. The consulting you provide would unquestionably be very useful. And you have a highly efficient promotional channel for your consulting—the help-wanted pages of local newspapers. But these clients don't have the money to pay for one-to-one consulting.

Client's Lack of Awareness of Need

This danger signal is as deadly as a client's inability to pay, but the death is slower and more painful. A good example is the reaction of prospering physicians in highly specialized fields to the offer of marketing advice. Because they have plenty of patients, they don't think seriously about marketing. On the other hand, physicians generally recognize their need for outside help in managing their practices. In fact, engaging a management consultant is considered fashionable in some physician circles, and some marketing advice occasionally slips in through the back door with these consultants.

Unfortunately, many physicians close the door to marketing consultants. They neglect to plan for dangers to their prosperity, such as socialized medicine, increases in malpractice claims, the growing impact of health management organizations (HMOs), or competition from specialists in their field. They don't feel the need to fine-tune their images to get exactly the kinds of patients they want. From long tradition, physicians are reluctant to consider self-marketing, and no small-practice consultant can afford to overcome such an obstacle. As the competition continues to increase, however, more physicians will consider marketing, just as more and more dentists have.

Value of Your Services

Sometimes your solution to a client's problem turns out to be exotic and untried. It may be the type of answer that could be recognized nationally if it is successful—or could make a tombstone of your letterhead if it isn't right. Perhaps your answer to low productivity and morale is to have workers' pay levels voted on by fellow workers. The effect of this innovation could mean quantum leaps in productivity and profitability or one small leap into bankruptcy. The chance of success is very slim, too slim to justify betting your client's interests and your own survival.

Instead of an exotic, untried approach, you might consider a more orthodox solution to a problem or even withdrawing from the project. The rationale for greater orthodoxy is simple. Without word-of-mouth momentum, not even the most sophisticated promotional campaign can help you grow as a consultant. Betting on the momentum of a highly experimental solution entails more risk than you need to take. Conversely, with so many opportunities available, a prudent withdrawal from an exotic approach does not mean a loss of business. If you happen upon some unusual, innovative approach that becomes widely and highly valued, that is fine. Not only are you likely to have a built-in patent on your ideas, but someone will probably write a book about you. The chances for this kind of success, however, are slim and probably not worth the risk.

Unsuitability of Your Talents or Temperament to a Client

With the abundance of consulting opportunities, you have no reason to deal with people you don't like. Sometimes the personality of a client group makes it almost impossible for certain consultants to work with them. Some consultants are free-wheeling, others controlled and careful. Different client groups are comfortable with different styles of consulting. Accountants, for instance, want to work with no-nonsense, detail-oriented people. Higher levels of management in low-tech companies are usually not interested in discussing the details of new discoveries in engineering or science. They are more comfortable with generalists. On the other hand, upper management in high-tech firms usually are uncomfortable with generalists, especially if they lack a high-tech background.

In spite of these personality differences, some consultants give their so-called unsuitability so much importance that they often pass up excellent consulting opportunities. Perhaps they mistakenly think that they don't have the necessary capability. Or maybe they don't have the courage to present themselves to a class of consulting clients with whom they are not socially comfortable.

Don't overrate this danger signal. You have to take only two precautions when you sense it. First, be certain that you don't pass up an opportunity because it calls for a talent you forgot you had. Some of your most powerful talents may be invisible to you. Second, don't pass up an opportunity merely because you doubt your own authoritativeness in dealing with a potential client group. If the clients are truly aware of the need for your consulting and if you are certain of its value to them, your fear is groundless.

The real factor to look for is the extent to which your potential clients don't like you—or you don't like them.

Inefficient Promotional Channels

A client group may have all the earmarks of a splendid market except for its accessibility. Yet if you can't reach it, you have no opportunity. In this age of seemingly endless market segmentation, specialized mailing lists, and the Internet, you aren't likely to find any market group totally inaccessible. If gaining access to a group and communicating with it is difficult, you might find a quick and efficient alternative promotional method. If you can't, you might be better off foregoing the opportunity.

Effective marketers, including successful consultants, select a reachable market and then package their services to be both attractive and desirable to that market. A *reachable market* is one that can be promoted cost-effectively and efficiently. Dentists, for example, are easily identifiable, limited in number, and inexpensive to reach. They represent a reachable market. Contrast that market with people interested in improving the interface between worker-machine systems in the workplace. They are everywhere, but they are hard and expensive to identify and reach.

Concentrating on a particular market can create tremendous opportunities. One marketing consultant had an unusual start in the consulting business. At the age of 29, he left a company where he had served successfully for four years as sales manager and later as vice president of marketing. He had studied marketing, lived marketing, thought marketing, and practiced marketing. And he was smart enough to realize that the world could survive without another marketing consultant. He systematically reviewed five industries in which he had an interest. He noticed that for one of these industries, there seemed to be no marketing authority. Granted, it was a new and young field but one filled with opportunity.

This consultant established a goal for himself—to be the nationally recognized authority in this industry within three years. He was successful! He writes a monthly marketing-advice column in the industry's leading trade magazine. He speaks at national and three regional industry conventions. He charges $2,500 a day for his services and at this writing has a backlog of 87 days of consulting services. He is quoted, interviewed, and sought after on a regular basis by the "powers that be" in his field.

How did he achieve this success? By systematically applying the proven principles of marketing strategy and theory to a specific situation and market. True, he is a generalist—but one smart enough to promote himself as a specialist!

Saying No to Bad Business

If any of the danger signals discussed above appear, you may have to turn away a client. You have hung out your shingle and are in business, so a flat turndown is not good promotion. It is almost insulting. There are several better ways to say no. You can adopt one or more that suit you.

One way to say no is to respond, "I would love to work with you, but I don't offer that particular service." Then give a referral, making sure that the referred person can handle the project. A bad referral is almost as bad for you as a mishandled project. When you do not have a sure referral, offer the client several names, and state that you are not certain of their abilities. That response throws the obligation of the evaluation onto the client.

Saying you are too busy can create a false impression about your fee. When you are too busy, clients and some consultants may infer that you will soon raise your fees. If you are truly too busy but would like to do some work for the client later, you may not get the chance. Word may get out to other clients that your fees are high and that you are too busy. That impression, however false, hurts your chances not only with the one client but with others as well.

If you *are* too busy, be sure that any attempted refusal will work. Don't use a refusal technique that might corner you into taking on more work—no matter how high the fee. The following techniques are designed to either avoid taking on a project or get the work on your own terms.

Redefine the problem and accept the job on your own terms. For example, a county office of education was hoping to start the third year of a federal grant for a curriculum development program, and it needed an external evaluation as federal programs often do. The project was about a year behind schedule, and the county office was concerned about getting funds for the third year. An outside consultant who was offered $3,000 to do an evaluation contract decided that too much had to be done for the money and that the evaluation was too late to do any good anyway.

Instead of refusing directly, the consultant decided that a pilot study contract would be more appropriate. He asked a series of questions calculated to embarrass the office director: What are you going to do about sample size? What are you going to do about the lack of a control group? These questions were deliberately designed to surpass the director's ability to answer. If he wanted to be hired for an evaluation, the consultant would never have asked such questions. In fact, he knowingly killed his chances of being hired for that contract.

Finally, the director asked the consultant what he would do. When the consultant answered, he was then asked if he would be willing to contract for a pilot study if someone else did the evaluation. The consultant received a $23,000 contract to do the field study, and the director did hire someone else to do the evaluation report. The consultant, in other words, had redefined the problem on his own terms.

The consultant in our example understood that the client did not know a great deal about the problem at hand. Such is usually the case. Look at it this way: When clients don't know a lot about their problems, they are likely to feel all the more compelled to maintain control. They must let the consultant know they are not going to be hoodwinked. In actuality, clients typically formulate their strategy for two minutes on the elevator following lunch, just before they meet with you. In such a case, the first thing that a client has to do is impress you with how much thought was given to the problem. Some consultants are intimidated by this strategy and fail to propose alternative solutions.

When face-to-face with clients, just tell them, in some way, that they will have control. All you have to do in most cases is say: "I hear you. . . . I understand you. . . . I know you want control." Then propose your alternative solution. As long as you have properly communicated your understanding of clients' need for control, they are usually willing to accept another solution. Without saying so, they think you're an expert—and they haven't given the problem more than two minutes of thought anyway. They have no confidence in their own approach. They just want to avoid being taken advantage of.

High-bid the project. This strategy is not suitable to pedestrian consulting assignments because you come off looking just plain expensive. The project should involve a technical element or a judgmental area. You have to render a conclusion on how the job is to be done or on the quality of the job. In such instances you can high-bid the work in order to turn it down. The desirable feature of this approach is that you can't lose. If you go high and the client still wants you, the high fee is a sweet consolation for having to take on the work.

Misdefine the problem. Again, this approach works only in technical areas. If you misdefine a routine problem, you look dumb. When you misdefine a technical problem, however, the client figures you have a different approach, judgment, or philosophy. In most technical fields, people misdefine technical problems all the time. Frankly, no one knows whether you are right or wrong. Everyone has a different approach to a problem. Misdefining a technical problem, therefore, should not reflect unfavorably on your competence as a consultant, though you should exercise this strategy with discretion.

Accept only a portion of a project. Sometimes clients want to make their managerial duties easy by hiring one consultant to do everything. As the consultant, you might take on the assignment if you are willing to hire other consultants, staff, or resources. If you don't enjoy managing other consultants and staff, suggest you take only a piece of the project. Suppose a client wants a marketing study that includes billboards, experimental designs, and the supervision of field staff. You might offer to take just the experimental design part of the project. You really can't lose. If the client turns you away to avoid having another consultant to manage, you have said no to the business. If the client accepts your counterproposal, you have business on your own terms.

Conflicts of Interest

Conflicts of interest crop up in a number of ways. Suppose you are working full-time for a business organization, and one of its customers asks you to do some consulting. You are a natural for the work, but you might be taking business away from your employer. In such cases you have to assess the potential conflict and the attitude of the organization. Some are very rigid, almost paranoid, whereas others have relaxed policies.

Another potential source of conflicting interests arises when you're working for two or more clients who are competitors. You have two ways to handle this situation. So long as there is no conflict of interest in your estimation, inform each client of your work for the other. Tell both that no information or advantage can leak from one account to the other. If you haven't already done so, insist on signing a nondisclosure agreement with each client.

If you have a consulting opportunity that could grow into a conflict, on the other hand, your ethical obligation is to turn down the new work. Inform your existing client that you have received an offer of work that you perceive as a conflict of interest. Usually the client agrees. State that as long as you are working for the client, you won't take on work from the competitor. These steps are necessary both for the client's protection and for yours. The best protection for your reputation is honesty with all parties concerned.

When You Don't Have the Resources

Consultants sometimes have to pass up good opportunities because they don't have the resources to properly execute an assignment. Perhaps they don't have a sufficiently high-powered computer, adequate staff, or the necessary facilities. If a project is actually beyond your capabilities, you can hurt your reputation by taking it on and botching the job. Some projects are so big that they require a large team of consultants. If you can't manage or assemble such a team, perhaps you can recommend a leader and work as a team member. Other projects may call for skills you don't have. You can recommend another consultant who can handle the job, or you can work with one and use the skills you have.

In general, don't let an opportunity pass because you lack the resources. Today, you can usually subcontract with other consultants to perform the work you can't do yourself and do so at very favorable rates.

A marketing consultant to utility companies, for example, was asked to undertake a market segmentation study for one of her clients. Although her background provided her the ability to conceptualize the project and determine its steps and requirements, she did not have the database capability nor the survey background necessary to conduct the project. Rather than turn down the engagement, she found a marketing survey specialist and subcontracted with him to design and conduct the survey. She used the Internet to research database alternatives and found one suitable—in applicability and in rental price—to drive the study. By extending her own capability through using other specialists as well as external resources, she was not only able to conduct the project for her client but also create a whole new specialty area for her practice.

Don't give up consulting jobs because you lack the resources to do the job effectively. Subcontract with others and rent whatever you need!

Add-On Opportunities

Following the guidelines in this book, you should have no trouble enlarging the size of your clientele. At the same time, selling additional services to your existing clients is the kind of opportunity you can handle more efficiently and that can produce greater profit than a new account.

With new accounts, consultants spend a great deal of time establishing relationships instead of handling the problem that they were hired to solve. With an existing client, you don't have to spend time on such preliminaries as familiarizing yourself with the client's operation, meeting the people affected by your proposals, or marketing your services. You can spend more time dealing with the problems and justifiably receive more money for solving them.

Even though an add-on opportunity accompanies every account to one degree or another, some clients require add-on services more naturally than others, including the following:

- Some consulting has to be done on a continuous or periodic basis, such as keeping a customized software program in step with an organization as its business processes evolve over time.
- Some clients have a number of problems that call for modifications of the same solution. For instance, a changeover from the English to the metric system might have been so successful that a client will call upon the consultant to handle a change in accounting procedures, customer relations policies, or other transitions.
- Sometimes a very large client organization has a widespread problem that manifests itself in piecemeal fashion, and a consultant might be called upon to apply the same solution repeatedly. If the consultant successfully teaches the middle managers of a headquarters corporation how to build effective work teams, that consultant might then be contracted indefinitely to train the middle managers of all the corporation's branches.

Add-on opportunities are the bread and butter of a consulting practice. Add-ons do not require the expense involved in marketing yourself to new clients, and they will enhance your reputation as a problem solver. You will be seen as someone who can tackle a variety of problems, and that makes you a real asset to any company that retains you.

☞ Tips

The opportunities in consulting presented in Chapters 4 and 5 offer a new perspective on how to identify and exploit a broad range of possibilities. Too many consultants look only at what they have done in the past as a guide to the future. They ignore the new possibilities and needs that arise every day with the result that they may never use their talents to the fullest. By identifying opportunities and testing them against the danger signals for viability, you can broaden your horizons in the business world almost overnight.

Once you have identified the opportunities that you want to take advantage of, you have to market yourself. The next chapter shows you how to set up an effective marketing strategy and sell yourself so that you can turn these opportunities into income.

CHAPTER 6

Low-Cost/No-Cost Marketing

In the consulting business, as in most others, billings tend to rise or fall in direct relation to the energy, enthusiasm, and creativity invested in marketing. Yet many consultants simply do not see the need for it. Why not?

Two attitudes toward developing a consulting practice prevent consultants from properly marketing their services. Some consultants rely on their reputations to attract clients. Others are fascinated with the technical side of consulting and simply don't care about marketing. These attitudes and inclinations, as natural as they may be, can nullify the benefits of all your other work. If you really want success, you must make marketing—active, aggressive, effective marketing—part of your practice.

Consultants who rely on their reputations for selling assume that if they simply take care of their reputations, their reputations will take care of them. This rule of thumb is partially true. A poor reputation can undermine all your other efforts to grow, so a good reputation is the foundation for increasing business. However, it is only a foundation. It cannot yield the results that an active marketing plan produces.

A reputation does not take care of itself. You must take care of it as you would a plant. Waiting for your reputation to develop as a natural consequence of your consulting activities will shortchange you in the following ways:

- Your reputation may become outdated, giving you a high rating on abilities that no one needs anymore.
- Your reputation spreads haphazardly, and it probably does not reach all the prospective clients you want to reach to be successful.
- Your reputation may become distorted through word of mouth. You may not be credited with the kind of expertise that best suits your marketing approach.
- The passive approach does not bring a new consultant those first crucial clients and keeps the established consultant from getting the most desirable contracts.

FIGURE 6.1   Marketing Strategies Used by Consultants

Marketing Strategy	All Consultants	Pretax Income Greater than $110,000	Pretax Income Less than $55,000
Cold personal calls	58.5%	14.4%	70.7%
Direct mailing of brochures/ sales letters to cold lists	70.6	20.8	71.3
Provision of no-charge diagnostic services to prequalified leads	42.7	19.8	58.1
Promotion to similar clients on basis of referrals or names obtained from clients	60.5	71.6	22.9
Lectures to civic, trade, and professional audiences	17.8	40.1	9.6
Writing articles, books, newsletters for trade, professional, civic audiences	18.2	37.6	8.3

Source: *Economics of the Consulting, Training & Advisory Professions, Consulting Fees, Incomes, Operating Ratios, Marketing Strategies,* May 1991. Reprinted by permission of National Training Center.

Marketing often takes a back seat to the technical aspects of a consultant's work. Challenged and energized by apparently insoluble technical problems, most practitioners are frustrated when confronted with basic marketing responsibilities. They tend to put off the marketing work because they are too busy at the moment or because they have plenty of work already.

To be a competent consultant, you must be technically proficient, but you don't necessarily have to be adept at marketing. To be a competent and successful consultant, however, you must learn to be effective at marketing. At the same time, your services cannot be marketed like Coca-Cola, aluminum siding, or PCs. You want to *sell without selling* so that prospects come to you instead of your chasing after them.

This chapter will help you meet the challenge of marketing. Fortunately, the most effective approaches to selling yourself are also the least expensive. We will see that the most successful consultants use these low-cost/no-cost techniques, which have an effective track record for building viable, profitable consulting practices.

Planning Your Marketing Approach

Marketing strategies that consultants use have a profound effect on their chances of success. As advocates of indirect marketing techniques for consultants, we believe that the hard-sell techniques some consultants use are not as effective as indirect strategies, which are more like public relations activities. As an added bonus, these indirect, low-cost/no-cost techniques are much less expensive.

In semiannual studies of the economics of the consulting profession that Howard Shenson conducted routinely prior to his death in 1991, consultants were always asked several questions about the marketing strategies they deployed. The results were then correlated with the consultants' income levels (see Figure 6.1).

FIGURE 6.2   Earnings Curves of Consultants

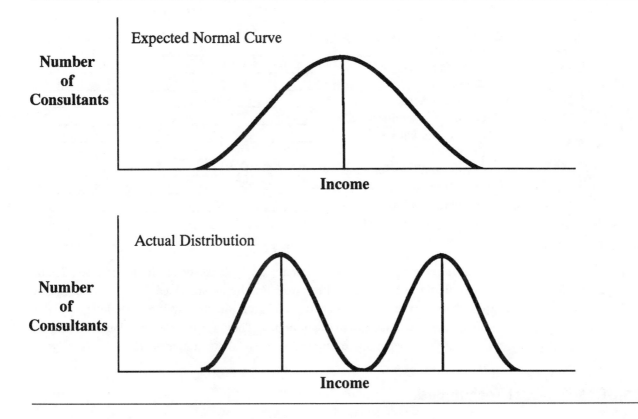

The data, which clearly demonstrate the value of different approaches to marketing, can serve as a guide to selecting the marketing strategies and techniques that are most effective for building your consulting practice.

We see significant differences in the kinds of marketing techniques used by consultants based on their income. Even though the data shown go back to 1991, very little has changed in the relationship between certain marketing techniques and consultants' income. The reason for these differences is related to the distribution of that income. You might expect that consultants would be distributed along a normal curve according to income, with a few having very high or very low incomes and most clustered in the middle of the income range. However, the actual curve is skewed (see Figure 6.2), with one large group clustered below the middle and another, actually smaller, group clustered well above the middle.

Consultants on the lower end of the scale seem to have a deprivation mentality. Lacking in self-image and self-confidence, they follow the very marketing strategies—cold calls and other direct types—that have been shown to be ineffective. Successful consultants, who have high self-confidence, rely on productive marketing strategies—the low cost/no-cost public relations techniques.

The degree to which different marketing techniques are successful is even more important as a guide to choosing your marketing approach than are the practices of other consultants. How would you rate the following different marketing strategies in terms of their productivity?

Marketing Strategy	How Successful Is This Strategy?		
	Very	*Somewhat*	*Not at All*
Cold personal calls	_____	_____	_____
Cold mailings	_____	_____	_____
Free diagnosis	_____	_____	_____
Cold phone calls	_____	_____	_____
Writing articles	_____	_____	_____
Giving free seminars	_____	_____	_____
Contact marketing	_____	_____	_____
Fee for diagnosis	_____	_____	_____
Giving seminars for a fee	_____	_____	_____
Prior client reference	_____	_____	_____
Newsletter publishing	_____	_____	_____
Speaking engagements	_____	_____	_____
Volunteering	_____	_____	_____

Cold contacts and giveaways, in fact, are the least successful techniques. Speaking, newsletter publishing, and referrals are the most successful. These successful approaches, also the least expensive, and activities like writing articles and giving seminars are low-cost/no-cost techniques. They are the indirect, public relations types of approaches to marketing that successful consultants use.

Low-Cost/No-Cost Techniques

Most of us are familiar with traditional marketing methods: ads in *The Wall Street Journal* or local newspapers or professional publications, direct mail campaigns, cold-call solicitations, country club membership, and the like. Although a few consultants have achieved success with such methods, we don't recommend them as primary marketing techniques. A less traditional approach—the low-cost/no-cost techniques—more closely suits the nature of consultants.

Most consultants are technicians who find marketing challenges frustrating. They don't enjoy the process and don't do well at it. To be successful at anything, you have to enjoy it. The low-cost/no-cost techniques help consultants enjoy marketing because they are lower key and more of a soft sell.

Pursuing clients in the traditional way puts consultants in an unfavorable position. Ideally, consultants should have potential clients come to them, but if a consultant does initiate a contact, the consultant is in a far better position if a client already knows about him or her—if the client is presold. Low-cost/no-cost techniques help either way by encouraging clients to seek you out or by paving the way for your acceptance when you approach them.

These techniques are more technical than traditional marketing methods, yet they have a profound impact on obtaining business. They bring the market to you and allow you to enjoy building a thriving practice. Here are the major low-cost/no-cost techniques:

- Requesting assistance in research
- The rubber chicken circuit—becoming a speaker

- Public and professional meetings
- Directories
- Newsletters
- Newspaper, magazine, and journal articles
- Using the Internet
- Letters to the editor
- Teaching
- Working the press
- Volunteering

Let's address these techniques one by one.

Requesting Assistance in Research

Because you are a consultant, the assumption is that you can bring a well-documented body of knowledge to the market of your choice. Remaining an effective consultant means staying current with developments in your field. You can turn this obligation into a three-step marketing tactic (see Figure 6.3):

1. List the important organizations and people in your field.
2. Write to each name on your list, asking to be kept abreast of any developments related to your field.
3. Publicize your research efforts, and market yourself and your abilities.

Several sources for your list would include those you already know or know of, news clippings about key people and organizations in your field, directories of associations, research organizations, publications, and rented mailing lists.

Once you have assembled your mailing list, send a letter to each individual on it to say that you are engaged in important research in your field and asking the person to assist. A letterhead with a prestigious, public service name will enhance your professional image. The most natural thing in the world is for recipients of your letter to keep you informed of their activities, even at some trouble and expense.

Beyond asking those on your list to send you information, you may ask to interview several that you see as potential prospects for your services. Most will oblige, ostensibly to provide service to the profession. In actuality, they will oblige because your request makes them feel important and reinforces their self-perception of being on the cutting edge of their field.

On the other hand, those you interview want to get information from you too. They expect an exchange with someone who is in touch with the latest trends in your area. They may get more information from the interview than they give you. This is acceptable because you want them to find out that you are competent and knowledgeable. Your aim is to establish yourself as an authority who offers the state of the art in your consulting specialization.

Your research efforts should be well publicized through press releases, newspaper or journal articles, and the like. When you make your knowledge and capability generally known, you are self-marketing. Your purpose is to make yourself and your abilities known to as many influential people as possible. As people begin to asso-

FIGURE 6.3 Requesting Assistance in Research Form

Important Organizations and People	Address and Phone	Date Initial Contact Made (Notes on Contact)	Dates Information Received	Date of Thank-You Letter Call/Sent/Made

ciate your name with your specialty, prospective clients will start coming to you. You can also achieve this result by using other low-cost/no-cost techniques.

You can let your list of information sources do double duty by pulling out the names of the most important sources—key company executives, trade association officers, trade publication editors, and the like. These key people tend to be the most influential names on your list. As such, they are also the busiest and least accessible.

If you contact these key people just to get general information or—worse—referrals, you are nothing to them but an unprofitable nuisance. On the contrary, if you approach them for their insights and thoughts for an upcoming article, book, or lecture, you become someone who can enhance their prestige and nourish their reputations. You are a source of important information who may be an authority with valuable insights to offer.

Your contacts become involved unwittingly in your future success. Because you will be delivering their thoughts to the world, they will make sure that those thoughts are properly recorded and that they receive the appropriate attention.

No matter how famous or important your contacts already are, they are flattered that their thoughts are important enough to be sought out for publication. Thus, they may even give you information that they might not dream of disclosing if they weren't enticed by the publicity your book, article, or speech offers.

Your key contacts may provide personal referrals to other important people, including potential clients. Their initial reluctance to talk with you is an attempt to avoid wasting time with unprofitable nuisances. Once you establish yourself and your particular manner of publicizing their views, they will do everything they can to help you—and themselves.

Two shrewd publishers recently launched a small textbook empire using these techniques. They had virtually no campus salespeople, and their competitors were giant publishing houses with scores of campus "reps." In producing their first college textbook, they sought the advice of dozens of prominent educators. They produced an excellent textbook and involved educators in its success. By the time the book appeared, the professors couldn't wait to get their hands on it. They talked about it with their colleagues, and they adopted it for their classes. It was, after all, partly their own creation! Within two years this text was the leading introductory text in the field—an incredible marketing coup.

The lesson is clear: When you involve influential people in your research efforts, they invariably become contacts. Whenever your contacts have the opportunity to recommend services of the type you sell, they are almost compelled to think of you favorably. They have a personal investment in your success.

The Rubber Chicken Circuit—Becoming a Speaker

Ours is an organized society. We group together on the basis of professions, business interests, and community affairs. Thousands of professional, technical, and civic organizations are in the United States. Hundreds meet every day. Every major hotel in this country rents its meeting rooms out each day to groups of professionals and business leaders for their weekly, monthly, quarterly, or annual meetings. Organizers of these meetings share two characteristics: They almost always serve chicken unless the group meets for breakfast, and they use a large number of speakers.

Consultants in the higher earnings brackets consider speaking and writing engagements powerful marketing tools. At least 30 percent of the most successful consultants are estimated to use these avenues frequently. Consultants in lower earnings brackets, however, report they rarely seek out or accept such opportunities, saying that articles and speeches are burdensome responsibilities. They are missing out on some powerful ways to sharpen their edge in the marketplace. Long after people have forgotten exactly what you said or wrote, they recall that you did it. Their natural assumption is that you are an authority.

Writing and speaking opportunities are two of the most effective ways for consultants to attract clients. Prospective clients are favorably impressed by a good performance, as are those in a position to refer business your way. Therefore, you should think twice before turning down these opportunities.

If you want to gain exposure to local business leaders and bankers, spend time talking before such organizations as a chamber of commerce or a Rotary or Lions Club. If you're interested in members of a particular profession, you can meet them at the appropriate professional and technical association meetings. Members who frequent these meetings are the most likely prospects for your services. They join certain associations and attend their meetings because they're looking for help, cooperation, and insight.

Speaking before these prospective clients is time well spent. People who speak to a group are presumed to be authorities! As a result, you gain a lot of professional exposure and stature. You also should get a lot of consulting business.

If you have ever belonged to an organization or, worse yet, been a program chairperson, you know how difficult it is to find good speakers who can say something of value to the membership. The demand for speakers always seems to outstrip the readily available supply. Perhaps the reason is not so much the dearth of speakers as it is the abundance of organizations.

In addition to professional, trade, business, and civic meetings, thousands of corporate and business training sessions are held each year. Being invited to make a presentation at a regional or national training session provides a golden opportunity to make contacts and get referrals. Speaking at a national meeting gives you the stamp of approval from the central office in the eyes of regional and local managers. And as a bonus, companies usually pay a fee for your work—sometimes a substantial one.

If you're not already in contact with organizations in your area that need speakers, look in the *Encyclopedia of Associations* or *National Trade and Professional Associations of the United States* (see the bibliography). These directories list the addresses of each organization's national headquarters. A call or letter to headquarters provides the names and addresses of those who head chapters in your community. Simply contact these local leaders and let them know about your interest and availability.

Invariably, you'll find ample opportunity to gain professional exposure before prospective clients. This exposure is enhanced if you're invited to speak at some of the many regional or national conventions, meetings, or trade shows.

At the local level, many organizations are unwilling to pay for your services as a speaker. But don't limit your exposure to only those organizations willing to pay you. If you want to use the lecture circuit to make money directly and immediately, other approaches would likely be more profitable. Then, too, when you're compensated for your efforts as a speaker, your tendency is to feel less free to market your services as a consultant.

When speaking to members of an organization, don't hide the fact that you are a consultant. Tell them what you do. Include descriptions of consulting situations with which you've been involved without disclosing confidential information. Let members of your audience see how they can benefit from your services as a consultant.

Hand out something interesting to the audience that contains your name, address, and phone number. Audience members may not need your services as a consultant today, and they may not need you for six months or a year, but anything that will help them remember you is to your benefit.

To be prepared at all times, create one or two talks about 15 to 25 minutes in length, keeping them ready for presentation whenever the opportunity arises. In selecting a topic, remember that broad, familiar subjects are more interesting to your listeners than a specific, time-sensitive, once-only kind of talk. Listeners almost always prefer to hear known information presented in a new fashion.

Public and Professional Meetings

You don't have to be the speaker at a meeting to create marketing opportunities—all you have to do is show up and circulate. If the meeting is in any way related to your area of interest, you can make your services known to other attendees. Some of them might be looking for your kind of consulting right then and there. The best opportunities, however, come from your active and significant involvement in the power structure of an organization.

Public meetings sometimes present business opportunities. These meetings include any get-togethers by local agencies, such as the school board, sewer district, or city council. Although you would probably be wasting your time by attending all of them, those that deal with issues and areas of interest to you are worth your attention. Even relevant meetings don't require your attendance from beginning to end.

To make the best use of your time at these meetings, confine your attention to the people who represent business opportunities. Professionals, for instance, show up at public meetings simply to satisfy themselves that their government is doing a good job. They can't be considered prospects. Entrepreneurs and small business owners, on the other hand, represent potentially rich opportunities. Don't make the common mistake of thinking that all consulting work comes from large corporations or big government agencies. Actually, a great deal of it is found with small businesses and entrepreneurs.

Professional organizations also provide an opportunity to make your services better known and to contact people who can benefit you professionally. As you work with other members, they come to recognize your skills and expertise. When they need consulting services, you're a natural in their minds.

Membership in organizations is a low-cost but highly effective self-marketing technique, yet worth little if you're not active. Merely joining and paying dues is not enough—you have to be a worker. Because you should plan on devoting time to the organizations of your choice, join only one or two. Then select the two most important active committees and become involved.

Membership in a professional association enabled one young training director in private industry to get his career started. Extremely introverted, he didn't come off well when he first met people, and he was having trouble convincing prospective employers of his worth. After bouncing around from one job to another, he considered leaving his hometown, Minneapolis, for a larger city where he felt that opportunities in his chosen field would be better. Instead, acting on the advice of a friend, he became active in the local chapter of the training professionals association, working on committees and participating in the association's affairs with a number of people. Potential employers got to know him and his skills. He overcame his introversion as he got to know these people and eventually landed a better job with one of the association members.

Which organizations are for you? Review such publications as the *Encyclopedia of Associations* (see the bibliography), and select organizations whose membership would likely include candidates for your services. Attend a few meetings, size up the group, and make your selection.

Directories

Another low-cost/no-cost marketing approach is a listing as a consultant in one or more association directories. In about 40 percent of cases, the listings are free. Roughly another 30 percent offer listings in the form of paid advertising spots about the size of a business card with a message about your service. Although the other 30 percent of directories don't offer either paid or free listings for consultants, they might accept general advertising, and you should consider a listing in these directories as well.

Most professional associations for consultants publish directories or rosters of their members. Perhaps the best known and most comprehensive directory of consultants is published by Gale Research Inc. of Detroit, Michigan—*Consultants and Consulting Organizations Directory*. There is no charge for being listed in its directory, which can be found in major public, academic, and corporate libraries. Updated periodically, the directory provides an excellent means of exposure for consultants (see the bibliography for more information).

Use the *Encyclopedia of Associations* or *National Trade and Professional Associations of the United States* (see the bibliography) to identify the associations related to your market. Then simply inquire about the nature and availability of their directory listings.

Newsletters

More than 25,000 newsletters are published in this country, many thousands of which are business and professional ones. As instruments of communication, they channel a great deal of information to large numbers of people—often at a low cost to both editors and recipients. As business enterprises, some make a lot of money for their publishers.

More than half of the newsletters published in this country are given away free as extremely effective, high-level marketing devices. Consultants often give them to potential clients, selling either single copies or subscriptions to others. Typically, consultants find a few hundred people who are good prospects and send each a free newsletter. With the newsletter they establish a medium for technical, professional dialogue about a variety of topics. As an added feature, the publication permits mention of their consulting activities.

Most newsletters are done on a personal computer with a simple word-processing program and shipped out for a quick, limited printing run. The most important consideration is that the news is relevant and highly interesting to readers. Usually, content bears more weight than appearance. See the sample newsletter in Figure 6.4.

Newsletters are superb marketing instruments that have worked for many consultants. If you feel that a newsletter is right for your consulting specialty, you'll want to select subjects that don't reveal any proprietary information. You can concentrate on subareas in your field of specialization—judicial decisions, legislation, new products and services, book reviews, and many others. If you feel that a newsletter is a good marketing tool for you, the next question is: How do I get started?

If you plan to use a newsletter as a promotional vehicle, just send copies to all groups who are prospective clients. If you want to make a profit on the publication, you have to identify a group that needs information that is currently unavailable from any other source. Scout out the competition by checking publication listings and the *Newsletters in Print* directory (see the bibliography). Get sample copies from publishers of newsletters and magazines in your area. Before starting a for-profit newsletter, make sure that the intended reader group is willing to pay for it and that they are easy to identify.

Because your newsletter will probably offer highly specialized information, your market will be narrow, allowing you to use articles on precise topics. If the material is too broad, it isn't likely to hold your readers' interest. By concentrating on such subjects as new books, research results, patent news, judicial decisions, and new legislation, you can provide information that is publicly available and yet not worth your readers' time to track down. You perform a service without giving away information that is a profitable part of your consulting practice. With this approach the topics and ideas will be easy to research and write.

Your newsletter should target those who are actually interested in its contents. Start with those who know you and are interested in what you have to say, then extend your readership by renting inexpensive mailing lists for a direct mail promotion. Consider obtaining prequalified leads from small-space ads in various publications.

The experience of some newsletter publishers suggests that the most effective way to market a newsletter as a profit undertaking is to provide prospective readers with one or more sample copies. You might send prospects sample copies once a month for three months. With the first two copies, simply solicit a subscription order. In the final copy, inform readers that this is their last chance to get the newsletter unless they subscribe.

Getting the News. You want to accumulate more news than you could ever use. Get on everyone's mailing list. Cull through every article and column, focusing on material related to your area. Then direct your attention to what you write down. If your newsletter deals only with legislation affecting the oil industry, select material concentrated in that area.

FIGURE 6.4   Sample Newsletter

The Professional Consultant

Issue # 1547

ISSN 0272-8559

Paul L. Franklin, Editor
National Training Center
123 NW Second Ave., Suite 405
Portland, OR 97209 USA
Telephone 503/224-8834
Facsimile 503/224-2104

The Professional Consultant newsletter serves as the official publication of the Academy of Professional Consultants & Advisors (APCA) and is included as a part of membership dues.

Issues of *The Professional Consultant* are distributed to members of the Association of Independent Consultants (AIC).

Subscriptions: $120 per year (12 issues) may be paid by Visa, MasterCard, American Express, Discover or check made payable to National Training Center. Air delivery beyond North America add $18. Single issues: Subscribers & APCA members $8, non-subscribers $12, Survey issue $29. Telephone and fax subscription orders accepted.

The Professional Consultant is available by fax. For information and pricing contact Faxitron, Inc. at 213/475-4901 or fax 213/475-1368.

Postage paid at Portland, Oregon. Postmaster: send address changes to: *The Professional Consultant*, Paul L. Franklin, 123 NW Second Avenue, Suite 405, Portland, OR 97209.

Momentum Plus Presence Equals Success

You meet. You talk about problems they are encountering. You are sure that you have found a prospect.

You send some information about your business and its capabilities. You even zero in on the benefits they can derive from engaging you.

You suggest they call to discuss their needs further. You hear nothing. So you call and call but are unable to connect. Finally, the prospect takes your call but is disinterested in addressing the issues you had previously discussed.

You get busy with other projects and give up trying to contact the new prospect. Time passes. The prospect decides to act and hires another consultant to handle the problems you helped him clarify.

I see and hear this scenario play out every day among the consultants I work with and talk to...Prospects failing to do what we want: **to act** on the needs we can help them address **when we think** they should act.

It is all too easy to take prospects inaction personally -- to believe that they don't like you, don't value your services, didn't like what you had to say and so on.

In reality, prospects -- like all humans -- act when they are ready to act...<u>not</u> when we want them to act.

There may be any number of reasons that someone doesn't act today, tomorrow or the next day but will move three weeks from now. Something provides *momentum for action* and they move.

The key for the consultant is to *be present* when there is momentum to action among prospects. That presence does not have to be physical. It can come through the use of a variety of media that keep you freshly in the mind of the prospect.

Establishing presence requires acknowledging that people move on <u>their</u> <u>schedule</u> not yours. It then requires a strategy for continuous, <u>tasteful</u> <u>contact</u> so that they do not forget about you.

Therein lies the challenge to consulting success: finding innovative ways to remind your target market of your potential value in ways that don't put them off <u>and</u> that will have them think of you when they are ready to act. ❑

FIGURE 6.4 Sample Newsletter (Continued)

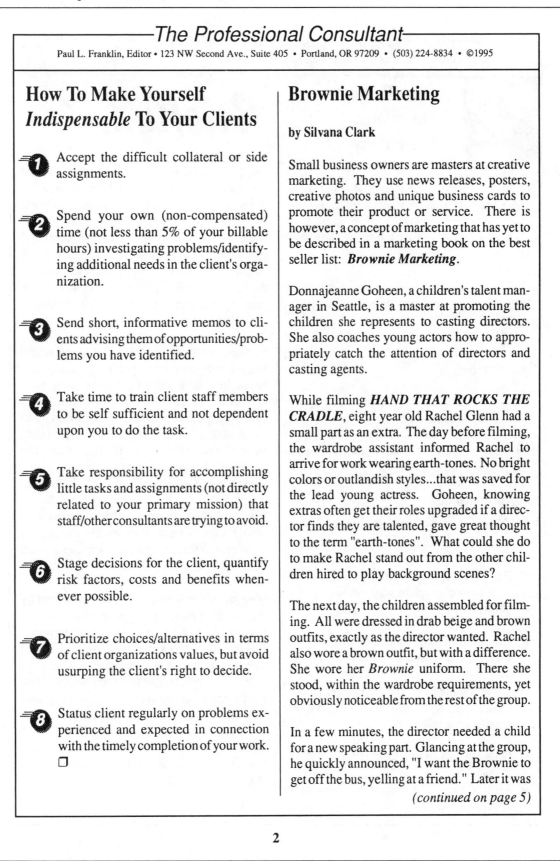

The Professional Consultant

Paul L. Franklin, Editor • 123 NW Second Ave., Suite 405 • Portland, OR 97209 • (503) 224-8834 • ©1995

How To Make Yourself *Indispensable* To Your Clients

1 Accept the difficult collateral or side assignments.

2 Spend your own (non-compensated) time (not less than 5% of your billable hours) investigating problems/identifying additional needs in the client's organization.

3 Send short, informative memos to clients advising them of opportunities/problems you have identified.

4 Take time to train client staff members to be self sufficient and not dependent upon you to do the task.

5 Take responsibility for accomplishing little tasks and assignments (not directly related to your primary mission) that staff/other consultants are trying to avoid.

6 Stage decisions for the client, quantify risk factors, costs and benefits whenever possible.

7 Prioritize choices/alternatives in terms of client organizations values, but avoid usurping the client's right to decide.

8 Status client regularly on problems experienced and expected in connection with the timely completion of your work. ❑

Brownie Marketing

by Silvana Clark

Small business owners are masters at creative marketing. They use news releases, posters, creative photos and unique business cards to promote their product or service. There is however, a concept of marketing that has yet to be described in a marketing book on the best seller list: *Brownie Marketing*.

Donnajeanne Goheen, a children's talent manager in Seattle, is a master at promoting the children she represents to casting directors. She also coaches young actors how to appropriately catch the attention of directors and casting agents.

While filming *HAND THAT ROCKS THE CRADLE*, eight year old Rachel Glenn had a small part as an extra. The day before filming, the wardrobe assistant informed Rachel to arrive for work wearing earth-tones. No bright colors or outlandish styles...that was saved for the lead young actress. Goheen, knowing extras often get their roles upgraded if a director finds they are talented, gave great thought to the term "earth-tones". What could she do to make Rachel stand out from the other children hired to play background scenes?

The next day, the children assembled for filming. All were dressed in drab beige and brown outfits, exactly as the director wanted. Rachel also wore a brown outfit, but with a difference. She wore her *Brownie* uniform. There she stood, within the wardrobe requirements, yet obviously noticeable from the rest of the group.

In a few minutes, the director needed a child for a new speaking part. Glancing at the group, he quickly announced, "I want the Brownie to get off the bus, yelling at a friend." Later it was

(continued on page 5)

2

FIGURE 6.4   Sample Newsletter (Continued)

—The Professional Consultant—

Paul L. Franklin, Editor • 123 NW Second Ave., Suite 405 • Portland, OR 97209 • (503) 224-8834 • ©1995

How To Answer Questions Effectively

Listen for both the content (what is asked) and the intent (what is meant) of the question.

Acknowledge the question; i.e., show that you understand it, or if necessary...

Ask for clarification from the questioner. Paraphrasing the question is one way of seeking clarification.

Answer the question: accurately, completely, briefly.

Verify the questioner's satisfaction. Has your answer been responsive?

Be ready to **Offer** proof, clarification or support of your ideas.

Avoid the following:

✔ Showing you feel that the question is stupid, or ill-conceived.

✔ Being unresponsive, or flippant. If you can't answer, explain why not simply and politely.

✔ Going off on long-winded diatribes. Keep your answers concise, to the point.

✔ Diverting the question needlessly. If you must divert it, be sure to try to give the answer later on.

✔ Going off on an unrelated tangent.

✔ Treating two questions as one. This can be confusing. ❐

Briefly...

Meal and entertainment deductions would go back to 80% if bill in House of Representatives goes through. Rep. Toby Roth, R. Wis., is pushing the Travel and Tourism Relief Act which would restore the meal and entertainment deduction from 50% to 80% of actual expenditure. Among other tax breaks, the bill would also broaden tax deductions for meeting attendance abroad and for promoting incoming international travel.

Directory of State and Regional Associations is a must if you want to pursue speaking and/ or writing as a means of promoting your services.   Over 7,400 regional and state associations are listed, including timing and location of meetings and conferences; the size, format and editor of publications; the membership composition; and more. Available for $60 from Columbia Books, 202-898-0662.

The American Institute of Small Business has a library of books on virtually any subject of import to starting and/or operating a small business. Call 800-328-2906 for a listing.

New business helpline has been initiated by the NFIB Foundation, an affiliate of the National Federation of Independent Businesses. The 900-line has a series of advice messages that each average about four minutes in length. Topics range from how to get a bank loan to cost cutting ideas to complying with various federal laws and regulations (e.g., independent contractor status). The first 15 seconds of each message is free. Thereafter the cost is 95 cents per minute. Call 900-820-6342. ❐

3

FIGURE 6.4 Sample Newsletter (Continued)

The Professional Consultant

Paul L. Franklin, Editor • 123 NW Second Ave., Suite 405 • Portland, OR 97209 • (503) 224-8834 • ©1995

Using Newsletters To Build Consulting Business

by Dr. Rick Crandall

Newsletters are an excellent low key marketing tool. They can build or sustain relationships and build your credibility. They keep you in people's minds and give them valuable information free. And if you do a really good newsletter, it can become a profit center in itself, by selling either subscriptions or advertising.

Keep Your Goal In Mind

Always keep in mind the purpose of your newsletter. It may provide some ego gratification in being able to broadcast your opinions, but its real purpose should be to build your image and cause people to want to talk to you further. It should try to represent you when you're not there. It should be your foot in the door. It should get you business! A newsletter is particularly useful to send to people you don't know. It starts a "relationship" by letting them know that you exist.

Two Ways to Offer A Newsletter

There are two general ways to have a newsletter to send out. One extreme is to buy a newsletter that is "franchised" to you. That is, another company writes a generic newsletter and sells it to many different businesses. Each of you gets an exclusive territory and receives copies of the general product specially imprinted with your company name.

For instance, in the printing industry, there are many people who send masters of a newsletter to printers. The printers then add their names to the top, print them and send them to customers. There are many companies that create such "stock" newsletters, but none are focused on consultants. (See the end of this article for a few sources.)

The other extreme is to produce the entire newsletter yourself. In between these two extremes would be hiring people to do various degrees of the work for you or getting some of your material from other sources (see source list at end).

Custom Newsletters

Many marketing, advertising or PR firms will create custom newsletters for you. They generally interview you to get ideas and then go away to write it as if they were you.

This approach can be fairly expensive. However, a few hundred or even a few thousand dollars may not be too much to have a professional marketing piece that doesn't take your time. If you are a larger company, you may even be able to have one newsletter that works for your combined customers, prospects, and employees.

The Best Newsletter Is Personal

Your goal for your newsletter should be to *keep* you in the minds of others, *build* your image, and *support* a relationship. The best way to do this is with personal letters each month to everyone in your list. In addition, you'd add articles or clippings just for them. Every month, or quarter, you'd send a different item in the mail. You could send an article you've written for another publication, or an interesting clipping that you thought would apply to their businesses. From the recipient's point-of-view, these non-newsletter pieces of mail are more personal because they are individually customized for each of them.

If you only want to contact 10 or 20 people a month, I recommend that you use this com-

(continued on page 5)

4

FIGURE 6.4 Sample Newsletter (Continued)

─────The Professional Consultant─────

Paul L. Franklin, Editor • 123 NW Second Ave., Suite 405 • Portland, OR 97209 • (503) 224-8834 • ©1995

(continued from page 4)

pletely personal approach. Only you will know that you're doing it systematically and some of the material may be the same for each recipient.

As soon as you begin to produce an official newsletter, it becomes a little less personal. You use a newsletter when you have many people to reach, and you can't write each of them a personal letter (with things that would be valuable to each of them).

In order to get the most out of sending out the newsletter, I highly recommend that you send a brief note--perhaps a Post-It note--personalized for as many people as possible. For instance, the first time you send it to someone you don't know, that personal note might simply be: "I thought you might be interested in this newsletter," and why you're sending it to them (e.g. because you saw their name in a particular place).

Your Image vs. Immediate Business
Newsletters are a general image-builder. When you speak to people, they'll often comment on having received it.

That's nice, and it can lead to a better relationship and more business in the long run. But most newsletters don't stimulate much direct business immediately. Remember, your object is not to produce a great newsletter, but to get more business long term *and* short term.

To make your newsletter stimulate business more directly, you have to write items that require people to call you for more details. For instance, for a short item, you can add a note to call you for more information, a free checklist, etc.

Remember that you don't want your newsletter to be viewed as advertising. And you don't

want to tease recipients. If you're writing an article about ways to manage a construction project, have a complete article. But you can mention at the end that you have two or three worksheets available if readers would like to call or fax you for a copy. This gives you information about an active interest of theirs, which can be the basis for a discussion and a possible offer of your services. In every issue, try to have a reason for people to call you to get more information or a free handout.

(EDITOR'S NOTE: Dr. Crandall publishes a number of subscription business newsletters. His company is considering offering a "stock" general business newsletter for consultants to send to their clients. He also has a new book out called "Marketing Your Services: For People Who HATE to Sell," $15.95, 415/924-1612. It has six pages of free editorial material readers can use in their newsletters.) ❏

─────────────

Brownie (continued from page 4)

announced, "Get the Brownie to be in front at the school assembly scene". Rachel found herself as a featured extra, complete with speaking lines and a higher pay scale.

Brownie Marketing. A simple concept overlooked by small business owners. What can you do to catch the attention of your clients? A subtle touch can get positive results, as shown by Rachel's choice of clothes.

(EDITOR'S NOTE: The above article was taken from, TAMING THE MARKETING JUNGLE, by Silvana Clark. Available for $6.95 plus $2 shipping from: Memory Makers, 3024 Haggin St. Bellingham, WA 98226 (206) 734-9506) ❏

5

FIGURE 6.4 Sample Newsletter (Continued)

The Professional Consultant

Paul L. Franklin, Editor • 123 NW Second Ave., Suite 405 • Portland, OR 97209 • (503) 224-8834 • ©1995

---

13 Tips For Getting Consulting Assignments From Seminars

Conducting seminars remains a very good strategy for marketing consulting services. One reason is that the right seminar topic properly promoted virtually guarantees that those in attendance are potential prospects for your consulting services.

Just conducting a seminar, however, does not guarantee that consulting work will follow. You must take some steps to nurture and increase the possibility of follow-up consulting work. Here's 13 easy steps you can take to enhance the likelihood of follow-up assignments.

1. Send participants at your seminar follow-up letters. For example, mail them a copy of a report of interest; or, your views on a new development in your field.

2. Display your phone number and tell attendees that they are welcome to call you with quick questions.

3. Make yourself available well before and after each day's session and during coffee breaks to answer questions and get to know attendees personally. Don't think of yourself as a paid lecturer but as a host to a group of professionals who value your presence.

4. Develop a systematic way of following-up with your alumni, such as a newsletter or a quarterly report.

5. Constantly relate to saving dollars, increasing revenues or improving productivity so that attendees know that you are results-oriented and practical in your thinking.

6. Have dinner and/or drinks with attendees.

7. Don't hold back information during a program. Share what you know. Attendees expect it and will resent the slightest hint that you are keeping certain information to yourself for use as a consultant.

8. Make certain the biographical information in the marketing material and handouts stresses your accomplishments.

9. Develop some handouts that you can occasionally update and distribute at the program to demonstrate that you are not only on top of developments, but constantly revising and tailoring the program for each group of attendees.

10. Display some of the reports, samples, or projects that you've consulted on. Be careful, however, to make sure they come across as educational and not a form of advertising.

11. Cite current developments, key people, recent figures, to demonstrate that you are really on top of developments in the field.

12. Dress conservatively. Dress styles vary throughout the country. Better to play it safe than to encourage attendees to focus on your dress rather than on your ability.

13. Do a superb job...and consulting will follow.

Finally, remember that seminar participants are just like any other group of prospects. They may not immediately follow the seminar with a consulting assignment for you. But, if you do a good job in the seminar and stay in touch with them over time, they are likely to think of you when they need help downstream. ❏

6

FIGURE 6.4   Sample Newsletter (Continued)

The Professional Consultant

Paul L. Franklin, Editor • 123 NW Second Ave., Suite 405 • Portland, OR 97209 • (503) 224-8834 • ©1995

THE PROFIT CORNER

by Chris Brandlon

There are five essential questions you can ask every business owner you speak with, questions that will help you uncover the fundamental opportunities that lie hidden in most businesses. Learning to ask these questions and interpret the answers is the most important skill you need to master in order to help your clients to greater success. Regardless of your consulting specialty, you will find new avenues for leveraging your value to clients by asking these key questions.

1. What business are you in?

The answer to this question, and the follow-up questions you ask to clarify, will tell you how clear the business owner is on his/her vision for the company. If she cannot give a clear and concise description of the company's industry and their place in it, she probably needs help with positioning her business for greater profits (developing a compelling Unique Competitive Advantage, for example).

2. How do you generate revenue?

Can the owner describe his sales process? Where does his income originate? Is the business oriented to the consumer market? Are they wholesalers or do they supply industry? What's their sales process? The answer to questions like these show points of leverage for improving sales results.

3. How do you reach your customers?

This self-evident question is aimed at developing a starting point for a discussion on how to leverage their marketing efforts. Follow up questions include what kind of advertising they use, whether and how much direct mail they send, whether and how they capture names and addresses of customers and prospects, etc.

4. What do you do to go back to your customers after they buy from you?

Even some of the best-run businesses don't do anything with their "back end." If anyone can give you a detailed accounting of how they continue selling to customers again and again, the chances are they are a very sophisticated marketer.

5. What is the "Relationship Value" of a customer?

Most business owners calculate their return on marketing dollars by figuring out whether they made money on the initial transactions resulting from any particular ad or direct mail campaign. In reality, however, the new customers generated by marketing will continue to buy for as long as the business serves them well. Knowing the dollar value of a customer over the life of the business relationship is crucial to making intelligent marketing decisions. This little-known figure is actually as important as profit margin to a business' future health.

Remember, the most successful consultant is the one who asks the best questions!

(EDITOR'S NOTE: Chris Brandlon offers advice to online marketers through his Portland-based business, ProfitAble Ventures. You can reach Chris at 13500 SW Pacific Hwy. #707, Tigard, OR 97223 or call 503/759-2030 or email to profitsa@IX.netcom.com) ❑

7

FIGURE 6.4   Sample Newsletter (Continued)

The Professional Consultant

Paul L. Franklin, Editor • 123 NW Second Ave., Suite 405 • Portland, OR 97209 • (503) 224-8834 • ©1995

MARKETING TIPS

Learn as much about your client's business as possible. Meet and get to know as many people as possible inside the company. <u>Really</u> listen and look for other consulting opportunities within the client's enterprise.

◆ ◆ ◆

Respond to your mail as quickly as possible. Set a time limit for your response to mail. Divide your stack between routine mail that does not require a quick response and mail coming from clients and/or prospects. Correspondence in the latter group should receive a quick response - at least within two days.

◆ ◆ ◆

Return telephone calls as quickly as possible. Again, have a rule for response and try to live by it. Example: all phone calls from clients and prospects returned within two hours. Other calls (deserving a return) within the day. More consulting business is lost due to failure to respond quickly to client and prospect inquiries than for any other reason. Do not let this one get you.

◆ ◆ ◆

Graphically demonstrate to clients that you are listening. Some behaviors demonstrate you are listening: taking notes; asking for clarification; restating; nodding in affirmation; open body language. Some behaviors that suggest you are not listening: finishing statements for the client; interrupting; rejecting directly or indirectly their statements/assumptions; closed body language, particularly folded arms.

◆ ◆ ◆

Subscribe Today:

Just one good idea is worth the investment.

Make *The Professional Consultant* a part of your professional development. Don't miss news about vital trends and strategies important for your professional success!

❑ YES! Please start my subscription to *The Professional Consultant* immediately:

❑ One year subscription (12 issues) for $120
❑ Two year subscription (24 issues) for $200
❑ Air Service beyond North America, add $187/year

Method of Payment: ❑ VISA   ❑   MasterCard   ❑   AmEx   ❑ Discover   ❑   Check

Card Number

Expires   Signature

Name

Firm/Organization

Address

City   State   Zip Code

Area Code & Phone

Paul L. Franklin, CPC
123 NW Second Ave., Suite 405 • Portland, OR 97209 • 503/224-8834
Fax: 503/224-2104

Paul L. Franklin
123 NW Second Ave., Suite 405
Portland, OR 97209

First Class Mail
U.S. POSTAGE
PAID
Portland, OR
Permit No. 637

8

Pay attention to people news. Readers love news about others in their profession who got promoted, demoted, born, "done in," ripped off, convicted, released, or otherwise caught in the limelight. Your subscribers are a great source of news, and they invariably enjoy the opportunity to assist you.

Writing the Newsletter. If you've done everything correctly up to this point, the rest is a downhill glide. Your news-prospecting tactics should have filled your mail with hundreds of potential news items. You have only to sort out those that will be of greatest interest to your readers.

Follow the following three rules:

1. *Select regular news categories as ongoing features in all issues.* Such topics as industry meetings, conventions, new products, and merger news are appropriate. Devote a half to a full page to each topic, and your newsletter will be organized and blocked out.
2. *Be terse and concise.* Use a crisp, catchy writing style.
3. *Design an easy-to-use format.* Keep it simple to give the impression that it is hot off the presses and to make your job easier.

Now that you are ready to go, start writing the news.

Keeping Readers/Subscribers Happy. After your readers have completed your newsletter, you want them to think: This was better than I expected. If the publication is supposed to promote your consulting practice, a sharp format with good information reflects favorably on your competence. If you are publishing for profit, keeping your readers happy attracts subscription renewals and new subscribers. Communicate with your readers. Find out what they like and what they don't. Give them what they want.

You need to set a competitive subscription rate on a for-profit newsletter. Because you are setting a price for a product, you must contend with the elusive volume-price relationship. In some markets the price has a direct bearing on the volume you sell. If the market is elastic, high prices can turn off part of your readership. If it is inelastic, it yields higher profits in proportion to higher prices and is comparatively insensitive to high prices. How do you find the right price? Unfortunately, no formula can give you the answer. You have to keep testing the market to find out the effects of various prices on your subscription volume.

Publishing Newspaper, Magazine, and Journal Articles

More than 9,000 technical and professional publications and 9,000 house organs are published in the United States. Many accept unsolicited manuscripts on topics of direct interest to their readers. These publications are usually desperately short of good articles and often pay a modest sum to writers. Take advantage of this scarcity. Newspapers are less likely to publish unsolicited articles, but they frequently will consider columns, although you'll rarely be paid for them. In addition, newspapers often seek expert opinions in various areas to add to the depth of stories. Make yourself and your area of expertise known to the reporters covering your special area of knowledge.

Publishing articles gives you valuable professional exposure and recognition. To gain actual consulting opportunities, however, you must place your articles with the right periodicals. In some cases an article might fail to generate business because it didn't contain any information of value. More likely, the article didn't work because it was published in a periodical that was largely or exclusively academic or theoretical—a readership that is just not in the market for consulting services. Few people other than professors and graduate students read the theoretical journals, so you can't expect much response to articles in these publications. Furthermore, with so many professors trying to get published, the backlog of articles is up to three years for some journals.

Instead of academic journals, publish your articles in periodicals and newspapers that are read by practicing professionals and businesspeople. Be certain your articles contain solid information of value to the readers. Let them know you are a consultant. To drive your point home, include actual experiences or cases (without disclosing names or confidential information). Include a biography of yourself with enough information to enable readers to get in touch with you. You might even express an interest in hearing from people who wish to pursue the topic in greater depth. Also include a picture of yourself—publications like to use photos to break up long blocks of type, and a photo with your article enhances your professional image.

Some writer-consultants get a lot of mileage out of their writing efforts. A consultant in one of my seminars recently provided me with an excellent case in point. He published 65 articles in various house organs in one year! Although that many articles might sound like a full-time job in itself, the fact is that he wrote only 4 basic articles. By changing the industries' and companies' names, he multiplied the 4 into 68, of which 65 were published. With each article he required his standard "bio" to be printed; it included his name, photo, address, the fact that he is a consultant, the kind of consulting he does, and some of his experience. He was deluged with more business opportunities than he could handle.

Success stories like this one give rise to the next question: Where do I get published? For professional and technical publications, try *Business Publications' Rates and Data* for the names of suitable publications. Also try *Encyclopedia of Association Periodicals, The Working Press of the Nation: Volume 2-Magazine Directory,* and *Scientific and Technical Organizations and Agencies Directory* (the latter lists and describes the organizations' publications). Some people find *Writer's Market: Where & How To Sell What You Write* an excellent starting point because of the list of technical and professional journals provided. For publishers' addresses and telephone numbers, consult *Literary Market Place* or *Publishers Directory.* All of these books are listed in the first section of the bibliography. When you have the names and numbers of the publications that suit your purpose, call or write each one to ask for a copy of its manuscript requirements.

Pay attention to what topics are being written about in your area. Write about controversial subjects or areas where there is a genuine need for information. With enough good material and a little persistence, you should be able to place several articles. To be published in a newspaper or quoted in a newspaper story, simply identify all newspapers, both paid circulation and free delivery, within the geographic area you select. Contact each with a sample column, some ideas of future columns, and your marketing package.

Using the Internet

Technology now allows you to reach your target audience with valuable information without printing and mailing a newsletter or finding a publication to carry your writing. The Internet provides a variety of alternative strategies for promoting yourself and your services beyond setting up your own World Wide Web page or being part of a listing of consultants (see Chapter 2 for details on these Internet options).

The best way to think of alternate opportunities on the Internet is to think of it as a massive, yet easily accessible, compendium of information and information providers. Just as there are thousands of published trade journals and periodicals, there are thousands of sites on the Internet that provide computer-accessible information in periodical form.

Do some research—some surfing on the Internet—and look for resources that are directing information, research, news, services, and the like to the audience(s) you also want to reach. Contact them and offer to write an article for their site or to share research or interesting findings from a recent consultation. In short, use the same strategy you would use to get an article published; just change the focus from journal editor to Internet site editor.

Do another surf to identify forums, "chat rooms," and other discussion venues—periodic or routine—that address your area of consulting specialty. Join these discussions. Showcase your capability and expertise without being overbearing or overzealous. Let other participants in the forum know you are a consultant but avoid "pitching" your services. See the process as one of developing relationships from afar. Let others conclude from the quality and value of your participation that your services might be useful to them.

If you can't locate an appropriate forum, set up your own, placing yourself at the center as the moderator while remembering it may cost money. Another, perhaps better, option is to try to set up a moderated forum for an established site on the Internet that is already reaching your target audience.

A marketing consultant who specializes in seminar and conference promotions, for example, scanned the Internet for sites that appealed to seminar and conference promoters. When he found a site sponsored by an organization of associations and other providers of continuing education, he approached the organization to suggest that he moderate a forum every month on their behalf and within their site on how to boost conference and seminar enrollments. The organization was more than pleased to have someone else to help keep conversation on their forum going and who they could also tout as a "guest expert." And, of course, the consultant was not only pleased to reach the organization's Internet audience but to get the organization's endorsement as an expert with their membership.

Newsletter producers may be able to eliminate the cost of mailings altogether or at least increase promotion of the newsletter through use of the Internet. If your consulting market is local, then the Internet is not appropriate. But if you have identified

FIGURE 6.5   Sample Letter to the Editor

March 8, 1997

Business Editor
The Oregonian
1320 S.W. Broadway
Portland, OR 97201
att: Letters to the Editor

Dear Editor:

While I thoroughly enjoy and find useful information in the columns and news stories in the Oregonian's business section, I must take exception to a story which appeared in Sunday's paper suggesting that small communities will never grow because they cannot support a labor force.

Undoubtedly true until recently, the fact now is that economic development can take place anywhere thanks to current technology. To illustrate this point, I offer for example my situation and the situations of many of my clients, nearly all of whom operate consulting businesses which are national in scope yet are housed in homes and offices in some of this country's smallest communities. I live in rural Clackamas County. I maintain both food and ornamental gardens in my home, have an office in Portland and am in regular contact with clients all over the country. Faxes, the Internet, e-mail, and the telephone allow us to enjoy the benefits of country living and the income of a successful practice. We try to spend the money we make at local stores, have our cars serviced locally, and dine at nearby restaurants. We pay local taxes, bank at local banks, and participate in town meetings. As more people realize the benefits of a rural private life and the profitable business life sophisticated communications equipment can create, the economy of small communities will grow, creating more business and employment opportunities.

Furthermore, the business we bring to our home towns is environmentally sound and unobtrusive, contributing to the small town image while bolstering its economy. Please remember the possibilities technology can bring to small communities when making future editorial decisions.

Sincerely,

Paul Franklin

---

a regional or national market, then developing a Web page may be a cost-effective and leading-edge way to reach potential clients. If your practice is in the computer technology field, you may want to send your newsletter on disk or CD-ROM rather than on paper.

Letters to the Editor

Letters to the editor have more effect than most people think. Exposure in newspapers, magazines, and trade and professional periodicals has benefited many consultants. Invariably, zealous readers—about 30 to 40 percent of the total readership—follow letters to the editor to keep abreast of what people are saying and thinking. Writing a letter is an excellent way to show off your good ideas. See the sample letter in Figure 6.5.

Teaching

If you're inclined toward teaching at all, this option deserves serious consideration. Although teaching opportunities at universities aren't abundant, many organizations—school districts, libraries, park bureaus, major corporations, YMCAs, and YWCAs, for example—have entered the field of educating adults. Small Business Development Centers (SBDCs) located throughout the country often seek business-related experts to teach workshops or classes, as do community colleges and continuing education departments. Don't pass up the chance to teach or to create such an occasion.

You often meet and develop prospects through teaching. If your prospects are former students, you have an advantage because they have seen your competence in the classroom. Doing business with students while they are members of a class can be compromising. Former and current students both, however, often discuss their classes with employers, who may seek the consultant for an assignment.

Seminars also provide tremendous potential for a consultant. Profit centers in their own right, seminars can be highly effective marketing vehicles. Consultants who regularly market their services in seminars report that they convert one out of every 11 seminar participants into clients. It is important, however, that you not waste participants' time by directly selling your services during a program. Effective marketing of consulting services through seminars requires a low-key, indirect, unobtrusive approach.

Working the Press

A passive approach to consulting—hanging out a shingle and waiting for business to walk in the door—presumes that potential clients know who you are and accept you as an authority in your field. Unless you are already a well-established authority whose contributions are widely known, however, this presumption is not likely to produce the desired results.

One way to increase your exposure and establish yourself as an authority at little or no cost is to become a newsmaker and thus stimulate media interest in your opinions and activities. Getting the press to notice you takes more than just handing out a few press releases. You need to be aware of how periodicals work, what reporters and editors are interested in, and what makes the news. Just like you, most publications are in business to make money. Editors want material that will interest readers and increase subscriptions. Even though some newspapers and magazines are predisposed toward sensationalism and controversy, the trade press generally prefers practical, how-to information—the kind of information that you, as a consultant, can provide.

The first step in becoming a newsmaker is to target the trade publications in your field. Study them for content and style. What issues and topics are currently being featured? What slants are given to the articles? What is their editorial policy? Specific knowledge of what the trade journals consider to be newsworthy and a feel for how this material is presented will help you create effective press releases that will enhance your reputation as an authority.

Using the information gathered during your review of the publications, you can prepare a press release using one of the following approaches:

- Discuss economic, political, and social trends and their significance for your field.
- Comment on the relevant research and opinions of economists, politicians, and authorities in your field.
- Present and analyze data collected in a survey or questionnaire. (This needn't be a sophisticated or lengthy treatment—just enough to stimulate discussion and get your name before the readers.)

Press releases, in and of themselves, may not generate new business. But they will help to give your name an aura of authority, to establish you as a prominent figure in your field. Your opinions will become sought after by both the press and other people in your field—you will become newsworthy. Offshoots of this free publicity are invitations to submit articles and speak to professional associations and civic groups, which should increase your exposure tenfold. This exponential effect of well-placed, carefully timed press releases is achieved at little or no cost—and should contribute to a profitable practice.

In making yourself newsworthy, you must be careful to create a positive image. If you are perceived as being too controversial, too far removed from the mainstream of opinion, you could be labeled as a pariah, reversing the positive effect of publicity. Instead of being helped by it, your practice could be seriously harmed. This is not to suggest that you should avoid controversy altogether. Indeed, one of the surest ways to get your name in the news is to take a firm position on a controversial issue. But these opinions should not stray too far from accepted norms and standards—or you may find yourself becoming the person everyone loves to hate. Look over the sample press release provided in Figure 6.6 and the sample article in Figure 6.7.

Volunteering

Arguments can be made, of course, that volunteering contributes to society, to causes you particularly believe in, and to a well-balanced life. If you also select volunteer opportunities with an eye toward business development, volunteering can also be a low-cost/no-cost technique. Such opportunities include, but are hardly limited to, work with Junior Achievement, working with schools to make teachers more computer literate, doing a newsletter for a favorite nonprofit organization, or organizing an event at a church that counts potential clients as members.

FIGURE 6.6   Sample Press Release

NATIONAL TRAINING CENTER, INC.
123 NORTHWEST SECOND AVENUE, SUITE 405
PORTLAND, OREGON 97209

TELEPHONE (503) 224-8834
FAX (503) 224-2104

Press Release—Use anytime

From: National Training Center (for INTER/ACTION Associates)
       123 N.W. Second Ave., Suite 405
       Portland, OR 97209
       503-224-8834, phone; 503-224-2104; fax; PFCONSULT@aol.com, e-mail

Contact: Steve Kaufer at INTER/ACTION Association, 619-322-9097
       or Paul Franklin, National Training Center, 503-224-8834

Money Available to Supplement Voters' Desire for Increased School Safety

School district administrators throughout the state now have available funds to add personal and physical plant safety features to existing school buildings or to incorporate such features in new construction.

Voters last year overwhelmingly passed Proposition 203 which has made available millions and millions for school remodeling and construction. "One of the hidden bonuses of these funds," said Steve Kaufer, a recognized leader in the design of security programs for educational institutions, "is that the money available for creating safe schools can be leveraged through several existing programs so that value received for dollars spent can bring a district far more than might be imagined."

Over $200,000 in contributions from the local utility company helped one California district with which Kaufer worked stretch its state funds, save energy and increase safety in its buildings. "Other opportunities are out there," said Kaufer, "once a district knows where to look and how to ask."

In fact, continued the security specialist, there are a lot of things a school district can do to increase the safety of its students, staff, buildings and equipment, which cost little or no money. "Consideration of plant layouts, lighting, alarms, motion detectors, and promotion of personal safety awareness can do a lot to promote safe work and learning places. I have a little booklet I'll be happy to share," said Kaufer, "which addresses these issues. It's '99 Tips for Safe Schools' and it's free. Just call my office, leave your request with your name and address and I'll get it right out."

Kaufer's number is 619-322-9097.

"The time has never been better for school districts to address the increasingly worrisome issues of student safety, staff safety and protection of buildings from theft, vandalism and the like. With funding support from voters, knowledge of how to expand those funds through existing programs and remodeling or new construction planning which must include a safety specialist," concluded Kaufer, "personal and physical safety can be a reality in California schools."

--30--

Editor: *For expanded thoughts in school safety, which may be a critical issue in your area, give Steve a call. He can be reached at his Palm Springs, Calif., office at 619-322-9097.*

☞ Tips

The principles underlying our 11 low-cost/no-cost techniques are the same. Each one establishes you as an authority in your field. They not only encourage clients to come to you, but also offer ways for you to contact clients you are informed about. The uncomfortable cold contact is eliminated. The economic payoff is that, compared with expensive ads or direct mail campaigns, these techniques are all low-cost/no-cost or even make money for you by themselves! And they work—any successful consultant will testify to that. If you're beginning your consulting practice or if you're interested in expanding, you may want to supplement your low-cost/no-cost marketing techniques with some form of advertising to get your name in front of as many potential clients as possible. The next chapter will show you how to get the most out of your direct marketing dollar by using the same principles that underlie the 11 low-cost/no-cost techniques.

FIGURE 6.7 Sample Article

Home-Based Business News

Right marketing mix can smooth work flow

My last column spelled out three key steps you can take to avoid the peaks and valleys of "busyness" in your professional consulting practice. This column looks at the fourth step and offers some thoughts on how to keep a steady business base.

Serendipity vs. Orchestration

The fourth critical step is developing a marketing approach and plan that has the right mix between the serendipitous and the orchestrated.

"Serendipitous" and "orchestrated" are my words for the way clients come to us. They reflect two very different marketing approaches — both necessary to growing a lucrative business but only in the right balance.

Serendipitous marketing is the fallout that comes from being good and being out there in the market, noticeable and effective. It is the person who calls you "out of the blue" after you give a speech and says they want to engage your services.

It is the client that comes by referral from someone from whom you frankly never expected a referral. It is business that comes through word-of-mouth".

Serendipitous marketing is largely outside your direct control. It happens because you are visible and good at what you do. Prospective users of your services act on their own initiative and figure out how to reach you and how to access your services.

The serendipitous is great because it comes along largely unexpected.

That, of course, is also its drawback. You can't rely on it in building quarterly cash flow projections. Nor can you build a lucrative business on serendipitous marketing alone.

Yet, it is surprising how many consultants rely on the serendipitous as the backbone of their marketing efforts. Giving speeches, writing articles, newslettering, networking — all good marketing strategies.

But, to use any of these strategies without follow-up marketing is to rely on chance — the chance that someone in your audience will be motivated and self-directed enough to contact you.

You don't need to be a great student of human nature to know that self-directed people aren't in the majority. Rely on serendipity, and you will miss all those who intended to call you and didn't; all of those who wanted to call but weren't sure what to say; all those who had questions about whether you could help but weren't motivated to call; and so on.

That brings us to orchestrated marketing. For every one part of serendipitous marketing, you need four parts of orchestrated marketing to avoid the lean times. Orchestrated marketing is proactive. It is giving a speech and following it up with a letter to members of the audience with a specific service offer.

It is including in an article some

The Professional Consultant
Paul Franklin

compelling reason — like something free — for readers to contact you so they can be turned into prospects. It is then staying in touch with these new prospects, mining business from them over time.

Orchestrated marketing is asking for referrals, not relying on whim or chance to create them for you. It is having a planned, routine process for staying in touch with previous clients, thereby nurturing repeat business.

It is developing profit centers that feed off of each other. It is doing a given activity — like giving a speech or doing a workshop — because it sets you up to go back to a new group with an offer for your services.

It is deciding to do something for free — or at less-than-normal price — because doing so showcases your abilities and sets up a bigger project — and higher returns — on the back end.

It is sending out five, 10 or 50 letters a week soliciting business...or setting up a meeting...or inviting people...or informing prospects...or...

Orchestrated marketing leaves little to chance. It is blending marketing activities

together that give you maximum control over the flow of your business.

Orchestrated marketing is the key ingredient for developing a consistent flow of clients. It's the straw that stirs the drink — the essential element in the formula for leveling out the peaks and valleys.

In the sum, my formula for keeping a steady business base is simple, really. It is beating back the belief system that the ups and downs are an inevitable part of the business.

It is never getting so busy that you can't market continuously and consistently — devoting at least 20 percent of your time. And, it is deploying the right mix of marketing strategies.

Following the formula will give you the control you need to make business flow more predictable, cash flow more even. Over the long haul, it will make your business more enjoyable not to mention more lucrative.

(Paul Franklin is editor of The Professional Consultant newsletter and author of several books and programs on marketing services. For a copy of his catalog of marketing and consulting resources, call 1-800-223-5085.) ■

CHAPTER 7

Effective Direct Marketing

Given the myriad of indirect, low-cost/no-cost marketing techniques available to consultants and their effectiveness in building a profitable practice, you may be tempted to ignore the whole issue of direct marketing. Yet direct mailing of brochures and/or letters, space ads in newspapers and magazines, and other types of direct promotion of your services do have a place in your overall marketing plan. Primary emphasis should be on indirect marketing techniques but not to the exclusion of such direct low-cost techniques as advertising.

Effective advertising resembles our low-cost/no-cost techniques by also keeping costs down as you achieve maximum results for your output of energy and money. This chapter discusses how you, as a consultant, can design and implement an effective, low-cost ad campaign by overcoming clients' fears about using a consultant.

Fears and Concerns of Clients

The 11 low-cost/no-cost techniques described in Chapter 6 help to establish a personal, professional relationship with potential clients. In using these approaches, you don't have to be too concerned with clients' fears about hiring a consultant, because they know you and respect you. If you sense that a client is afraid of retaining a consultant, you can deal with that concern directly in a face-to-face meeting.

In advertising, you're at a disadvantage because those who read your ad don't know you and therefore may be influenced by concerns and fears about consultants. You have to anticipate and dispel those fears if your promotional campaign is to be successful.

Clients' nine major fears and concerns about using the services of a consultant, listed below in order of priority, were determined by a survey of 576 clients conducted by *The Professional Consultant* newsletter:

1. *Fear that the consultant is incompetent.* Many respondents indicated that consultants talk a good line but may not have the know-how to back up their talk.

2. *Fear that the consultant is incapable of being properly managed or directed by personnel of the client organization.* Some respondents perceived consultants to be competent but too controlling, too self-directed. Those respondents were concerned that they would lose control of their management prerogatives if they engaged a take-charge consultant.

3. *Fear that the consultant's fee will be too high.* While less than 21 percent of the respondents shopped or compared fees, many were concerned that they might be paying too much for the services being provided.

4. *Fear that the consultant is too busy with other client work to expend the time required or provide the resources necessary for doing the job right in the time allotted.* Some respondents indicated that consultants spend a great deal of time in the marketing stage of the consultant-client relationship trying to impress the client with how busy they are and how important their client list is.

5. *Fear that the need for a consultant is an expression of the client's own failures or limitations.* In some fields it is fashionable to use consultants. In others, needing a consultant is still viewed as an admission that something is wrong.

6. *Fear of the disclosure of sensitive proprietary data to a relative stranger.* A serious concern, especially among small corporate and high-tech clients, was that consultants would not be discreet with information they obtained from interaction with the client organization.

7. *Fear that the client organization itself has not properly diagnosed the problem.* Interestingly, it was not the consultant's diagnosis that concerned some respondents but rather their own. These clients were concerned that their own incorrect or incomplete information would result in the consultant's spending a lot of expensive time without results.

8. *Fear that the consultant will not be impartial.* Of the two issues of concern here, the obvious one is that the consultant will have some priority other than the client's interest that will color his or her objectivity. But true professionals never allow their evaluations and decisions to be governed by any objective other than the client's best interests. However, even the most ethical, disciplined consultants are prone to seeing the solution to all problems in terms of more consulting—the second issue of concern. This tendency is so pervasive that a consultant may recommend unnecessary add-ons without being aware of this bias.

9. *Fear of developing a continuing dependency on the consultant's services.* Respondents expressed a minor concern that they would never rid themselves of the need for the consultant's unique service.

Virtually all clients have fears and concerns. The good news is that few have all the fears we've listed, at least at any given moment in time. Don't make the mistake, however, of thinking that a denial of these concerns is all that is required to be successful in selling your services. Laying these fears to rest is just the beginning of marketing. This chapter will show you how your direct marketing campaign can reduce fears and induce clients to come to you.

Approach to Direct Marketing: The Free Offer

Direct marketing of consulting services requires a special approach suited to the nature of your services and the needs and concerns of your clients.

As a small or medium-sized consulting practice, you are not competing in the same market as sellers of shampoo and tires. Your goals, sales points, and target audience are all different. You can achieve your results with a relatively small budget, perhaps even more efficiently than with larger expenditures.

Your goal in direct marketing is very simple—to get prospects to contact you. Having prospects come to you obviously is preferable to pursuing and persuading them. Your direct marketing promotions should sell without selling, obliging prospects to think of your name when the need arises. On one level you must assure prospects that you are not selling consulting services. On another, albeit unspoken, level, you must compel them to seek those very services.

Achieving the delicate balance between selling and subtlety requires a special type of promotion that prompts prospects to contact you without arousing their anxieties about retaining a consultant. One effective technique is a direct mail piece or space ad in a newspaper or magazine asking readers to get in touch with you for free advice on some matter or free help with a minor problem. Usually, your promise is to provide the information or advice in printed form. You respond to the requests with a short booklet or brochure that solves the problem and gives the reader ample reason to contact you for more help and information—without obligation, of course.

This approach, known as the *free offer,* draws clients to you because it sells without selling. All that a free offer sells is the suggestion that readers contact you for assistance on some matter that you happen to know about. If the free offer has to do with your field, fine. Just be sure not to give everything away. Save a few items, and sprinkle the free offer with references to these items. Suggest that if readers need more information, they should call you. Almost anyone who can be considered a potential client will find some question to call about.

A space ad or direct mail piece merely asks readers to take a small, inconsequential, nonthreatening action. The promise is simply to solve a problem for free, with no implication that your consulting is needed to help the solution along. Your ad or mailing should offer a solution that is complete and self-contained.

You must be careful not to offer to solve too big or complex a problem. If you do, your readers simply won't believe it's possible to offer so much for free. Figure 7.1 contains examples of potential free offers.

FIGURE 7.1 Sample Free Offers and How They Work

The Free Offer	Help You Can Offer
For groups seeking to block federal funding cutbacks, a booklet, *How To make Your Congressman Aware of Your Federal Funding Needs.*	People in Washington to call with information requests. What to do when there is no meaningful response to a communication with a congressman. Where-to-buy service that facilitates mass mailings.
For small businesses with cash flow problems, a report, *43 Things You Wanted to Know about How to Behave Around Your Banker But Were Afraid to Ask.*	Where to get information on federal small business assistance. What to look for in your accountant's work to increase your loan-worthiness. Loan sources that have been lending money recently to small businesses.
For firms seeking to improve the morale and prestige of their sales forces, a booklet, *How to Attract a Better Class of Applicants for Your Sales Openings.*	Which local employment agencies have been doing work on sales jobs recently. How to tell if a job applicant is lying. The most frequent employment interview violations of the federal equal employment laws.
For small businesses confused by the rapid introduction of the Internet, a free short-term subscription to *The Internet Digest,* a monthly digest of new-product announcements.	Product introductions that are reliably rumored to be coming soon (from your inside sources at the companies) that have not been officially introduced. How to handle delivery backlogs. How to handle user satisfaction survey results.
For firms manufacturing expensive computer-based prosthetics for handicapped people, a booklet, *How to Keep Current on Federal Aid for the Handicapped.*	How to fill out a particular kind of grant application form. Where the federal money has been going lately in this area. What private sources of money have been doing lately in this area.
For real estate developers seeking to sell condominiums as professional offices, a research report, *How to Get a Doctor to Open the Mail You Send Him.*	Names of successful office condominium developers for developers interested in expanding into that area. Names of banks and bank officers heavily involved in office condominium deals.
For small companies seeking free publicity for their new products, a survey report, *The 22 Best Outlets for Free Product Publicity.*	Success stories in the reader's own industry. The best advertising or public relations agencies for the reader's particular situation.
For corporation executives facing hostile media, a booklet, *How Six Prominent Executives Handle Hostile Journalists.*	How your clients handle hostile journalists. How six prominent corporations prevent hostility from arising in the first place. Names of the best public speaking coaches.

By using a free offer like the ones in Figure 7.1, you may attract as many as 50 inquiries for every $100 you spend on advertising. This level of response broadens your prospect base, providing you with additional marketing opportunities. In sum, a free offer should have the following characteristics:

- The offer is free.
- The offer provides a solution to a prospective client's problem.
- The problem is related to your consulting area.

- The problem does not appear too difficult to solve.
- The solution is complete and self-contained.
- The offer encourages people to call you for more advice.

Why the Free Offer Works

A properly designed free offer communicates to a prospect that you will not deliver a high-pressure pitch for your services. Most prospects realize that you are not spending money for the benefit of humankind, but they will be more apt to contact you if you assure them that you're just giving away a bit of valuable knowledge. Of course, you don't say this directly. Your offer of some useful information in a booklet or brochure in itself assures the reader of your professionalism and low-key approach, encouraging potential clients to contact you for additional information.

Prospects can call you with the confidence that they can back off without hesitation or compunction. They know that you are selling your services, but they need the comfortable fiction that the call is only for information. Once they respond, your ad can be considered a complete success.

After the initial contact, both you and the potential client can conveniently forget the suggestions in the ad. Your prospects can talk with you freely without the threat of a sales pitch and pressure to close a deal. With this understanding, the client very often leads the conversation to buying your services. You should not be surprised if you're asked to take on a large, complicated, and expensive assignment at the initial meeting.

Developing Your Free Offer

The purpose of your free offer is to make a client contact, generally leading to a face-to-face meeting. Therefore, it should avoid any topic that evokes clients' concerns. It should seem to define in general terms only what can be done for the client. It should raise clients' confidence in themselves and in you, encouraging them to ask for your services.

Although most free offers are made in a brochure or booklet, you should not limit yourself to print. If your speaking voice is a vital ingredient in your presentation, your "booklet" might consist of an audiocassette tape. A consultant in the computer field might program a message on a floppy disk or offer to download a computer program or file. Give some thought to all the media.

A free offer consists of the following three parts:

1. Delivering the goods
2. Involving the client
3. Providing necessary information

As we review each of these parts, a free offer example will be outlined. You can use the worksheets in Figure 7.2 to develop an offer related to your consulting specialty.

Keep the nine fears and concerns of your clients in mind as you construct your free offer. The first fear—that the consultant is incompetent—is an opportunity to display your expertise. If your services involve creativity, your offer should show imagination and flair. If you are a graphic artist, for example, the graphics in your booklet had better be good. You are showing off your talents, so make it good, and the client will believe in your competence.

Delivering the Goods

In your ad or letter, state that you will produce valuable information on some worthwhile and interesting subject. Begin your booklet by outlining a problem and providing the promised information.

If you don't deliver the goods, potential clients will lose respect for you and expect the same kind of frustration in dealing with you. Make sure that whatever you offer is valuable, even though it relates to a limited topic, and that you provide useful information. You want the reader to believe in you and trust you.

A consultant who writes grant proposals, for example, wants to make a free offer. Because many proposals are written for government grants, the consultant wants to get inquiries from potential clients without offering too much and without giving away services.

If the offer is for a booklet entitled *How to Write Winning Proposals in Five Easy Steps,* prospects simply won't believe it. They've had enough experience with the government to know that it can't be that easy, and they will expect either a useless collection of generalizations or a direct sales pitch. The other problem with this offer is that the consultant would be offering to tell readers how to do what he does for a living. If he could actually deliver on the promise, he would be giving away his services.

The topic of *Finding Unclaimed Federal Grant Money* has a much better chance of succeeding. Potential clients are interested in finding grants, and the offer sounds plausible. The consultant can deliver the information without giving away free work. This is an interesting and credible free offer.

The booklet on unclaimed federal grant money can begin with a short outline, describing how hundreds of millions of dollars' worth of federal grant money is left unallocated because no one applies for certain grants. Then the consultant can describe how easy it is to locate these grants, which are matters of public record, and list the written sources to look up and agencies to contact along with listing a few unclaimed grants. At this point the consultant has delivered the goods; he has made good on his promise.

Now, pick a possible free offer connected with your consulting specialty— something that is interesting and limited in scope like the one in the example. Write it down on the worksheet in Figure 7.2, then list the information that will fulfill your promise. Concentrate on offering help and information that is not identical to your specialty but is interesting to potential clients. As you write down the actual information to be included in the booklet, make sure that it is valuable to your clients and fulfills the promise in the ad without giving away proprietary material.

FIGURE 7.2 Worksheet for Free Offer

Delivering the Goods

Your Free Offer

The Information That Delivers the Goods

FIGURE 7.2 Worksheet for Free Offer (Continued)

Involving the Potential Client

Obstacle to Using Your Advice	*Solution to the Obstacle*
Obstacle to Using Your Advice	*Solution to the Obstacle*
Obstacle to Using Your Advice	*Solution to the Obstacle*
Obstacle to Using Your Advice	*Solution to the Obstacle*
Obstacle to Using Your Advice	*Solution to the Obstacle*
Obstacle to Using Your Advice	*Solution to the Obstacle*

FIGURE 7.2 Worksheet for Free Offer (Continued)

Involving the Potential Client

A Vignette Describing How You Helped Someone

Another Vignette

FIGURE 7.2 Worksheet for Free Offer (Continued)

Involving the Potential Client

A Related Item or Area of Interest

A Related Item or Area of Interest

A Related Item or Area of Interest

A Related Item or Area of Interest

A Related Item or Area of Interest

A Related Item or Area of Interest

Involving the Client

After you have delivered the goods, you want to involve your potential clients by giving them a reason to contact you. The reasons should relate to the free offer alone, not to your consulting specialty.

One way to involve potential clients is to describe a couple of vignettes in which clients contacted you for help related to the free offer. The consultant in our example could describe two occasions on which clients came for help in finding grant money and were successful. This approach builds the client's confidence in your ability to be helpful by providing evidence of your track record. You want to depict clients as competent and independent, not as helpless and in constant need of your advice. Do not specifically identify clients as this may seem a breach of confidentiality. Use terms like a major manufacturing company or a national accounting firm. Your discretion will not go unnoticed.

Another way to involve potential clients is to list some obstacles to using the advice you gave in the first part of the booklet. These obstacles should relate to clients' lack of confidence in their ability to be creative or use new resources. In telling potential clients they have all they need except confidence, you are building them up by emphasizing how much they already have. You then provide the solution to the obstacle, which involves contacting you and getting a little advice or help. If the prospects lack confidence, you can show them how to use the information in your free offer to get the most out of their abilities and other resources. The solution should involve only an hour or so of your time. Anything more than that implies that you are already beginning a major consultation—an impression that you want to avoid.

The consultant in our example could list some obstacles to tapping into the millions of dollars in grant money that are waiting for the right organization. One obstacle could be matching available talents with existing grants. An organization could have hidden talents or might not see how its business could be applied to a particular grant. This technique builds a prospective client's confidence by focusing on potential and hidden talents rather than on incompetence and failure.

Another possible obstacle could be not knowing the right people to talk to in some government agencies. After all, who has enough time to run a business and know the ins and outs of thousands of government agencies? Our consultant, however, can give guidance and support in the difficult process of finding the right people to contact, providing a prospective client with the benefit of experience in working with the government. This does not imply that the prospect is incompetent but rather that the demands of real-world business don't leave enough time to do everything.

A third way of whetting a prospect's interest is to add an enticing comment or two on a related subject. For example, the free offer on unclaimed federal grant money could also raise the issue of unallocated money available from private non-profit organizations and from state and local governments. In mentioning these sources, our consultant can suggest and/or offer consultation availability on these matters without giving any details. Thus the promise on federal grants is fulfilled and new possibilities are raised, giving prospects a reason to make personal contact.

On the remaining worksheet in Figure 7.2, outline some potential obstacles to using the information you have provided in your free offer. Sketch several vignettes that show how you helped those who contacted you for information—without mentioning your consulting specialty or saying that these contacts signed up for your services. Finally, write down some areas related to your free offer that would also interest potential clients. In effect, these are additional free offers requiring face-to-face contact.

Keep in mind that you want to build clients' confidence and allay any fears of their becoming permanently dependent on you for help. You are simply giving clients an opportunity to get in touch with you for a little more advice and guidance on your offer.

Combine the vignettes with the obstacles and solutions by listing the obstacles and solutions first (of course, all the solutions involve a consultation with you—again at no cost) followed by a vignette in which someone contacted you and had a satisfactory outcome. As part of the vignette, you don't want to say that the prospect became a client of yours. Simply outline the free advice you dispensed and describe how it was useful. Emphasize as well that the information was delivered in a short time. Potential clients are not going to believe that you gave away a day of your time just to improve the economy.

Include related additional items as part of a vignette or separately as further information you can give. A vignette describing how a company contacted our consultant for more information on federal grant money could also state that the matter of private grants came up and leads were developed that led to valuable contracts. The obstacles and solutions, vignettes, and additional items give prospects a reason to contact you in person—and that is where the actual "sale" will take place. In the first section you delivered the goods, and in the second you gave prospects a reason to contact you. Having completed the contract you made in your ad, you created a sense of incompleteness to give potential clients a reason to contact you.

Providing Necessary Information

Your booklet should conclude with basic information about yourself and your services: your address, phone number, and a short description of the kind of consulting you do. You can also list your policies on billing, contracts, confidentiality, and so on. You might say you believe that consulting should be cost-effective, or you might declare your willingness to enter into performance contracts. Basically, you want the client to know you are a businesslike professional.

This section about yourself should be short—preferably one page. Too much personal information makes the booklet look more like a sales pitch and less like a simple offer. Clients who write for more information can get your brochure listing your accomplishments and abilities.

The procedure for developing a free offer is similar to that for producing a brochure. After you have written your copy, you need to consult a printer and/or design specialist to set up the actual format. You may want to engage professional help for writing the brochure as well as designing the layout and possible graphics. Remember that this booklet is a display of what you can do, and you want it to show off your abilities.

The expense involved in quality printing on good stock with good graphics is more than offset by the result in potential sales. With a successful offer you will probably be sending out only a few hundred brochures or booklets, perhaps fewer.

The response to your offer need not be massive to be successful because those who do inquire are very likely to need and want your services.

Following Up on the Free Offer

Paradoxically, a free offer may be too effective, cutting prospects off from easy accessibility to a consultant. Prospects may be disappointed in a sense to find that the consultant has kept the promise made in the ad. The offer turns out to be exactly what the ad said it would be—a self-contained solution to a modest problem. At the end of the piece is simply a line that reads: For more information or a consultation, contact _____. If prospects are still interested, they have to contact the consultant cold, just as if there had been no ad. They are up against the same old uncomfortable feelings. This free offer has failed in its essential purpose—opening the way to a face-to-face meeting between prospect and consultant.

An effective free offer provides some valuable information and shows that the consultant is competent or even creative. However, it only hints at or outlines part of the solution. To get the whole story, a prospect has to make contact with the consultant. That way, if the prospect is interested, it's easy to call and ask for more information.

Writing the Ad Copy

After you have selected your topic and have your booklet ready to go, you need to compose your ad or direct mail piece. The rules for composing a free offer ad are the same as for any good ad. And the same rules apply to crafting a direct mail piece or, for that matter, an ad for a free offer distributed over the Internet. If you decide to use more conventional ads, you can use this section as a guide. But the focus here is on constructing an effective ad for a free offer.

Gauging the effectiveness of advertising for an immediate response is very simple. For each ad or for each mailing, the question is the same: Did the dollar value of the immediate responses exceed the cost of the ad by enough to make the desired profit?

This emphasis on immediate response means that you won't have to use complex and expensive devices which may result in delayed responses (which you probably can't afford anyway). It does impose a harsh discipline on you, so harsh that perhaps the best frame of mind for writing advertising is desperation. Imagine that you are drowning. The 50 to 100 words you have left will be the last ones you utter—unless you get the lazy, indifferent, impatient reader to act now. You don't have time to be funny or clever, to glorify your business, or to justify your appeal. You have only enough time to clearly describe the benefits of responding immediately. You do this by

1. using the present tense and the second person (you);
2. appealing to the reader's senses by giving as physical a description as you can of the benefits of responding;
3. using short, simple words in short, simple sentences; and
4. urging the reader to respond.

If this advice strikes you as extreme or overly simplistic, observe how you read ads in a newspaper. Notice that a strong, simple, direct appeal is much more likely to make you stop scanning and actually read the ad.

As a professional offering a high-quality service, you may have developed a dislike for advertising, finding it crass or distasteful. As a result, your own ad copy may read like an announcement in a church bulletin. But any reticence or self-effacement in your copy is apt to undermine the purpose of your ad—and that is to get responses. Direct mail professionals attest to this on the basis of their experience with hundreds of millions of pieces of mail—each designed to get a simple, immediate response. Even when they are appealing to the most jaded, sophisticated audience, these professionals are bold and straightforward. Follow their example by being as direct as possible in your advertising, without resorting to hype or obvious overstatement.

Designing Your Ad

Especially when you are using small newspaper or magazine ads, where every square inch must earn its keep in direct responses, mail-order style is apt to be most effective. In mail order, an ad, a direct mail piece, or an entire advertising campaign can be judged quickly and easily by the number of responses it produces. Through thousands of scientific tests, direct mail professionals have discovered that you attract attention with white space, headlines, boxes, and pictures. See the sample in Figure 7.3.

Headlines should be short and punchy, promising the reader a quick, easy-to-understand benefit. Use words like *new, now, how to, announcing, at last* and *free.* Using a specific date in the headline is often effective.

A picture of your free offer is an excellent attention-getter. You should test it to see if it's worth the money you pay for the space it requires.

Layout

The slightest visual obstacle may prevent readers from completely reading your ad. In your layout use the following:

1. *Short paragraphs:* Indent the first line of each paragraph. Use six or fewer lines even if you have to break the formal rules of paragraph structure.
2. *Ordinary, popular typefaces:* Use serif type if your audience generally is older than 35. This book is printed in serif type. Use sans serif for an audience under 35. The type should be at least as large as that used in articles in the publication where the ad is appearing.
3. *Boldface words and phrases:* Impatient readers look at boldface first to get the gist of your ad.
4. *Small pictures:* Photo captions are the best-read parts of most printed matter. The captions need not explain the pictures, but they should give your sales message.

FIGURE 7.3   Sample Ad

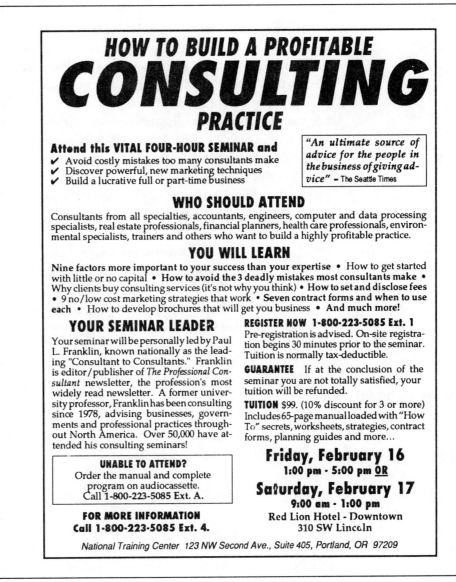

5. *Subheadings:* Plan subheads so that someone who reads nothing else gets enough information to respond to your ad.
6. *Easy ways to respond:* A reply coupon, toll-free 800 number, or a toll-free fax are the surest ways to get responses.
7. *Logos:* Even if your ad is not read, a distinctive logo increases your prestige and acceptability in readers' minds.

You want to avoid artistic effects, such as white type on a black background—except for a headline of no more than four words. Avoid help from anyone who seeks self-expression through your ads. Fancy special effects make your ad hard to read and turns off readers.

Placing Your Ad

Ad placement in the right newspaper or magazine gets two to five times as many responses per advertising dollar as placement in the wrong one. You can find productive media by checking Standard Rate and Data Service (1700 Higgins Rd., Des Plaines, IL 60018). Commonly referred to as SRDS, this service provides a number of different books for media and mailing lists, which can be surprisingly specific. You can select business executives of companies of a certain size range or hospitals with a certain number of beds. If, for example, you're interested in reaching firms with problems resulting from employees postponing their retirements, you will find the following:

> Magazines: *Business and Health, HR Magazine, HR News, Human Resource Executive, Personnel Journal* (from *Business Publications Rates and Data*)
>
> Mailing lists: 92,000 personnel executives; 80,000 personnel administrators; 27,000 personnel and benefits executives (from *Direct Mail Lists Rates and Data*)

With this kind of guidance, you can target the most appropriate periodical or newspaper in which to advertise or the best mailing lists to use for direct mail campaigns.

The Rules of Advertising

Years of experience with advertising, both good and bad, have taught us four rules of thumb that you may not find in textbooks.

Effective and Cost-Efficient Advertising Is Specific Advertising

Advertising can be effective but not cost-efficient. It may bring in prospects but may cost too much to do so. Targeted advertising costs less because the audience is smaller, and you can concentrate on magazines that reach your audience or use a small mailing list. An ad in *The Wall Street Journal* costs a lot more than an ad in a professional journal.

Test, Test, Test, and Test Some More

Careful testing is the only proven avenue to success in advertising. Testing provides the feedback you need to develop ads and to protect yourself from the whims of inspiration.

If you're located in a major metropolitan area and elect to try newspaper advertising, test your ad in a smaller neighboring community before investing big dollars in the local metro daily. You can save up to 80 percent of the money needed for a test in a metropolitan area. Pick a community that resembles yours demographically and has a newspaper with similar reader characteristics. You can exercise the same caution with radio, magazine, and direct mail campaigns. For example, send out

1,000 direct mail pieces, not 20,000. This market test enables you to determine whether it is worthwhile to spend money on a larger campaign.

Extensive testing may be required because a number of variables are involved, including the following:

- The frequency with which advertising appears
- The dates and times when advertising is run
- The promotional message being used
- The size or length of advertising
- The media in which advertising is placed
- The price or fee charged

With so many variables, if one attempt fails, it doesn't mean the idea is bad. It might work with a different combination. Testing enables you to find out at minimal expense.

Keep track of the variables that affect the response to your ads. Placement on the page, size of the ad, the headline, the absence or presence of a coupon can all affect results. Record the response by ad and date so that you know how long it takes to get the full response to an ad. You might discover that for a daily paper, 60 percent of the ad's total response comes within two days after it is run, 20 percent on the third day, and 10 percent on the fourth. With this type of information, you can tell within a few days whether an ad is a winner or not. You can then purchase your advertising accordingly.

If you are running ads simultaneously in different publications, make sure that you can tell which ad is responsible for which responses. If you offer a free booklet, one way to trace responses is to code the request in a specific publication with a line such as: "Ask for booklet NP-3."

If your early ads don't pull their own weight in immediate billings, don't abandon the whole concept of advertising. Experiment with different media, themes, free offers, graphics, and other methods. If you keep at it, you will learn which combinations produce results. Treat each failed ad as a valuable investment in knowledge. You can then build on your successes and avoid failures.

Emphasize Immediate Response When Your Budget Is Limited

If your budget is limited, design ads that produce an immediate, direct response. This kind of ad proves or disproves itself quickly. The cash flow also may be improved because immediate-response ads usually turn revenue more quickly, reducing the amount of cash that has to be tied up in advertising.

Spend Only Enough to Get the Job Done

Consulting almost always requires individualized, one-on-one selling, so most consulting advertising is designed to create an inquiry, not a sale. Because consultants must talk with potential clients before making a sale, you need not make a large investment in advertising space to sell your services. It's cheaper to advertise for contacts than for sales.

☞ Tips

If you follow our 11 low-cost/no-cost marketing strategies and use an effective free offer in combination with a good brochure, you'll probably find yourself inundated with contacts. Once a potential client is in your door, you have to make the sale. Selling involves the same indirect strategy that you used to generate contacts—to sell without selling. At the same time, you need to be skilled at asking a potential client to commit.

The next chapter will show you how to win contracts from your face-to-face meetings. An important element in entering negotiations and making a sale is knowing what the project will entail. If you can't make reliable estimates, you'll end up badly underpricing or overpricing yourself—and either practice will hurt your consulting business. A good estimate leads to a good proposal—and a good proposal is an excellent way of selling yourself.

CHAPTER 8

Selling Your Services

The very notion of selling is anathema to many consultants. It conjures up an image of a sleazy man in a checked suit haranguing customers with an obnoxious sales pitch. The traditional hard sell, which turns off many people and has given selling a bad name, certainly has no place in the sophisticated arena of the consultant.

Modern selling strategy eschews the hard sell in favor of a client-oriented approach. Rather than cramming a product or service down consumers' throats, today's sophisticated sellers determine the needs of their target markets and dovetail their product or service to fit those needs.

This modern approach is particularly well suited to consultants, whose services are built around clients' needs. Emphasis is placed not on imposing services on unwilling prospects but on providing solutions to problems and enabling clients to take advantage of opportunities.

During the selling phase of your marketing plan, you present yourself face-to-face with a prospect. The skill and confidence with which you handle the presentation will determine the eventual outcome—either a lost opportunity or a contract and the possibility of additional business.

Controlling the Presentation

The key to a successful interview is *control,* which is your ability to exercise subtle restraining or directing influence over your prospect. The purpose of control is not to overpower the prospect but to exercise authority. Without control your chances of getting a contract are significantly decreased. In fact, control is the essence of *selling,* which can be defined as helping the prospect identify his or her needs and demonstrating that you are in a unique position to satisfy those needs.

Most clients want to speak with you, a consultant, because they have a problem. They may or may not have given the problem much thought, even though they claim to have done so. Your ability to assess the problem quickly and succinctly will establish you at the outset as an authority, placing you in control of the situation. Don't wait for your prospective client to tell you when you can start exerting control. Instead, make controlling statements and requests, such as: "Could you sit over there, sir?" "I will first demonstrate the outcomes that will be achieved. Then I will show you how . . ."

Ask your prospect questions; start to give directions; keep control over your sales literature or examples. Show them to your prospect when *you* are ready.

Speak forcefully and with confidence. When your behavior indicates that you know what you're doing, your prospect will believe it and relinquish control to you. A weak voice or tentative manner will undermine your authority. Don't say, "I want to give you some information." Say instead, "I am going to . . ." Don't say, "I think." Say, "I know." Don't say, "This might." Say instead, "This will." Just remember that confidence should not be confused with boastfulness or arrogance.

Here are some tips on controlling a presentation:

- *A good first impression:* A strong and forceful (but not too forceful) greeting is a good start. Be firm and confident from handshake to opening statement. Your dress and style should suggest command and authority without being intimidating.
- *Use your personality:* Don't be someone you're not! It won't work. Figure out your unique strengths and let them work for you. Be comfortable with who you are, and display your satisfaction with yourself. It's been said that the true sign of maturity is an acceptance of who and what you are. This maxim doesn't mean that you can't change or that you're not interested in change. It does mean that you accept yourself for what you are at the present time and that you can capitalize on it.
- *Think positive:* Have you ever gone to see a prospective client saying to yourself: "I hope to get a contract?" That mental posture, while not necessarily wrong, does not predispose you psychologically to making a sale. You are not as apt to succeed if you think in terms of *hope, might, maybe, perhaps.* Instead, think in terms of *can* and *will.* Always say to yourself: "I'm going to get this contract. This person needs my services, and I intend to close the sale."
- *A smooth sales presentation:* Your prospect won't be as likely to interrupt if your sales presentation is logical and flowing. A smooth presentation reduces your need to exercise outward control. It's always in your interest to maintain an aura of control without actually having to exert it.

A well-planned presentation answers all of a prospect's major questions and objections. It demonstrates that you are in control and reduces the prospect's objections and concerns. Dragging out a presentation or meandering detracts from the main point and gives your prospective client a chance to ask questions out of sequence. When that happens, you lose control.

The Inexperienced Interviewer

Going into a meeting with a prospective client can be a disaster through no fault of your own. The prospect who doesn't know how to conduct a proper interview may receive a poor impression despite your best efforts.

The interviewer who slumps in the chair across from you and says, "Well, tell me about yourself," has just set the course for disaster. What do you talk about? What can you say to lead the prospect to your services? You don't know what the client needs, so you can't speak to anything in particular. In such an open-ended void, simply say that you will be glad to talk about yourself but that you would first like to ask a question.

After the prospective client agrees, ask him or her to describe the specific outcomes, benefits, and results required for the project under consideration. Next, ask the prospect to describe the specific qualities that he or she is looking for in a consultant to handle the assignment. While both questions are being answered, take careful notes, either mentally or in writing. You can then formulate your response to the original question should it arise again. Now you can match your specific capabilities to the client's needs.

You also want to know what experiences the client has had with other consultants in the past. Fundamentally, the question is whether the relationship was a good one. If not, what specifically did the client dislike? In what fashion have past consultants been compensated? The next thing to determine is whether the client expects to compensate you for this initial meeting.

Payment for the First Meeting

Consultants often have difficulty deciding whether to ask clients to pay for the first meeting during which a proposed project is discussed and before a contract is signed. Maybe that's an unreasonable expectation, and maybe it's not. Experience shows that roughly 20 percent of clients anticipate they are going to pay for the first meeting, so determine the client's attitude on paying during that initial meeting. Clients who have not used consultants before may expect to be billed fully for the meeting; those who have may realize that the first meeting has a marketing objective and thus payment would be unreasonable.

The main drawback to requesting payment for the first meeting is that the client usually expects tangible results immediately instead of waiting for the consultant's plan of attack. We recommend that you inform the client the initial contact is an opportunity to get to know each other and to explore the project under consideration and that it is customary not to charge for this initial session. In the cost calculations presented later in this chapter, an initial contact is computed as part of your marketing expenses so that the client is paying for the initial meeting as part of your overhead.

Focus on the Problem

Of course, the main piece of information you will elicit during the interview is the client's understanding of the problem to be solved. Don't ask the client to tell you what you ought to do. The solution is your job. Instead, ask clients about their experience in working on the problem or situation. The emphasis is on the client's observations.

Ask the client what is supposed to look different after the consultation? What question is going to be answered? What situation is going to be changed? What thing is not going to be happening anymore? Try to uncover the client's concerns. Suppose the client says that the company would like to get personnel turnover down from 44 percent to 20 percent a year. You now know what's troubling the client and what would prove that the consultation was a success.

All these techniques set the stage for working with clients. You let them know you are interested in their situation, you understand their problems, and you want to deal with them in a way that has meaning for them.

Making the Sale

Consultants have a hard time getting clients to say yes. The reason is usually that consultants are good technicians but rarely good salespeople. However, you can decide to do *one* thing at an appropriate time with the client—ask for the contract.

Asking is one of the most important techniques in sales. A major midwestern university conducted research into professional sales techniques. In an analysis of the behavior of sales personnel, the study revealed that the 15 percent of the salespeople who were most effective, the ones who wrote the most orders and had the biggest "book," were the ones who asked at least eight times for an order while giving their sales pitches. They repeatedly found different ways to ask: "When would you like this installed?" "Will it be all right with you if we install it next Wednesday?" They keep taking an aggressive role. On the other hand, the 19 percent who represented the least successful sellers never asked for an order. Some comment by the prospect during the sales presentation would indicate to them that the prospect didn't want to buy. Rather than risk being turned down, they never asked for the order. The study concluded that the most effective way to get an order was to ask for it in a number of different ways on a number of different occasions.

Asking is a good way to overcome a prospect's inaction. Press the point with statements like: "I think we have a good understanding of what needs to be done." "I will start a week from today, and I'll stop by tomorrow with a letter of agreement for your review and signature." With such statements, you've asked for the contract. You have made a definite proposal. The client has to either accept your offer or refuse it.

Inaction can be deadly. It can kill an otherwise lively deal. If a decision hasn't been made, you want to concentrate your efforts on getting it made in your favor. Keep selling. If the client has decided to buy your services but for some reason postpones implementation, don't spend any more time trying to sell the client. Concentrate instead on finding out why the prospect won't implement.

Usually, clients fail to implement a decision because they don't know how. They want you, and you want them. They like what you're going to do, but they don't know the mechanics of getting started. Many people who retain consultants don't have to actually write the checks or write purchase orders. When they need a widget, they ask for one, and someone else writes a purchase order. You have to be prepared to implement the decision for them while easing their embarrassment at not knowing how. You develop the contract or letter of agreement. You specify the wording for the purchase order.

Another reason that clients may postpone implementing decisions is a lack of funds. You may have to help them find the funds—maybe a grant—to get the contract. Or you show them how they can generate the money internally. If funds are in an organization's coffers but not available for your project because it doesn't seem important enough, you might demonstrate how the project has a higher priority than the client thinks.

Finally, some clients fail to implement their decisions simply because they get cold feet. Everyone hesitates before making a major purchase. People who buy consulting services experience the same last-minute reluctance. The only thing to do is to reassure clients that the decision is the right one and recall all the benefits of the consultation.

Body Language

Many sales authorities take careful note of nonverbal communications. Below are some typical nonverbal signals and what they communicate:

- *Folded arms*—Very defensive: "Prove it to me."
- *Crossed legs*—Bored and defensive
- *Hand stroking the chin*—"I'm thinking about it. . . . I haven't reached a decision."
- *Putting something (e.g., a pencil) in the mouth*—"Give me more information. . . . What's in it for me?"
- *Touching or rubbing the nose*—"I doubt it. . . . I don't believe you. . . . Doesn't make sense."
- *Rubbing the eyes*—"Convince me. . . . I really don't know. . . . Tell me I should."
- *Sitting on the edge of the chair*— "I'm interested. . . . I'm cooperative."
- *Unbuttoning coat/jacket*—"I'm opening up to you. . . . I believe you."
- *Tilted head*—"I'm still interested."
- *Short in-and-out breaths*—Frustration and disgust: "Get out of here, now!"
- *Tightly clenched hands*—"I'm tense . . . not relaxed. . . . I'm getting hostile."
- *Palm to the back of the neck*—Defensive, uncertain, and apprehensive: "Are you through?"
- *Clearing throat*—Uncertain and apprehensive
- *Fingers positioned to make a church steeple*—Confident: "I'm very sure of what you're saying."
- *Tugging at ear*—"I want to say something. . . . I want to talk."

By paying attention to body language, you can sharpen your sales skills. The key to sales is control of the situation. If you know what your prospect is thinking about you and your presentation, you have a definite advantage.

Ego and Control

Letting your ego control your reactions to clients can have an adverse effect on your sales efforts, as illustrated by the following example. A university professor received a call from a consulting firm interested in having three smart graduate students do an image study of the firm. The students, who didn't know very much about image study, were flattered and worked to become conversant in the subject.

In a meeting at the consulting firm, the president and vice-president explained what they wanted done. The students in turn explained their enlightened approach. The president and vice-president said that was not exactly what they had in mind, and they again explained how they wanted things done. The students became insulted and left without the consulting job.

The students let their egos get involved. They wouldn't compromise their professional standards (so newly acquired) for the "crass" approach suggested. If they couldn't be in control, they refused to be associated with the job. If you think a client is denying you sufficient control over a project, ask yourself whether you really don't trust the people in control—or is your ego getting in the way? Most often, you will find that it's your ego.

Consulting can be defined as the art of the possible. Realistic, successful consultations result from shared objectives and approaches between clients and consultants. An unwillingness to subvert your ego to the requirements of the job can only end in disaster.

Estimates and Sales

The foundation of your relationship with your clients is your ability to accurately estimate the needs of each client and each situation. This estimate guides your proposal and your estimate of costs to the client. Without a thorough understanding of what is involved in a particular assignment, you'll be unable to draw up an effective and fair contract. Your estimate and description of a given project form the basis of your proposal, which can be a very effective sales instrument. If you can't make solid and believable cost estimates, you can hardly expect to impress prospects with your efficiency and professionalism.

Estimating is a matter of time and discipline. It calls for thought, work, and calculation. If you take the time and do the work, you should be able to come up with very accurate estimates. Admittedly, the first one or two estimates may not be as close to the actual costs as you might like. But as you do more of them, you collect detailed feedback, and you can be more accurate on future estimates.

Seventy-six consultants polled by *The Professional Consultant* were asked questions about fee setting, contracts, and estimates. They were asked to cite the cause when costs exceeded estimates. In reply, 73 percent of those who used a fixed-price contract and 59 percent of those who used a daily-rate contract reported poor estimating as the cause (see Chapter 10 for elaboration of fixed-price contracts).

The consultants working exclusively on fixed-price contracts also evaluated their ability at estimating. Of those who ranked themselves as very good, costs exceeded the original estimates in only 14 percent of the cases. Of those who evaluated themselves as being not very good, the percentage of overruns was 29 percent.

The key to profitability in fixed-price contracts is reliable estimates. Preparing a reliable estimate entails

- mapping out the entire project to identify its components;
- assigning detailed cost estimates to each component;
- totaling the costs for all components; and
- applying the overhead rate and profit.

The Functional Flow Diagram (FFD)

To visualize a project as a whole, construct a pictorial flowchart of what must be done. Review it, revise it, and redraw it until you can't think of anything else that can be done. If you're uncertain about your comprehensiveness, ask someone to review the diagram. Sometimes a fresh pair of eyes see things that you don't.

Suppose a client needs a training program in sales and product maintenance for branch office personnel. Your first step would be to construct what is called a functional flow diagram (FFD), such as the one shown in Figure 8.1.

An FFD is made up of a series of lines and boxes:

- *Each box represents a major component of project activity, indicated by a label in the box.* These labels should begin with action verbs, such as *administer, analyze, compute, design, determine, tabulate.*
- *Every box must have an input and an output.* See Figure 8.2. In the course of designing your FFD, additional activities may have to be added. In Figure 8.2, for example, you may decide that the names of persons to be surveyed will have to be determined. The result of this activity or step would have to feed into Box 2.

Figure 8.3 indicates how you would make this addition. The added symbol is called a *connective.* There are two kinds of connectives: *"and" connectives* and *"or" connectives.* In Figure 8.3, the "and" connective is used to demonstrate that the result or output of both Functions 1 and 4 is required to proceed with Function 2.

The "or" connective indicates either a *choice point,* when used on the input side of a function, or a *branch point,* when used on the output side of a function. Suppose that in this particular project you could modify the survey instrument used by the client last year rather than design a new one. The benefit of doing so remains to be studied. Figure 8.4 describes this future option.

Consider using such options liberally. They anticipate decisions so that you don't have to make up your mind suddenly on the basis of limited data. These options enable you to demonstrate to your client that full consideration is given to all viable alternatives. This point may be particularly useful in a competitive situation because it demonstrates that a part of your bid, estimate, or fixed price includes a series of decisions involving choices between viable alternatives.

FIGURE 8.1   A Typical Functional Flow Diagram

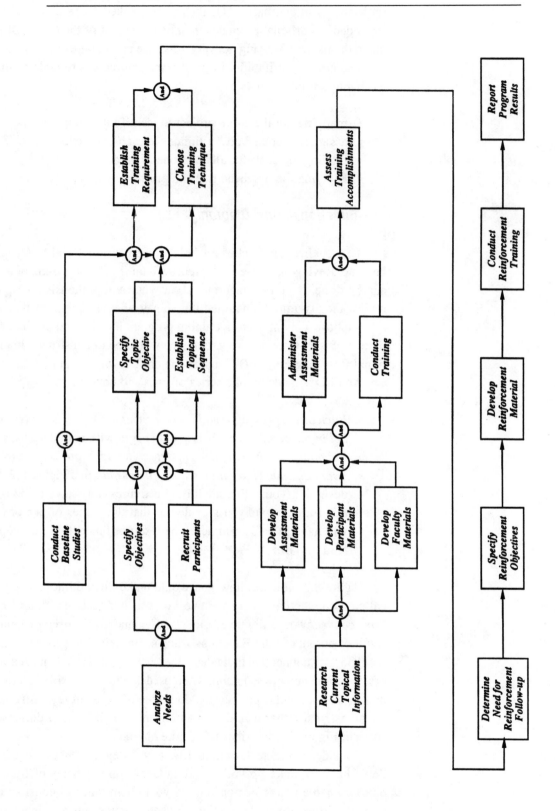

FIGURE 8.2   Example of Input/Output Elements

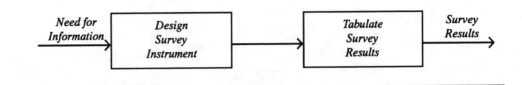

Itemized Estimates

As you review Figure 8.1, you can foresee having to

1. determine trainee information requirements;
2. assess the competence of trainees relative to information requirements;
3. develop training objectives;
4. select indicators/measures that ensure objectives have been met;
5. determine training requirements;
6. formulate training outlines; and
7. create training agendas.

If you've done similar projects before, perhaps this degree of detail is enough. If not, you probably should itemize each activity further. A detailed breakdown of the first task, for example—to determine trainee information requirements—might require you to

1a. develop management interview guides;
1b. create branch office survey instruments;
1c. conduct test of face validity for interview guides/survey instruments;
1d. modify interview guides/survey instruments;
1e. interview management personnel; and
1f. write a report of your preliminary findings.

Although this degree of detail is usually enough, you can break each of these items down even further. Requiring you, for example, to create branch office survey instruments, as in 1b, might make it necessary for you to

2a. determine the type of questionnaire to be used;
2b. select questionnaire items;
2c. develop scales or measures;
2d. write questions to be used; and
2e. develop survey instrument shell.

You may continue to break down the components of a job until you feel familiar enough with the subdivisions to make reasonable "subestimates." For subcomponents that are still difficult to estimate, ask for some advice. Perhaps a business acquaintance or someone you work with can help you with that part of the estimate.

FIGURE 8.3 Example of "And" Connective

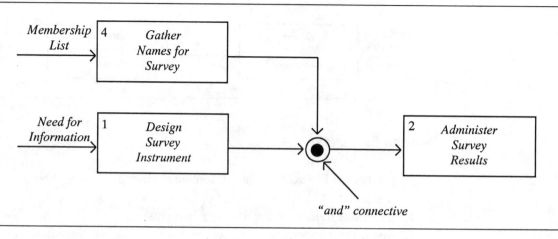

Assigning Costs

For each component assign precise, detailed estimates, using a pricing sheet such as the one shown in Figure 8.5. This form enables you to cover all possible sources of cost for each component of the project, even the smallest or most remote. It also makes estimating easier by enabling you to work on one relatively small part of the project at a time. For example, estimating an engineer's time on one inspection tour is much easier than estimating time on the project as a whole.

On the pricing sheet, costs are categorized as either *Direct Labor* or *Direct Expense*. Because your needs may require additional or different classifications, you can make up your own sheet, modeling it on this illustration.

To calculate labor, estimate the time in hours or days that each personnel category is likely to spend on the subcomponent. Then note the rate to be applied for that type of employee. If you have a specific individual lined up for a job, use that employee's or consultant's rate.

FIGURE 8.4 Example of "Or" Connective

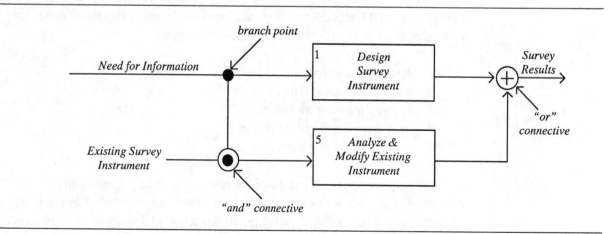

FIGURE 8.5 Pricing Sheet

Project Title _____

No. _____

Component _____

Direct Labor	Days/Hours	Rates	Total
Senior Consultant(s)	_____	_____	_____
Junior Consultant(s)	_____	_____	_____
Clerical Personnel	_____	_____	_____
Drafting Personnel	_____	_____	_____
Subtotal			_____

Direct Expenses	Units	@	Total
Auto (in miles)	_____	_____	_____
Phone	_____	_____	_____
Postage	_____	_____	_____
Air	_____	_____	_____
Hotel (per day)	_____	_____	_____
Rental Car (per day)	_____	_____	_____
Printing/Photocopying	_____	_____	_____
Subtotal			_____
Overhead			_____
General and Administrative Expense			_____
Profit			_____
Total			_____

Do the same for direct expenses as for labor. In some cases you can estimate units, such as the miles driven in an auto. In other cases you simply have to put down a lump sum. Let's say that you're estimating for the final report. When you get to "Printing/Photocopying," you know that the report has to be roughly 50 pages and that you need 25 copies. If you pay $.10 a copy for your photocopying, your cost here is $125 (50 pages × 25 copies × $.10).

Let's say the project calls for three plane trips to the factory. Under "Auto," you would insert three times the mileage to and from your local airport, as you'll have to drive your car to the airport and back three times. The cost of the three plane tickets goes into the box for "Air." And if the client does not provide transportation at the airport near the plant, insert under "Rental Car" the cost of car rental for three days.

As you can see, very few, if any, costs can escape this system. Having a stack of preprinted pricing sheets makes the estimating process all the easier. The breakdowns for our training program are shown in Figure 8.6.

FIGURE 8.6 Estimates by Components

1a. Develop Interview Guides

Direct Labor	Days	Rate*	Total
Senior Consultant(s)	¼	$400	$100
Junior Consultant(s)	¼	250	63
Clerical Personnel	¼	80	20
Drafting Personnel	½	125	63
Subtotal			$246

Direct Expense	Unit	@	Total
Auto			$ 0
Phone			10
Postage			0
Air			0
Hotel (per day)			0
Rental Car			0
Printing/Photocopying			4
Subtotal			$ 14

*Note: Rate refers to daily salary, not billing rate. See Chapter 9.

1b. Create Branch Office Survey Instruments

Direct Labor	Days	Rate*	Total
Senior Consultant(s)	½	$400	$200
Junior Consultant(s)	1	250	250
Clerical Personnel	½	80	40
Drafting Personnel	½	125	63
Subtotal			$553

Direct Expense	Unit	@	Total
Auto			$ 0
Phone			10
Postage			0
Air			0
Hotel (per day)			0
Rental Car			0
Printing/Photocopying			4
Subtotal			$ 14

1c. Test Face Validity

Direct Labor	Days	Rate*	Total
Senior Consultant(s)	0	$400	$ 0
Junior Consultant(s)	½	250	125
Clerical Personnel	0	80	0
Drafting Personnel	0	125	0
Subtotal			$125

Direct Expense	Unit	@	Total
Auto	75 mi	.27 mi	$ 20
Phone			10
Postage			0
Air			0
Hotel (per day)	1	120	120
Rental Car	1	100	100
Printing/Photocopying	1	50	50
Subtotal			$290

FIGURE 8.6 Estimates by Components (Continued)

1d. Modify Guides/Survey Instruments

Direct Labor	Days	Rate*	Total
Senior Consultant(s)	¼	$400	$100
Junior Consultant(s)	¼	250	63
Clerical Personnel	¼	80	20
Drafting Personnel	¼	125	31
Subtotal			$214

Direct Expense	Unit	@	Total
Auto	75 mi	.27 mi	$ 20
Phone			25
Postage			0
Air			120
Hotel (per day)	1	120	100
Rental Car	1	100	50
Printing/Photocopying	1	50	10
Subtotal			$325

1e. Conduct Interviews

Direct Labor	Days	Rate*	Total
Senior Consultant(s)	1½	$400	$600
Junior Consultant(s)	0	250	0
Clerical Personnel	0	80	0
Drafting Personnel	0	125	0
Subtotal			$600

Direct Expense	Unit	@	Total
Auto	75 mi	.27 mi	$ 20
Phone			25
Postage			0
Air			120
Hotel (per day)	1	100	100
Rental Car	1	50	50
Printing/Photocopying			10
Subtotal			$325

1f. Write Report

Direct Labor	Days	Rate*	Total
Senior Consultant(s)	2	$400	$ 800
Junior Consultant(s)	3	250	750
Clerical Personnel	2	80	160
Drafting Personnel	½	125	63
Subtotal			$1,773

Direct Expense	Unit	@	Total
Auto	75 mi	.27 mi	$ 20
Phone			20
Postage			5
Air			0
Hotel (per day)			0
Rental Car			0
Printing/Photocopying			135
Subtotal			$180

Totaling the Pricing Sheets

This step is simply a matter of arithmetic. Take a blank pricing sheet and label it "Total Pricing Sheet." Then go through all your subcomponent pricing sheets and total each type of expense. In the example in Figure 8.6, you would add up the number of days spent by senior consultants on the whole project:

1a.	Develop interview guides	¼ day
1b.	Create branch office survey instruments	½ day
1c.	Test face validity	0 days
1d.	Modify guides/survey instruments	¼ day
1e.	Conduct interview	1½ days
1f.	Write final report	2 days
	Total senior consultant's time	4½ days

You would repeat this step for all the pricing sheets for all the subcomponents of the job. The 4½ days for component 1 (a through f) would be added to the subtotals for other parts of the project. When you have collected all the hours for senior personnel, place the total in the appropriate box on the total pricing sheet. Then multiply that figure by the daily labor rate (in our example, $400) for the total labor cost for senior consultants. Repeat the process for all personnel. Add the totals for each labor category to derive the cost of all direct labor for the project. Next, enter the total costs of all direct expenses (auto, phone, and so on), and add these figures to obtain total direct expenses.

In our example, the total for direct labor totals $3,511, while direct expenses total $1,154. The cost of the job to you (including your own daily labor rate) is therefore $4,665.

Applying the Overhead Rate and Profit

This calculation is simple. The overhead rate is applied to the direct labor rate. The profit percentage is applied to the total charges. In our example the calculation is as follows:

Direct labor	$3,511
Overhead rate (85%)	2,984
Direct expenses	1,154
Subtotal	$7,649
Profit (18%)	1,377
Total	$9,026

With this estimate you need to be sure that you have broken down your project into sufficiently specific segments and that your overhead is really 85 percent. If these two points are firm, then you should be quite safe in assuming that the $9,026 will yield the profit you seek.

Normally, a client sees only the total figure; that is, the client knows that the total fixed price for getting the job done is $9,026. Your labor rates, overhead, and rate of profit are confidential. However, if the client is a government agency, it may require that your proposal include a line-item budget. If so, you can then enter the figures in a spreadsheet, which gives you an overview of the entire project and clearly demonstrates to the client that you have not produced your figures out of thin air. One concern of clients is that a consultant's fee is based more on imagination than reality because there's no solid product like a car or a building. For clients the entire consulting process is a little mysterious, and a spreadsheet with figures you can explain and justify lends an element of reality to an otherwise mystifying activity.

Flexibility

One major advantage of our approach is its ability to allow you flexibility in dealing with clients. Let's assume that you've presented your proposal to a client, who likes everything about it except the total fixed price. Your client informs you that its budget for this training program is only $8,000. The worst thing you could do is agree to do it for $8,000, which is like telling the client that your estimate contains at least $1,026 worth of fat.

Instead of agreeing to the client's price, go back to your bid sheet and pick out some less important item(s) that could be cut from the project. Then go to your client and say, "If we eliminated the testing for face validity of the questionnaire and survey instruments and cut the follow-up training to two days rather than three at each branch office, we could do the project for $8,000." Now the decision is with your client. Making such changes is easy when you have done a good job of estimating with a bid sheet.

In a larger consulting practice, a number of individuals are likely to contribute to a given project. In such a case, perhaps the bid sheet should be put together through the joint efforts of several individuals. The person responsible for the components of the project should usually bid it. However, one person, probably you, should coordinate and control the efforts of the bidding individuals. You want to ensure that those responsible for bids don't pad their estimates and that the estimates of others aren't unrealistically high.

Padding the Estimate

Beware the *creeping pad* when more than one person contributes to an estimate. Example: You ask a staff member (Joe) to estimate the labor for part of a project. Joe asks a second staff member (Jane) to provide an estimate to him. Feeling that Jane may have estimated low, Joe pads it a bit. When the estimate comes to you, you feel that Jane may be "light," so you too pad her estimate—hence, the creeping pad. Before long, what was supposed to take 7 working days is increased to 12 because everyone feels that Jane has not provided any slack.

Nothing is wrong with padding estimates to compensate for the underestimates of others. Only one person, however, should be charged with the responsibility of padding. If not, you may become the unwitting victim of the creeping pad, and you may grossly overprice your services. For a much more detailed discussion of estimating, see *How to Strategically Negotiate the Consulting Contract* by Howard L. Shenson (see the bibliography).

The Written Proposal

The written proposal is an important part of selling your services. It shows a client what's needed and how you can supply it, without giving away or underpricing your services. If a sale has already been closed, the proposal becomes an outline of the project and does not need to emphasize the qualities that would convince a client to sign.

This section will show you how to produce a proposal that will sell your services. A simple working proposal is quite similar to a selling one and can also be based on the outline here. For an expanded, step-by-step guide to writing winning proposals and samples/examples, see *The Consultant's Guide to Proposal Writing* by Howard L. Shenson (see the bibliography); also see Figure 8.7.

A proposal should be developed only when you believe that a good opportunity for success justifies the expenditure of time and effort. The proposal must communicate your ideas so that the reader (the decision maker) is convinced that you can achieve what you propose within the budget estimate or fixed price you quote.

You must convince a client that the need for a consultation is important. This involves showing that not having nor implementing a consultation will harm the client's interests and that your goals and objectives will correct the problem and take care of the need. The client must be convinced that the procedures you propose are the best and only alternative for rectifying the problem or meeting the need. And you must accomplish these objectives without giving your services away.

A proposal is divided into three sections: the front section, the main section, and the conclusion.

The Front Section

The front section of the proposal communicates your understanding of the purposes of the consultation and the needs it is intended to fulfill. If your services have been sought by the client, you will show your understanding of those needs. If you are seeking to inform the client of the need for using your services, you need to show what undesirable consequences will develop if you're not retained.

The front section establishes objectives and goals that will direct the services you'll deliver. *Goals* are statements of broad direction or intent. *Objectives* are specific statements of outcome presented in a format that will enable the client and consultant to determine when they have been met. This section also establishes a mandate for action, such as compliance with existing or expected laws, cost-effectiveness, warding off adverse publicity, and increased profits.

FIGURE 8.7 Sample Proposal

Date

Name
Company
Address
City/State/Zip

Dear _____ :

    I enjoyed our telephone conversation of _____. AAA has an excellent marketing opportunity for its video seminars as public seminar programs, and this letter is designed to serve as a proposal to define the steps that I believe should be undertaken to evaluate and capitalize on the marketing potential. When we spoke, I had received only the video introduction, leader guide, and participant materials for _____. Following our conversation, I received your letter of _____ and enclosures. The enclosures were particularly beneficial in the preparation of this proposal, and I apologize for taking your time on the telephone to answer questions that were handled by the enclosures.

    In my estimation the decision of how to distribute should be based upon a recognition that AAA brings to the market for distributors a significant and very valuable asset. Accordingly, the analysis of options should carefully determine the market value of the programs to ensure that the full profit potential be realized. Careful attention needs to be given to potential outside distributors relative to such factors as:

> Market experience and capability;
> Financial viability and resources;
> Importance of the AAA opportunity to their business; and
> Credibility and capability to perform at a high level.

    I believe that the following steps should be undertaken to evaluate and capitalize upon the marketing (as public seminars) of AAA seminars in general and _____ , specifically.

1. Determine the relative advantages and disadvantages of self-distribution in comparison to obtaining one or more established distributors.

    This step would include a competitive analysis of distributors, a determination of their marketing capabilities, and their financial viability/future plans. It would also include an estimation of expenses and revenues (a pro forma) for self-distribution and would evaluate various self-distribution models, such as licensing, franchising, and establishing an independent dealer network. Particular attention would be paid to operating practices and distribution models of successful and less-than-successful operating practices and distribution systems of established seminar companies, including such organizations as . . . . Further, the evaluation would concentrate on emerging learning methods that may, in time, prove more efficient and effective than live seminars and the consequences that such technological changes might have on AAA programs in general and _____ in particular.

2. Identify and select potential outside distributors.

    Step 2 would build on the work already accomplished in Step 1 and would serve to identify those organizations that might serve as a suitable distributor for AAA programs as public seminars in general and _____ specifically. The result of this activity would be to identify a list of candidate organizations that might be solicited by AAA for that purpose. It is anticipated that such candidates would include established seminar providers, as well as other organizations not currently involved in the seminar business with strong, related marketing capabilities who would be in a position to serve as a viable distributor.

FIGURE 8.7   Sample Proposal (Continued)

3. Establish requirements for performance by outside distributors.

This step would establish minimum requirements that distributors would have to meet to be acceptable to AAA and would be based on marketing and financial information gained about providers in general and candidate distributors as a result of the analysis undertaken in Steps 1 and 2. It is anticipated that such requirements would be quite specific about the nature and extent of marketing efforts to be provided by potential distributors to ensure that distribution proposals submitted in the future by such candidates could be adequately evaluated relative to self-distribution options.

4. Structure offering package to outside distributors.

On the basis of minimum requirements for distributors established as a result of the completion of Step 3 and the determination of the profit potential for self-distribution determined as a part of Step 1, the specific offer(s)/proposal(s) to be made to potential distributors would be developed.

5. Solicit outside distributors.

Offer(s)/proposal(s) developed in Step 4 would be forwarded to candidate distributors.

6. Review outside distributor responses.

Responses received from interested distributors would be reviewed, and acceptable respondents would be interviewed and evaluated.

7. Decide on method of distribution/select outside distributor(s).

Acceptable distributor offers/proposals (as modified as a result of Step 6) would be evaluated and compared to self-distribution options, and final decision would be made with respect to the distribution for _____ , specifically and perhaps for other AAA programs as well.

I believe that the above activities can be accomplished quickly as follows:

February 17–March 6, 1997
1. Determine the relative advantages and disadvantages of self-distribution in comparison to obtaining one or more established distributors.

March 2–March 13, 1997
2. Identify and select potential outside distributors.

March 9–March 20, 1997
3. Establish requirements for performance by outside distributors.

March 9–March 20, 1997
4. Structure offering package to outside distributors.

March 16–March 27, 1997
5. Solicit outside distributors.

March 30–April 17, 1997
6. Review outside distributor responses.

April 13–April 24, 1997
7. Decide upon method of distribution/select outside distributor(s).

FIGURE 8.7   Sample Proposal (Continued)

I would be pleased to provide my services in connection with the above to AAA on either a per hour fee basis or on a fixed-fee plus expenses basis, as you determine to be in your best interest. Listed below is my estimate of the hours that I anticipate would be required on my part to complete the above activities. Also, please find the fixed fee that would be charged for the completion of each activity. If it is your preference to work on an hourly fee basis, the charge would be _____ dollars per hour.

1. **Determine the relative advantages and disadvantages of self-distribution in comparison to obtaining one or more established distributors.**
   Estimated number of hours   30–40
   Fixed-fee charge $_____

2. **Identify and select potential outside distributors.**
   Estimated number of hours   12–20
   Fixed-fee charge $_____

3. **Establish requirements for performance by outside distributors.**
   Estimated number of hours   10–15
   Fixed-fee charge $_____

4. **Structure offering package to outside distributors.**
   Estimated number of hours   14–19
   Fixed-fee charge $_____

5. **Solicit outside distributors.**
   Estimated number of hours   1–14
   Fixed-fee charge $_____

6. **Review outside distributor responses.**
   Estimated number of hours   10–30
   Fixed-fee charge $_____

7. **Decide on method of distribution/select outside distributor(s).**
   Estimated number of hours   15–25
   Fixed-fee charge $_____

In addition to the above, AAA would be charged for direct expenses incurred for travel and nonroutine communications, if any. The above estimates are based upon a total meeting time with you or others you might designate in amount equal to 15 hours. Should it become necessary to meet for a duration or frequency in excess of 15 hours, additional meeting time would be billed at $XXX per hour. There would be no charge for the first 25 hours of travel time, if any.

There is no requirement on my part for AAA to contract for all of the services indicated above. If you prefer, they can be taken one at a time, and you could reach a decision at each stage as to the wisdom of further retention of my services. In the event that you were to find it advisable to contract for all or several of the services outlined, please understand that AAA would be provided with the right to terminate my services at any time during the course of the consultation.

I hope that the above information is sufficient to meet your requirements. If I may provide further information, please don't hesitate to let me know.

I look forward to the prospect of working with you on this very challenging project.

Personal regards,

_____

In some cases, particularly in smaller projects, the front section may be a page or less. In larger projects and usually government proposals, the front section typically includes the following:

- A letter of transmittal
- The proposal cover
- The proposal title page
- An abstract
- A table of contents
- A statement of assurances
- A statement of objectives
- A statement of need

In addition to indicating that the proposal is being delivered to the client organization, the letter of transmittal also conveys your availability and high level of commitment to the proposed project.

The cover should be of professional quality. The title page may include limitations on distribution. The abstract is a one-page, single-spaced summary—brief and to the point. The table of contents is a road map through the document. It should make the reader want to go on by arousing interest in the same way newspaper headlines do.

The statement of assurances communicates the following:

- Your proposal is, in your estimation, the most cost-effective possible consistent with needs.
- There are no lawsuits or judgments pending against you.
- You do not discriminate in hiring.
- You self-insure and hold your client blameless and will defend any lawsuits.

This statement should be signed by the highest official of your consulting practice and dated.

The statement of need and statement of objectives are the two most important parts of the front section. The statement of need enables the reader to independently assess the extent and validity of the needs that the proposal addresses and creates a sense of obligation to respond to the needs you have identified. Be sure to describe the problems in terms that are meaningful to the client. Avoid the use of soft terms, such as *a substantial number, a high degree,* and *a downward trend.* Use hard and quantifiable terms—the more numbers the better.

Each objective that you formulate in the statement of objectives must convey some specific information to the reader. Each objective should do the following:

- Describe the outcome you intend to produce.
- Provide a means of measuring the results.
- Set the level or quality of outcome necessary to carry out the project.

The Main Section

The main section of the proposal contains the *functional flow diagram (FFD)*, a timeline communicating when the work will be done and a written narrative explaining the results and benefits to be achieved by each activity outlined in the FFD.

We have already discussed how to formulate the FFD. The timeline gives dates or periods of time needed to complete each stage of the project. The timeline can be expressed as a line with the dates and project stages marked on it. Don't be too concerned about having exactly the right amount of time between events; just be sure that you have them in order and that you have left sufficient time for necessary client reviews and approvals.

The written narrative communicates to the reader the outcomes, results, and benefits of a consultation. It shows how the FFD will achieve the objectives and communicates that the client will have the opportunity to manage you, the consultant. For each activity box in your FFD diagram, write a one-paragraph or two-paragraph statement about the activity, and describe in general terms which procedures will be used. Your written narrative should be specific enough to communicate the type of work you'll be doing but general enough to prevent your client from using your work to get a free or lower cost consultation from someone else. Focus on what you will do but not exactly how—to avoid giving away valuable proprietary techniques.

The Conclusion

The concluding section of the proposal may include the following:

- Evaluation plan and procedures
- Reporting and dissemination plan
- Consultation/project management and organization plan
- Consultation/project price/bid
- Consultation staff statement of capability

Not every proposal will require all these elements. Sometimes clients will tell you which they want, either directly or through a published Request for Proposals (RFP). In other cases, you will have to gauge the importance of each to selling your project. The evaluation plan, when required, is important to the client by providing some type of measurement of the quality of your work and the viability of your proposal. The evaluation plan is the means by which the client can hold you accountable for funds that have been spent.

The project management plan contains information that enables the reader to assess your qualifications. The plan must show that the consultation will be conducted by one or more individuals who have an understanding of client needs and can work with the client's administrative structure. The management plan also demonstrates that the consultant has management and administrative skills as well as creative ideas. Many people are creative but have trouble getting results because they're poor managers.

The management plan should describe the administrative structure of the project, including the following:

- A detailed list of any key positions with their responsibilities and duties
- A description of the connective link between project consultants and the client's organization
- Estimates of the number of people needed to complete the project (a personnel-loading analysis)
- A description of the background and qualifications of personnel to be assigned to the project
- A description of any outside individuals or organizations needed to carry out the project, if necessary

The personnel-loading analysis provides the distribution of work hours or days for each element of the project. If you find that certain elements require too many people or hours, you may reorganize the timeline to spread out functions more evenly over time.

The fee or bid is most often introduced in the proposal at this point. Depending on the distribution of your written proposal, you may wish to include the price/bid here or put it in a confidential letter delivered separately with your formal proposal.

The statement of staff capability usually includes a statement of the organization's resources, the talents of its personnel, and résumés of key personnel who will contribute to the client's project. Have staff members prepare their own résumés according to your standard format, and make sure they update them at least every six months.

In packaging the proposal, consider using index tabs or dividers and keying the table of contents to the index tabs. If the client gives you a specific format, follow it as closely as possible. If you're sending examples of previous work that are more than five or six pages long, put them in an appendix that can be detached from the main body of the proposal.

Don't be afraid to spend a few dollars on the package. Use good-quality cover stock, colored paper, and comb binding to enhance the appearance of your proposal. You don't wish to appear lavish and wasteful, but you can produce a superior-looking document that is both cost-effective and worthwhile.

The written final report has become commonplace for many client organizations, and as many as 100 or more copies may be disseminated.

☞ Tips

This chapter has taken you from the initial stages of selling in a face-to-face situation to estimating the requirements of a project and drawing up a proposal. Part of the estimate is your daily billing rate. The next chapter will go into detail about setting your fees and determining your billing rates. When you go into a sales session with solid figures of your costs and fees, as well as confidence in your worth and understanding of the needs of a particular project, you have a much better chance of "making a close" and getting a contract with which you can work.

CHAPTER 9

Setting Your Fees

A successful marketing plan will bring more calls than you can handle. After sifting through many of them, you've lined up a number of appointments with the most suitable prospects. You've driven to a potential client's place of business, you've been ushered into the office, and you've been made comfortable with a seat and a cup of coffee. Over the next hour you discus one or two very interesting and challenging assignments. The prospect seems all but ready to become your client. At this point she smiles and asks how much will your proposal cost. That is not the moment to start thinking about fees.

The time to set fees is at the very outset of your business. Your fees are based on your skills, the need for your talents, and the assumption that you will give your clients state-of-the-art services.

This chapter will introduce you to the basics and philosophy of setting fees. For a more detailed description of the process, see *The Contract and Fee-Setting Guide for Consultants and Professionals* by Howard L. Shenson (see the bibliography).

State of the Art

Business people don't contract with consultants to get the same tired, old solutions and approaches. They want and deserve the benefit of the state of the art. You want to be able to present your clients with computer-generated reports that you can fax or download to them and get back their comments. At times it may be appropriate to deliver computer disks or CD-ROMs to clients so they can review your initial reports on their computers.

Having an e-mail address adds another dimension to communicating quickly. And using the Internet not only shows that you are technologically up to date but it can deliver reams of information at the press of a button. Having voice mail and a pager or cell phone also suggests you are in step. Being limited by not having state-of-the-art technology is a disservice to your clients and reflects poorly on you in the long run.

Asking clients to pay for cheap, shortcut, or outdated methods is as unethical as overcharging them for top-notch processes. The compilation of field survey data, for example, is best done on a personal computer or by using a computer service. The extent of your computer use depends on the amount of data you have and your processing requirements as well as on the budget.

The same principle applies to human resources as to computer use. Given an opportunity to use an assistant who's going to charge you a low fee and enable you to make a greater profit, your concern must be whether you are shortchanging a client. If the same talent and ability can be purchased at lower cost, so be it. No one suffers, and you prosper. If your judgment indicates that lower-priced talent does not meet the specifications of a contract or your own requirements, however, you are not giving your client the state of the art in human resources.

Name Your Price

Don't be afraid to talk about your fee. If you select one or more of the fee-setting methods in this chapter or so long as you arrive at your fee through a reasonable calculation, you should not allow that amount to be negotiated. Given a change in requirements or specifications, which in turn lowers the amount of time or the level of expertise required, the cost of a particular contract is certainly negotiable—but not your base rate and not your underlying calculations.

As a consultant, you may find yourself about to lose a contract award to a competitor on the basis of price. In general, bidding lower to keep the assignment is not good policy. Doing so gives the impression that your original bid was inflated in the first place. The logical and probably unasked question in the client's mind is: Why didn't I get this price the first time? From your point of view, if your fee contains a reasonable profit in the first place, you should not settle for a less-than-reasonable profit.

Competitors who underbid you dramatically tend to have short business lives. They might have a secret formula that enables them to survive, or perhaps even thrive, on lower fees. If so, they deserve their contracts. More likely, they're underpricing themselves just to get work, which often turns out to be less than satisfactory for clients. Even if these lowball competitors stay in business, they can become your best advertising. In such cases you'll see their clients again. Don't be afraid to stick by your fee—so long as it's reasonable.

Determining Your Fee

If you feel you should be earning, say, $600 a day, you might have to bill out at $1,100 or $1,200 a day. The difference is explained by accounts for something many consultants forget about—overhead and profit. You can't price yourself like a day laborer because *you* have an office and other costs to support.

Large firms have a lot of overhead. A typical management consulting firm breaks down its fees into thirds: One-third covers the cost of a job, one-third non-marketing overhead, and one-third marketing overhead and profit. If such a firm is charging $1,000 a day, a member consultant is earning $333. The other $667 is split between the two types of overhead and affords a reasonable profit.

Going into business as a consultant means just that—going into business. Expenses must be controlled and accounted for, and profits must be calculated and monitored. If you were the owner-operator of a product-oriented business, you would be concerned with inventories, raw material costs, depreciation, and other expenses related to manufacturing or shipping. In a service-oriented business, you must be just as concerned about expenses and profits, even though both take a different form.

Setting fees, or a price, for your services involves the following steps:

1. Establishing a daily labor rate—the expense of your time
2. Determining your overhead—the expense of being in business
3. Fixing your profit—the value you place on the risk you take by being in business

Your Daily Labor Rate

Figuring your daily labor rate starts with deciding the yearly amount that you're worth and then converting that annual figure to a daily amount. Before calculating your daily rate, it's very important that you are realistic in assessing how much you want to make annually and what your services are worth in the marketplace. Don't underestimate either your value or what you want to make. Doing so will find you setting your fee too low—a common mistake made by many and one from which recovery is very difficult.

The median daily rate charged by consultants in some specialties is shown in Figure 9.1. These figures represent the findings of a national survey conducted by *The Professional Consultant* to determine the overall economic status of the profession. Median rates have held stable through the 1990s, largely because of the influx of people into the consulting profession. For the same reason, average rates in most specialties have held at somewhere between $1,100 and $1,500 per day.

The influx into virtually all consulting specialties has resulted from restructuring in the marketplace. Downsizing, reengineering, and the flattening of organizations have left many thousands out of work. Many have entered the ranks of consulting reluctantly. The laws of supply and demand apply to consulting, too, and the significant increase in supply has seen average consultant rates stay stable.

This stability of consultant rates doesn't mean that top consultants are charging less for their services. Rather, it means that there are more and more neophyte consultants who are charging less for their services and causing average consulting fees to stay flat. Many of these new entrants are reluctant entrepreneurs who would really rather be working for someone else but find it difficult to find positions equivalent to those they held in the past. They often mistakenly set their rates based on what they were making in their last jobs without regard for the overhead associated with starting and running a practice.

FIGURE 9.1 Median Daily Billing Rate and Income of Consultants by Specialty

The Professional Consultant ©199., HOWARD L. SHENSON • 20750 VENTURA BOULEVARD
WOODLAND HILLS, CA 91364 • USA • TELEPHONE 818/703-1415

FEE MEDIANS BY GEOGRAPHIC MARKET LOCATION, MARKET POSITION, SIZE OF CLIENT

Field/Specialty	MajMkt	SmlMkt	Top10	Low10	BigCli	SmlCli
All Professionals	$1,218	$ 899	$1,994	$ 486	$1,173	$ 891
Accounting	$1,197	$ 915	$2,012	$ 495	$1,218	$ 604
Advertising	$1,280	$ 921	$2,513	$ 583	$1,224	$ 992
Agriculture	$ 815	$ 713	$1,187	$ 366	$ 823	$ 685
Aerospace	$1,095	$ 968	$1,490	$ 671	$1,222	$ 947
Arts & Cultural	$ 852	$ 633	$1,224	$ 319	$ 767	$ 645
Banking	$1,185	$ 967	$1,756	$ 601	$1,254	$ 898
Broadcast	$1,103	$ 851	$1,595	$ 660	$1,121	$ 873
Busn. Acquisition/Sales	$1,002	$ 832	$1,891	$ 456	$1,035	$ 840
Chemical	$1,256	$ 890	$1,955	$ 543	$1,156	$ 946
Communications	$ 914	$ 665	$1,312	$ 401	$ 838	$ 752
Construction	$1,049	$ 856	$1,744	$ 696	$1,059	$ 847
Data Processing Conslt	$1,159	$ 857	$1,715	$ 613	$1,190	$ 955
Data Processing Progrm	$ 861	$ 553	$1,098	$ 440	$ 913	$ 642
Dental/Medical	$1,338	$ 906	$1,993	$ 597	$1,231	$1,001
Design (Industrial)	$1,088	$ 762	$1,239	$ 556	$ 959	$ 848
Economics	$1,128	$ 899	$1,678	$ 639	$1,077	$ 972
Education	$ 836	$ 581	$1,306	$ 412	$ 855	$ 670
Engineering	$1,351	$ 992	$1,723	$ 667	$1,332	$1,044
Estate Planning	$1,001	$ 720	$1,777	$ 554	$1,014	$ 835
Executive Search	$1,087	$ 783	$1,780	$ 586	$1,101	$ 919
Export/Import	$1,199	$ 937	$1,678	$ 641	$1,075	$ 987
Fashion/Beauty	$ 635	$ 456	$ 983	$ 354	$ 569	$ 548
Finance	$1,267	$ 956	$2,231	$ 605	$1,179	$ 980
Franchise	$1,013	$ 937	$1,688	$ 546	$1,126	$ 929
Fund Raising	$ 910	$ 753	$1,456	$ 500	$ 888	$ 759
Grantsmanship	$ 812	$ 585	$1,190	$ 433	$ 759	$ 681
Graphics/Print Trades	$ 850	$ 649	$1,451	$ 522	$ 778	$ 662
Health Care	$1,378	$ 994	$2,142	$ 738	$1,312	$1,001
Hotel/Restaurant/Club	$ 975	$ 686	$1,415	$ 539	$ 872	$ 763
Insurance	$ 846	$ 723	$1,368	$ 511	$ 834	$ 680
International Business	$1,234	$ 967	$1,974	$ 686	$1,256	$ 997
Investment Advisory	$1,033	$ 792	$2,112	$ 451	$ 968	$ 853
Management	$1,195	$ 981	$2,210	$ 535	$1,113	$ 976
Marketing	$1,173	$ 915	$2,034	$ 513	$1,288	$ 966
Municipal Government	$ 914	$ 679	$1,201	$ 544	$ 859	$ 680
New Business Ventures	$ 919	$ 750	$1,387	$ 487	$ 944	$ 742
Packaging	$ 957	$ 901	$1,399	$ 581	$1,024	$ 757
Pension	$1,067	$ 816	$1,655	$ 641	$1,087	$ 747
Personnel/HRD	$ 935	$ 744	$1,986	$ 535	$1,146	$ 773
Production	$1,136	$ 855	$1,824	$ 533	$1,198	$ 731
Psychological Services	$ 809	$ 638	$1,446	$ 452	$1,010	$ 550
Public Relations	$ 970	$ 711	$1,552	$ 499	$ 998	$ 648
Publishing	$1,234	$ 783	$1,577	$ 636	$ 941	$ 736
Purchasing	$1,058	$ 812	$1,629	$ 539	$ 992	$ 824
Quality Control	$1,056	$ 963	$2,088	$ 590	$1,283	$ 899
Real Estate	$ 952	$ 686	$1,930	$ 542	$1,126	$ 659
Records Management	$ 733	$ 626	$1,391	$ 476	$ 924	$ 541
Recreation	$ 832	$ 677	$1,116	$ 450	$ 874	$ 584
Research & Development	$1,301	$1,065	$2,211	$ 805	$1,438	$ 967
Retail	$1,113	$ 799	$1,564	$ 613	$1,214	$ 770
Scientific	$1,301	$1,224	$2,256	$ 843	$1,395	$1,082
Security	$ 891	$ 734	$1,486	$ 644	$1,180	$ 657
Statistical	$ 880	$ 723	$1,392	$ 655	$ 888	$ 661
Telecommunications	$1,215	$ 910	$1,597	$ 671	$1,210	$ 791
Traffic/Transportation	$ 946	$ 781	$1,539	$ 547	$1,094	$ 672
Training	$ 959	$ 774	$1,652	$ 668	$ 996	$ 586
Travel	$ 675	$ 588	$1,244	$ 512	$ 854	$ 482

Don't fall prey to this style of fee setting. Like those who purposefully lowball bids to get consulting work, you'll find your life in business a short one.

Calculating Your Daily Rate

Let's take an example to calculate a daily rate. Jane Smith is resigning her position as a computer systems analyst with a major firm to become a consultant. Her position paid $65,000 a year, and she would like to earn at least that much as a consultant to start—her determination of her annual worth.

Although there are 365 days in the year, there are only 261 working days (365 days less 104 Saturdays and Sundays). To arrive at her daily labor rate, she divides her desired annual salary by the number of working days:

$$\$65,000 \div 261 = \$249.05$$

Her daily labor rate can be rounded off to $250.

How Many Hours in a Day?

How many hours constitute a workday? As an employee your workday is clearly defined. In our society 8 hours is the commonly accepted workday. Yet even in a so-called 9-to-5 position, a conscientious professional often puts in more time than the prescribed 8 hours.

Like other professionals, consultants sometimes have to work more than 8 hours a day but will bill for just a day. You can expect to do that occasionally and chalk it up to goodwill. You'll probably work less than an 8-hour day at times for the same client and bill that as a day. In most cases, the "give" washes out with the "take."

Sometimes clients may take advantage of you, either deliberately or inadvertently. You find yourself working 10 to 12 hours a day for a certain client on a steady basis. Regardless of the client's culpability for the overtime, you should take measures to account for your time. One measure is better planning of the daily work agenda. Perhaps you haven't been realistic about how much you can accomplish in one day; if so, you need to reevaluate your daily agendas. Another measure is to bill on an hourly basis. To calculate your hourly rate, simply divide your daily rate by 8 hours. Jane's hourly labor rate would be $31.14 ($249.05 ÷ 8 hours), which could be rounded to $35.

Overhead

Consultants incur two types of expenses. One type includes the expenses you have regardless of how much work you do. They are fixed at one level whether you're working on one project or fifty. These expenses include office rent, lease payments for a photocopier, an office assistant's salary, Internet charges, an accountant's fee, and the like. These are your *overhead expenses*.

The other type of expenses, called *direct expenses,* varies with the work you do. These expenses are related directly to and arise from work on a particular project. Direct expenses might include the daily labor rates of associates, travel expenses on an assignment, long-distance phone charges, materials, supplies for mock-ups or presentations, and the like.

Between these two expense types is a gray area that could be classified either way. Travel expenses may constitute a direct expense if they're incurred on a particular contracted assignment. On the other hand, let's say that you traveled to meet with a prospect or two without the assurance that you would actually get a contract. In this case, the travel expenses would become part of your overhead. In general, the nature of the expenditure does not determine how it is classified, but its purpose does. The discriminating question is: Can this expense be related directly to an assignment?

Each type of expense, overhead or direct, is handled differently. Overhead is best converted to a fixed percentage and added to your daily labor rate. It is not recalculated for each job. As a general rule of thumb, overhead usually falls between 65 and 150 percent of your daily labor rate; although in some cases, it will be higher. Only rarely will it be lower than 65 percent, for reasons you will soon see. Direct expenses are calculated for each job and added to the amount that reflects the daily labor rate plus fixed overhead and profit. The total of all of these expenses is the project's cost.

Calculating Overhead

The percentage of overhead expenses charged by consultants depends on costs or expenses incurred. Although the amounts charged differ from one consultant to another, Figure 9.2 shows a realistic rather than contrived or theoretical example. Clerical expenses are billed partly as direct expenses and partly as overhead. About two-thirds of the clerical work is charged directly to clients for such activities as word processing and producing survey data. The rest of the clerical expenses are for tasks like answering the phone that have to be done routinely and are part of overhead.

Office rental is clearly part of overhead expenses. Even if you work at home and avoid paying rent, your daily rate should include the amount of rent that normally would be paid for an office as part of your overhead budget. Otherwise, you'll seriously underprice your services. The same holds true for any other overhead expenses for which you don't actually expend money.

Telephone bills are divided, like clerical expenses, into overhead and direct expenses. The overhead part is for telephone calls from just being in business, whereas the rest are charged to clients directly.

The charge for automotive expenses covers leasing and maintaining an automobile for business purposes. When the automobile is used on behalf of clients, the clients are charged directly by the mile. Most consultants bill the per-mile charge permitted by the IRS.

FIGURE 9.2   A Typical Overhead Calculation

Jane Smith, Full-Time Consultant
Daily Labor Rate = $250
Overhead (Monthly)

Clerical ($1,525)...	$ 525
Office rent...	700
Telephone...	225
Postage and shipping	80
Automotive...	350
Employment taxes	575
Personnel benefits...	450
Insurance...	200
Business licenses and taxes	95
Marketing	
Direct $ 275	
Personnel 1,000	1,275
Professional development..	100
Dues and subscriptions	35
Printing and photocopying	80
Stationery and supplies...	85
Accounting and legal	150
Practice management	250
Other expenses	250
Total Overhead	$5,425

Personnel Benefits

Because you go into business on your own doesn't mean you aren't entitled to fringe benefits. Your overhead budget should therefore contain a charge for such expenses as

- a paid vacation;
- health insurance;
- life insurance;
- paid sick leave; and
- a retirement plan.

These expenses are normal and routine in American business. Their cost usually falls between 21 and 33 percent of direct salaries.

Marketing

In Figure 9.2, consultant Smith charges $1,275 to overhead every month for marketing expenses. The $1,000 amount is categorized as "Personnel," and the balance of $275 is called "Direct." The total amount represents what this consultant feels she must spend to market her services.

The larger amount—$1,000—represents four days' worth of income to Ms. Smith at her $250 daily labor rate. She plans to spend those four days on marketing

FIGURE 9.3   The Feast or Famine Cycle

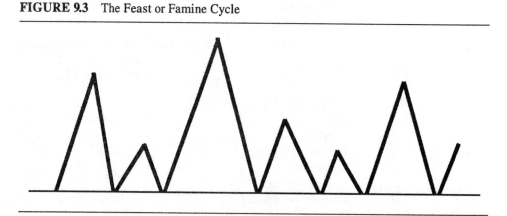

projects of her choosing. Somehow, those days have to be included in her overhead as a cost of doing business. She must account for the days on which she is not billing clients so that she can get paid and attain her annual income goal of $65,000.

Some consultants, in contrast, charge each client for marketing costs they incurred to get the client. And they also bill for some of the marketing money spent on prospects who didn't become clients. Besides being very unfair, these practices are neither wise nor recommended. They usually produce poor and rushed marketing. You might regard allocating four days as a marketing expense to be too much. It is not. You should give marketing the same time and care that you give your most important client. No matter how busy you become with client work, you must religiously set aside time each month for marketing. Failure to do so inevitably results in a kind of yo-yo cycle in which you go from financial feast to famine.

Figure 9.3 shows how this feast or famine cycle works. At the low points, you have no clients and no business. What do you do? You spend time marketing. You do so well that you become overloaded with work. Your schedule of client work becomes so heavy that you have no time to market. As a result you come back to a low point of no work. And so the cycle repeats itself.

A yo-yo cycle is not only a poor business practice, it is also psychologically unsettling. Far better to discipline yourself to market in a consistent and regular fashion to create a business cycle that looks like the one in Figure 9.4. The latter type of cycle gives you a smoother cash flow and greater peace of mind.

FIGURE 9.4   A Smooth Business Cycle

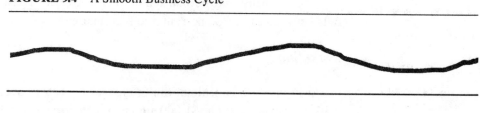

Professional Development

To maintain and improve your professional standing, you normally have to spend money and time to pay for courses, seminars, books, audiocassette training programs, and the like. These expenses arise either from legal requirements or from a professional's need to keep abreast of the state of the art in his or her field. These expenses are almost always treated legitimately as overhead. Clients must expect to share the costs much as they would when visiting the family doctor.

The Overhead Rate

In the field of professional services, overhead is always expressed as a percentage of the labor rate. To determine the daily dollar value for overhead, divide the total overhead amount by the number of days that you expect to be billing clients. The resulting dollar amount must be added to the daily labor rate for each day a client is billed. Ms. Smith's overhead rate in Figure 9.2, for example, is calculated by taking the total dollar amount for her monthly overhead, $5,425, and dividing that by the number of days she expects to bill clients each month, 15 days. Dividing $5,425 by 15 days gives $361.67, which is her daily overhead.

To find the overhead rate as a percentage, simply divide the daily dollar value for overhead by the consultant's daily labor rate. In our example, Ms. Smith's daily labor rate is $250. The overhead calculation is $361.67 divided by $250 = 1.45 or 145 percent. An overhead percentage rate is then applied to the daily labor rate charge for each day. One day of Ms. Smith's time would be billed at her daily rate plus 144 percent for overhead plus whatever percentage of profit she charges, say 20 percent.

Daily Labor Rate	$250.00	
Overhead (144%)	361.67	
Subtotal	611.67	
Profit (20%)	122.33	
Total		$734.00

Because the number is usually rounded to the nearest $50, Ms. Smith's daily billing rate would be $750.

Adding Goodies

Goodies are the not-so-necessary but very appealing items that you feel can be paid for as part of your overhead. You may want a fancy office or additional vacation time. These are nice to have, but take care that you don't price yourself out of the market by living too well. Be reasonable before loading something onto your overhead rate.

Bureaucratic Growth

As your business ages, it tends to grow. And with growth comes a higher overhead. Increased overhead is a reality of business life. As a practice becomes larger, it requires more labor to meet client demands.

On the surface, business growth seems obvious and even more profitable. Lower-paid people may be used to handling less demanding tasks. Yet the sheer addition of personnel requires more management, more supervision, more communication—and more risk. A larger practice has more of a reputation to protect, and controlling it is less direct than when it was founded. Additional expenditures have to be studied, supervised, and controlled. Many of these added expenses might well be judged as wasteful or indicative of poor management to all but the most seasoned bureaucrat. With growth, organizations tend to accumulate flab in their overhead rates.

Watching Overhead

To keep your overhead at a level appropriate for your size, you should compare your current actual expenses with those in the past. Where did the money go? Where did expenses decrease? What new expenses appeared? Which ones dropped off the list? During your first year in business, the absolute longest you want to go without checking your actual expenses is six months. For better control, you should check each quarter.

After the first year, expenses should be checked once or twice annually. If sudden or radical changes take place in your practice, more frequent comparisons are warranted. If you're expanding your practice and taking on new partners and employees, you should have more frequent audits of expenses to keep overhead under control.

Profit

Over and above your daily labor rate and overhead, you should charge a profit. Many consultants overlook the need for profit, rationalizing that because they're charging for their labor, charging a profit would be immoral or improper.

Another reason profit is overlooked is that it has acquired a negative connotation in some quarters. Somehow it has become associated with the supposed evils of "Big Business." Most people resent the huge profits of the oil, utility, and phone companies, and this resentment carries over into small business. Yet one more reason for overlooking profit is that most people don't really understand how the free enterprise system works. Profit is the whole purpose of running any kind of business. Consultants who don't understand this seem to think that all they have coming to them is their labor rate.

Profit is the reward for the risk of being in business. Even if consultants invest little or no capital in their businesses, they are still investing their time, which translates ultimately into money. They place their valuable time at risk, and they deserve to profit from that risk.

Consultants must distinguish between their labor rates and profits. They deserve their labor rates whether they work for someone else or for themselves. Their profits belong to them by reason of their being in business.

Typically, consultants charge between 16 and 24 percent of the combined sum of their daily labor rate and overhead charge as profit. Some consultants charge more and some less. The percentage depends on whatever a consultant judges to be fair and appropriate.

The Government Client

To get a government consulting contract, you have to be sensitive to the special requirements, policies, and attitudes of different agencies. Often you find yourself dealing on two levels: the official and the realistic. Officially, you may be entitled by policy or law to only a specified profit or a specified labor rate. Realistically, program managers for a government agency may recognize that you simply can't adequately or profitably perform your services within a policy's limits. They are caught between rocklike agency policy and the hard place of getting programs going.

We can describe only some of the practices that result from this dilemma. They are not recommended because, officially, they are improper. To be a well-informed consultant, however, you should know that a few consultants report that they do make use of such tactics even though they are unethical or even illegal.

With a government agency as a client, unique rules often govern disclosure of a consultant's fee to the client. Given the legal and procedural considerations that govern procurement by government agencies, you sometimes have to make your responses strategic. Your chief considerations are

1. the maximum labor rates,
2. the client's understanding of overhead,
3. the acceptability of overhead charges, and
4. the acceptability of profit.

Maximum Labor Rates

Some government agencies have maximum allowable labor rates. Whether established by executive decision or legislative mandate, these rates allow agencies to pay only so much per day. In such cases, consultants should be sure that the labor rates they disclose to a government client do not exceed the allowable maximum. If an agency is not permitted to pay any consultant more than $300 per day, for example, a consultant would not want to even hint that his or her daily labor rate is $350.

You might assume that the solution to maximum rates is to work on a fixed-fee contract. Unfortunately, working on a fixed-fee contract is usually not possible because most government agencies require full disclosure of all estimated price breakouts, even if contracts are fixed price. In the private sector, those who hire a consultant on a fixed-price contract usually are not told anything other than the total dollar amount of the contract. But most government agencies work on line-item budgets. The entire pricing sheet must be shown to the government client.

Suppose that you can't work on a fixed-price contract and that your labor rate exceeds the limits of acceptability. Some consultants rearrange work responsibilities so that their lower-compensated staff can do more of the work. If principal consultants are obliged to work at a lower rate, they need not do so for as many days as a result. The total billed amount will then come out the same, but the distribution of the workload changes to meet the agency's requirements. This practice is illegal and should be avoided.

What about the propriety of accepting a lower labor rate and rearranging the workload? Officially, this practice is neither recognized nor advocated, particularly by fiscal personnel in government agencies, although some program-management people accept such adjustments to get projects through.

Client's Understanding of Overhead

Because consultants must reveal their pricing details to a government client, they must be sure that the client's program personnel understand the nature of overhead and the process by which it is calculated.

In government agencies, many staff members are not experienced in buying consultant services. They may regard your charges as excessive and unreasonable, so you may have to instruct them about the nature of overhead and its method of calculation.

Acceptability of Overhead Charges

Some government agencies don't accept certain expense items as overhead charges; such expenses as marketing, entertainment, and interest are typical. If your contract is subject to certain audit provisions, these expenses will not be accepted. Always inquire about the acceptability of certain items before submitting a bid for services.

Acceptability of Profit

Some agencies have policies governing the allowable rate of contractor profit. Others lack specific policies, but their employees have attitudes about such matters. You must ensure that the profit you charge conforms to the client organization's policies or is acceptable to the client's representatives.

To learn about policies covering profits, you might use precise questioning or fact-finding. Or you might ask the client to provide you with a copy of one or more prior consulting contracts that were awarded in a similar situation.

However you get your information, suppose that profit rates of 5 or 10 percent are required or expected. Should you work at such low rates of return? Technically yes, but in reality no. Do consultants really work for government clients for such low returns? Some do, some don't. Fortunately, workers in many government agencies have realistic attitudes about contracting for services. They recognize the economic need for legitimate profitability. Some consultants often hide extra profitability in a budget while the profit line shows a low percentage. Profit may be hidden by showing a higher labor rate than was actually paid, more labor days than were actually expended, higher direct costs than were actually incurred, or the like.

If a contract is auditable, of course, consultants take greater care to ensure that the expenses claimed are supported by evidence. If you anticipate substantial work on auditable government contracts, study the subject in detail.

Some consultants get their additional profit without showing it on the profit line by creating an additional category of expense, such as General and Administrative (G&A), that government agencies are often used to paying but that small consulting practices rarely have. G&A is an expense that is handy for large businesses to account for things like corporatewide auditing and communications.

Although paying consultants for G&A expenses certainly won't be found in the policies and procedures manuals of government procurement agencies, it is relatively widespread. Whether the fiscal personnel within government agencies recognize the practice is not really known. Most program personnel who seek out consultants' services know about it, even if they don't generally admit it, and some government agencies even make half-hearted attempts to police the situation.

Fee Collection

As in any business, consultants sometimes have trouble collecting their fees. A number of precautions can help you avoid this problem, and several tactics can solve difficulties when they occur.

Mutual Understanding

There is no substitute for having a good understanding with clients. No contract and no agreement can substitute for it. If you and a client can't see eye-to-eye up front, your contract is going to run into trouble at some time in the future. Make sure that you and the client both look at the written contract in the same way—a strong mutual understanding can be an important asset when collecting the fee.

A Good Contract

With an adequate and clearly written contract in hand, you and your clients know just where you stand. A written contract is usually enough to make *your* obligations more legal in their minds. For small billings, a wave of the contract is usually enough to shake a payment loose. For large fees, litigation may become necessary; if so, a detailed contract is invaluable. A contract with an arbitration clause might ensure you get your money and keep you out of court.

Progress Payments

Most clients are quite willing to pay on a progress basis, either at prescribed intervals after a certain percent of the work is completed or when specified "deliverables" are submitted by the consultant. Don't be afraid to ask for progress payments. If you can arrange accelerated progress payments, you can always be working on the client's money. In this case, the payments are larger up front and smaller at the end. The earlier payments cover the work already performed and part of the remaining work, which helps your cash flow and requires only a little ingenuity in dividing up the invoices.

Even if you don't ask for progress payments, you should ask for immediate reimbursement for direct expenses, such as getting something printed or leasing a special piece of equipment.

Withholding Output or Resources

Sometimes a client has withheld payment in the past or seems likely to. In such a case you might consider withholding the results or product of your service. One accountant holds his client's books until he's paid. He even writes out the checks and has the clients sign them!

Factoring/Receivables Financing

Occasionally, you'll do business with large, solvent organizations that pay—but pay slowly. The money will come, but your cash flow needs an injection right away. *Factoring* (lending money, with accounts receivable as security) is sometimes a handy solution, although it won't work if you're working for relatively small or unknown clients.

Once work is billed to a large, well-known client, take the invoice to your bank and ask an officer to advance a percentage of the bill. Typically, you can get up to two-thirds of the invoice amount right away and pay it back with interest when the check comes in. You might even ask the client to let you submit invoices early so that you can get them factored.

Collection Proceeding

You may at times have to resort ultimately to collection proceedings. Unfortunately, collection agents are not suitable for collecting consulting fees. They charge a lot, and all they can do is send out a series of letters, each one a little more threatening than the last. When they run out of letters, nothing happens.

Instead of a collection agency, you have to use your ingenuity. Consider why it will be important to the organization that owes you money to pay you. Don't be vindictive. Being vengeful could cost you business in the future, not to mention referrals. But explain to the client why it's in its (the organization's) best interest to pay you—preserving the relationship so you can continue to assist it and it can avoid finding its name in the collections section of the local business newspaper and can continue to keep its credit rating good.

☞ Tips

Some consultants feel that by submitting a lowball estimate on the first assignment from a client, they can buy some business. Their rationale is that they'll work their way into the good graces of the client and eventually make back their losses on the low estimate. The fact is you don't buy any worthwhile business that way. Your client will be eager to tell everyone what great work you do for a low price. Getting rid of that image may take a very long time. Moreover, you have already established your value and you'll be hard pressed to get the client to pay you more for the second, third, or fourth engagement than for the first.

On-the-Spot Estimates

Telling clients your hourly or daily rate is one thing. Quoting a whole job on the spot is quite another, even if you know right away. Go back to your office, reflect on the client's needs, think about the job, do an estimate of your own if necessary, and then submit a reasoned estimate. Clients will be more impressed with a considered estimate that you provide two days later than with a snap judgment.

Increasing Fees

Increasing your fees is necessary and expected because prices are always on the increase. Your increases, however, shouldn't occur too frequently. You don't want to create an impression that every time a client turns around, your fees are up again. Limit your increases to once or twice a year at most. Your increases should be substantial enough to last 6 to 12 months. Informing regular clients by letter 90 days before a fee increase will serve ample notice for client planning and spur those considering your services to do so now rather than later.

When informing clients that fees will be increased, provide a letter explaining why. Point out all the factors that have led to increased costs: rent, utilities, secretarial assistance, increased self-employment taxes, and so on.

Now that you know how to make a sale and have set your fees and gotten what you're worth, you're ready to handle the actual consulting work. The next chapter covers negotiating the job with the client, setting up a contract, and handling client relations.

CHAPTER 10

Contracts and Client-Consultant Relationships

The cornerstone of a good relationship with your clients is a solid contract. Although this document is advisable for legal protection, it is nothing more than the reflection in black and white of the meeting of minds between two parties. The practical value of the contract depends on the quality of the relationship between you and your client. The contract becomes a tool that both parties can use for mutual benefit. If the contract is the product of mistrust, it becomes a two-edged sword. We'll look next at different kinds of contracts and the underlying relationship each embodies.

A complete treatment of the topic of contracts requires much more space than is available in this chapter. You can find a more detailed and extensive coverage of the topic, including examples and sample contracts, in *How to Strategically Negotiate the Consulting Contract* by Howard L. Shenson (see the bibliography).

The Form of the Contract

The contract can be in the form of a simple letter of agreement or it can be a formal instrument with clauses, subclauses, and other legal trappings. A verbal contract is usually legally binding, but it is hard to enforce and suffers from the well-known vagaries of human memory. You can always take a written contract out and look at it, but when two or more people are trying to remember what was said weeks or months ago, the result is nearly always conflict and confusion.

For most consulting jobs, a simple letter of agreement is sufficient. It outlines the project, sets the milestones and deadlines, and establishes the way in which the consultant will be compensated. It can also deal with such matters, for example, as the support the consultant will receive on the job, performance expectations, and the handling of unexpected problems. Because a letter of agreement is a contract, it is legally binding.

For large or complex projects, you may need to draw up a more formal contract, often with the help of a lawyer. If several consultants are involved in executing a project, a formal contract is essential, and you'll probably need one to avoid confusion and establish clear lines of authority on a major project.

Whether you use a letter of agreement or a formal contract, a number of standard arrangements, which are listed and discussed below, are possible. You want to choose the kind of arrangement that is appropriate to the project and the client. When you begin work with a clear understanding of responsibilities and financial arrangements, the job will be done more smoothly and will almost always end with both parties feeling satisfied. See the appendix for sample contracts.

The relationship between consultant and client can take a number of forms, including the following:

- Fixed-price contract
- Fixed-fee-plus-expenses contract
- Daily-rate contract
- Time-and-materials contract
- Cost-reimbursement contract
- Retainer contract
- Performance contract

Each type may be useful at one time or another, depending on the situation and the demands of a particular project.

Fixed-Price Contracts

The fixed-price contract is very simple. After ascertaining a client's precise needs, state that you can perform the services required for a flat dollar amount of your choosing (see Chapter 8 for details on estimating a fixed fee). Once the fixed price is accepted and a contract is drawn, you are bound to deliver the services for that amount. If you handle the work efficiently and the services cost you less than you estimated, you make more profit than expected. If your expenses are higher than estimated, you lose some profit.

Payment is linked to your performance. If the contract has not been fulfilled by the consultant, at the conclusion of the work, not only could the final payment be withheld but the progress payments, if any, might have to be returned. Clients run little or no risk with a fixed-price contract. It is the consultant who assumes nearly all the risk. Why, then, would you agree to this type of contract? The reason is that a fixed-price contract is usually more profitable than other types of contracts.

Not all fixed-price contracts are the same. They can fall into one of the following categories:

- Firm fixed-price contract
- Escalating fixed-price contract
- Incentive fixed-price contract

- Performance fixed-price contract
- Fixed-price contract with redetermination

Firm Fixed-Price Contract. This kind of contract offers a firm, fixed price for specified work and is not subject to change except when the scope or character of the work is changed. All risk is with the consultant, whose opportunity for profit in assuming this risk is greatest under this type of agreement.

Escalating Fixed-Price Contract. This kind of agreement is similar to the firm fixed-price contract except that it has provisions for upward or downward adjustments of the fee on the basis of predetermined contingencies, such as the cost-of-living index.

Incentive Fixed-Price Contract. This type of contract has an adjustment formula designed to reward efficiency and penalize inefficiency. If costs are below the ceiling price, the consultant gets the extra profit. If the expenses exceed the ceiling price, the costs are divided according to a predetermined schedule. Both parties might agree that additional expenses are to be borne by the client at a rate of 75 percent and by the consultant at a rate of 25 percent, reducing the consultant's profit by one-fourth.

Performance Fixed-Price Contract. This type of agreement is similar to the firm fixed-price contract except that it compensates the consultant for special performance. The consultant might get a bonus for bringing the contract in early or as a result of some other special achievement.

Fixed-Price Contract with Redetermination. This contract is the same as a firm fixed-price contract except that it has a provision allowing both the consultant and the client to redetermine or reset the price after the contract has been signed. This contract is most useful when the nature of the task is so vague, uncertain, or unknown that an accurate estimate cannot be made. At the time the contract is signed, both parties agree on a future time for redetermining the price on the basis of their experience with actual costs and expenses. They determine by agreement whether the change in price will affect prior work, future work, or both.

This kind of contract usually benefits a consultant who is working on some blind or unknown task for which the costs may be much higher than anyone would have conceived. But the redetermination may also be downward. If actual costs are a great deal less than anticipated, this contract may be to the advantage of the client.

Fixed-Fee-Plus-Expenses Contracts

When direct expenses are difficult or impossible to foresee, the consultant can submit the direct labor charge, overhead, and profit as a fixed fee, but the client is liable for the direct expenses.

Daily-Rate Contracts

Working on a daily-rate basis may be safer than submitting a fixed price. Some consultations smack of hidden pitfalls—too speculative or unpredictable for the consultant to guarantee either services or expenses. The client's personality may even create an element of uncertainty, and sometimes a situation just looks as if it might have surprises. You might pad the fixed-price contract you're going to submit. A little padding shouldn't hurt; however, a lot can not only dull your competitive edge but can also border on the unethical.

In daily-rate contracts, consultants submit an estimate of time and expenses, but they are not responsible for overruns. Clients assume all risk for overruns in both cost areas while they enjoy all the benefits of underruns.

Time-and-Materials Contracts

This type of contract works exactly like the daily-rate contract with a couple of exceptions. One is that the consultant pays expenses but adds a handling charge, normally at the same rate as profit. Because the consultant then bills the client for the total, the client doesn't pay expenses directly. Another exception to a daily-rate contract is that clerical support is not built into daily rates; instead, this work is usually charged as an expense.

A time-and-materials contract is a kind of fixed-price contract in that labor and overhead rates are fixed. What the client winds up paying, though, is far from fixed. However, the amount of time the consultant may spend is not predetermined. Hence, a time-and-materials contract is an incentive for consultants to be anything but efficient—the longer a project takes, the more money they earn.

Cost-Reimbursement Contracts

Cost-reimbursement contracts focus on costs rather than on fees. Under these contracts, consultants are reimbursed for costs they incur. Even in those contracts that call for fees—not all of them do—the fees are emphasized less than the costs.

The underlying assumption for these types of contracts is that clients pay all costs or consultants cease performance. Whereas consultants act as principals in a fixed-price contract, they act as agents of the client in a cost-reimbursement contract. They run no risk of loss but don't earn the added profit normally associated with fixed-price contracts.

Cost-reimbursement contracts are used when consultants can't accurately estimate costs and their cost accounting systems enable clients to monitor costs. Clients, as a rule, don't favor these contracts because they have to expend a lot of effort keeping track of consultants' costs.

The success of these contracts depends on the definition of costs. At the outset, both consultant and client must agree on allowable costs. Perhaps the consultant considers the cost of capital an allowable cost, whereas the client doesn't. Other costs, such as automobile transportation or entertainment, might also be disputable. If you enter into a cost-reimbursement contract, you must carefully define what you mean by cost.

Several different types of cost-reimbursement contracts are used by consultants; they include the following:

- Cost contract
- Cost-plus-fixed-fee (CPFF) contract
- Cost-plus-incentive-fee (CPIF) contract
- Cost-plus-award-fee (CPAF) contract

Cost Contract. With this type of contract the client agrees to reimburse the consultant for all allowable costs but pays no fee. It's used most widely when a nonprofit consulting agency has the opportunity to learn technology that will benefit it in the future. Cost sharing, in which the client agrees to cover a part of the costs or to share the costs, is another alternative.

Cost-Plus-Fixed-Fee (CPFF) Contract. This type of contract is the most frequently used form of a cost-reimbursement contract. Its popularity in general consulting developed as a result of its widespread use by the federal government. Here the client and consultant agree on all estimated costs of the consultation. They further agree on the allowable fee or profit to be earned by the consultant over and above cost. If actual cost is lower than estimated, the consultant earns a higher percentage fee on the costs.

In theory, the consultant is motivated to keep costs down and thus earn a higher percentage return. In practice, this isn't always the case. Consultants are largely assured of reimbursement for all allowable costs. They are normally not required to spend funds in excess of the agreed-upon amount even though the project or consultation has yet to be completed.

Cost-Plus-Incentive-Fee (CPIF) Contract. Similar to the CPFF contract, CPIF is designed to provide greater cost-saving motivation for the consultant. Rather than a fixed fee, this type of contract has a minimum and maximum fee. The minimum may be negative or zero. Clients and consultants may also share costs in some contracts.

If actual costs turn out to be lower than estimated, the consultant gets a bigger fee—up to the maximum. If costs run over the estimate, the fee is smaller and may even be reduced to zero if the overrun is great enough. In theory the risk for the client should be equal to that of the consultant. In practice each party tries to gain as much advantage as possible during contract negotiations. Frequently, CPIF contracts involve multiple incentives—one for early completion, another for cost efficiency, and so on.

Cost-Plus-Award-Fee (CPAF) Contract. A cross between the CPFF contract and the CPIF contract, this one was first used in federal procurements to handle technical items that were too difficult to estimate in contract negotiations. Under CPAF, unlike CPIF, an external third party awards the minimum or maximum fee based on an objective evaluation of the consultant's cost efficiency and compliance.

Evaluations are not required to take place at the end of contracts and are often scheduled on a monthly or quarterly basis. One advantage of frequent evaluations:

They provide feedback that may enable consultants to perform more in line with clients' expectations and thus earn higher fees.

Retainer Contracts

Although the term *retainer* is used in many ways, it generally implies an open-ended agreement between client and consultant that the consultant is available to the client for a specified amount of time or scope of work. Usually, additional work is billed out at some preestablished hourly or daily rate. From the consultant's viewpoint, the retainer contract makes good sense only when the consultant is able to predict with strong accuracy the amount of time needed by the client. From the client's standpoint, a retainer agreement is valuable because the client can tap quickly and easily the specialized talent of the consultant without extensive formal arrangements.

Availability-Retainer Agreements. In availability-retainer agreements, which have become more common in recent years, consultants make themselves available in the event that clients need their services. Consultants agree to reserve a specified block of time for clients in case of need. Because this reservation reduces the flexibility of consultants' time, consultants are awarded a portion of the value of the reserved time even if it's not used by clients. Usually, this amounts to between 20 and 30 percent of the value of their time.

Time-Retainer Agreements. Consultants perform a specific activity on a periodic (usually monthly) basis in this kind of agreement. Occasionally, they find themselves spending more time with some clients than a retainer is worth. Yet they put up with the overwork because the up-front money is a kind of insurance policy.

After a while time-retainer arrangements tend to break down because the consultant starts to cut corners and output suffers. The client becomes dissatisfied, and the relationship is no longer fruitful for either client or consultant.

Making Retainers Work for You. A retainer will work if it's for a specified scope of work or a specified number of clock hours or days for a specific fee. Suppose that the consultant is to train all new sales personnel about product competition. An analysis by the consultant suggests that such items as anticipated sales, production capacity, turnover rate, and knowledge of new sales personnel will result in four days of work per month. If the consultant's daily billing rate is $1,200, the retainer could be set at $4,800 per month.

If the amount of time to be expended is variable, the retainer can be tied to the clock. Suppose the client's technical staff needs high-level engineering data and resources to meet the requirements of specific customer applications. Neither you nor the client knows how much help will be required. You figure your time at $100 per hour and agree to provide the client with 40 hours a month of such time for a fixed amount of $4,000. If the client needs only 30 hours, you still get your $4,000. If the client needs 50 hours in a given month, you'll collect $5,000.

With everything clearly specified under a retainer contact, clients are well aware of what they are getting, and consultants don't feel as though they are being taken advantage of. In such cases, a retainer is a smart idea.

If you decide that an up-front payment is best for you, obtaining it generally depends on how well you can exert your will on others. In American business, most people expect to pay for services rendered, not for services to be rendered. If you ask for a retainer, you're cutting across the grain of that tendency, so you must be very firm. If you give the impression that you might make an exception, if you seem afraid to lose the client, you won't get your way. Be firm, be insistent. Your only risk is that you will encounter an equally strong-willed client or one whose employer policy forbids up-front payments.

Performance Contracts

In any contract providing that the payment of your fee depends on performance, make sure you and your client both agree on what performance means. A performance contract is not one with a clause that says: "If the client is happy, that client will pay the consultant." Performance has to be something measurable, such as a 10 percent increase in sales volume, a 4 percent increase in gross volume, or a 3 percent decline in personnel turnover. That's the type of performance that you can prove in court if need be. The performance-related contract is valuable when there is high-gain potential, and it can help overcome client resistance.

High-Gain Potential. In a situation with high-gain potential, you see that a client will reap substantial and perhaps ongoing financial benefits from the consultation. A performance contract enables you to participate in those benefits. Perhaps the most important point to remember about performance contracts is that you should never assume more risk than you have to.

Almost as important: Never share in profits. At the flick of a pen, profits can be either created or turned into losses. A less-than-honest client could leave you with nothing. Even a perfectly honest client is put into an uncomfortable spot by sharing in profits. To reduce taxes, the client has to show a reduced profit, but doing so reduces your fee.

Negotiate instead for participation in gross sales, gross margin, or some aspect of cost savings. Share in anything that is easily measurable and that is defined by accounting standards.

Client Resistance. If your client simply doesn't believe that you can do what you say you can, you might offer to work under a performance contract. That way, the client regards you as someone who is sure enough of success to take a share in the risk. Your offer is an effective way to overcome the uncertainty of a client who otherwise might hesitate to sign a contract.

Surprisingly, the contract the client does sign is likely not to be a performance contract even though you offered one. Client organizations are simply not disposed to deal on a performance basis. From a legal viewpoint, organizations generally don't have standard performance contracts at the ready. They have to either confer with the legal department, which may mean a weeks-long delay, or hire outside legal help, which means a fairly heavy cash outlay.

In addition, client organizations under a performance contract might have to design special accounting procedures for handling your account. Finally, although the people you deal with may be able to approve a check for a flat payment, they may not have the authority to encumber their employers with a performance-related obligation. Getting that authorization may draw more attention to their consulting needs than they want. All in all, you're likely to get a contract if you offer to work on a performance basis, but the ensuing contract may be one that entails less risk for you than would a true performance contract.

You're more likely to enter into performance contracts with small businesses than large ones. In most cases, a small-business owner will be handling the negotiations and can authorize performance payments. Small businesses may not have the money available to pay for your services as you deliver work, so making part of the payment dependent on future events should facilitate payment. It may cost the business more in the long run, but the increased business from your services should offset the expense.

Enforcing a Performance Contract. Occasionally, clients may not follow through on a consultant's recommendations. Although the consultant may design and develop a system for improvement in performance, the client may fail to implement it. Or the client may implement the plan haphazardly or ineffectively. No savings are realized, no volume increases effected—and the consultant gets no performance fees.

The solution to the problem of poor or nonexistent implementation, which is all too common, lies mainly with foresight. A clause in the contract should stipulate that the client is to pay you a certain flat fee if the plan is not implemented fully and as mutually agreed. With such a clause, you have some protection. Without it, you may be out of luck.

Relations with a Client Organization

The contract embodies your relationship with the individual you call client, but, in a broader sense, you may have a contract with a client organization. Even though your contract is agreeable to the individual or small group that negotiated the deal, you often have to build a good relationship with other members of the organization—particularly employees. The rank and file can determine your success or downfall, so a close rapport with a company's employees is also essential to the success of the consultation.

The Consultant Perceived as Hatchet Man

Perhaps the biggest threat to success in building rapport with personnel is the common perception among employees that consultants pose a threat to their jobs. You become the efficiency expert who is going to put in new equipment and cut jobs. A quick note from the boss to employees that you're going to be coming around on a given day usually only heightens those fears.

The key to keeping employees on your side is communication. More specifically, have the boss spend a day with you at the site of your consultation. Get introduced, become familiarized, answer questions, and let people get to know you. Informally, you can brief them on what you're doing and why. If too many people are involved in the consultation for you to work face-to-face in small groups, organize a briefing session. Send a memo on your own letterhead that is copied and distributed by the client. At the briefing give a short presentation, leaving plenty of time for questions. Then when you show up at the site unannounced after the meeting and as the consultation progresses, you can expect much more cooperation than you would had you not worked at early communication.

Keep the employees as involved as possible. Usually, some information has to be kept confidential. Yet, to the extent possible, get employees to contribute to the consultation and share the output with them. You not only make the project easier on yourself, but you may also receive some unexpectedly helpful input.

Disagreement within the Organization

Sometimes an employee will set out to torpedo your project. Some old-timers in a client company can sabotage your work by simply creating a lot of disagreement over what has to be done. In such situations, you have clear orders from the signers of the contract but are up against endless confusion on the site.

You can deal with deliberate, employee-engendered confusion two ways: with a meeting or with a memo. You can bring the disturbing employee and the client together in a meeting with you. You might be able to iron out the differences face-to-face. In most cases, however, the client will not attend the meeting because he or she usually knows what the employee is doing but doesn't want to confront the problem. Very likely, that confrontation is the underlying reason for retaining you. If a meeting doesn't work out, try a memo. Whether the organization is large or small, you protect yourself with a memo on the record. More important, you can follow up with a polite insistence for clarification of your role.

"Free" Consultation

Whether negotiating a contract or executing it, consultants often realize suddenly that they are giving away services for no compensation. Most free consulting results from subconscious tendencies to provide additional services. You can avoid giving away your services by being aware of those tendencies and avoiding them. Aside from giving away valuable information in your proposals, you should be wary of the free-consulting tendency in at least three other situations:

1. The follow-up consultation
2. Diagnostic work
3. The add-on assignment

The Follow-up Consultation

The follow-up consultation consists of services or advice rendered to the client after a project is completed. Invariably, this kind of freebie takes the form of a phone call from the client "just to ask questions." If the client does indeed need only a call to straighten out a wrinkle in the original consultation, courtesy and good business sense dictate that you consider the call part of the original fee. On the other hand, when one call leads to so many others that you find yourself giving away time and fresh advice, several options are open to you. You could put the client on a per-call basis. Bill a certain amount for phone consultations and another amount for on-site follow-ups.

Another possibility is to negotiate a retainer agreement. One of the following two kinds might be appropriate.

The Time Retainer. With this type of retainer contract, you complete a specified quantity of work or a discrete activity on a regular, periodic basis, perhaps monthly. You might agree to conduct a psychological screening of all new employees of a client organization. Given the client's size and rate of personnel turnover, you assume that you'll need to spend two days each month to fulfill this obligation. Because your daily rate for consulting is $1,000, you sign a retainer agreement with the client for $2,000 a month, each and every month, for conducting this psychological screening.

The Availability Retainer. Under this type of agreement, you contract to make yourself available to a client for a specified amount of time during a designated calendar period to perform a certain job—for example, analyzing the client's financial statements and interpreting them for management. You calculate it will take you three days. At a daily rate of $1,200, you are paid $3,600 for each month that you're retained for this assignment.

The client doesn't want you to perform this service every month but does want you to be available for the three days when the need arises. Because being available three days in a given month reduces your flexibility and freedom, you collect a fee for this availability. You may set your fee at whatever you wish, but most commonly it would be about 25 percent of the value of your time. If you follow the 25-percent guide, you would charge the client $900 a month simply to be available.

What do you get paid if you actually do the work? Our research demonstrates that 44 percent of consultants working on an availability basis would credit the $900 against the $3,600, and the rest would charge a total of $4,500.

Diagnostic Work

Many clients know exactly what their problems are and have set expectations for the precise accomplishments they are seeking from a consultant. Some clients, however, are not even aware of their problems, much less appropriate solutions. In these cases, a consultant often decides that undertaking a diagnostic evaluation for a client is a profitable investment of marketing time. The consultant develops a proposal that not only identifies problems or needs, but also specifies a particular plan of action. The psychology of this approach is that the client is sufficiently impressed with the consultant's diagnostic powers that a contract is awarded to implement the action plan.

At times, however, you, as the consultant, feel that no matter how good your diagnosis is, a client will not retain your services to implement your action plan. Perhaps the client has a brother-in-law in the consulting business, or maybe the client won't be motivated to do anything about the problem even if it's identified. Whatever the reason, undertaking a diagnosis in such a situation probably will result in your giving away valuable time without compensation. How do you handle such a situation?

You could just walk away, telling the client that you have no interest. If the prospective business is too good to pass up, you could propose that the client award you a diagnostic contract. This contract would compensate you for your analysis and the action plan you propose. When complete, the client may either select you or another consultant or do nothing about your findings. In some cases, you may inform the client that if you're selected to implement your action plan, the charge for the diagnostic work is deducted from the total charges incurred.

Add-On Assignments

In some situations, a client, in effect, says: "As long as you're doing X, why not do Y too?" Your contract covers X, but you know not a cent is available for Y. Although you are concerned that you won't be compensated for the extra work, you may not be sure just how serious the client is about really doing it, but you hate to make it an issue. How do you handle this situation?

Too frequently, consultants ignore a client, hoping the idea will be forgotten. It isn't. The best approach is to pick up on the client's suggestion. A very effective response to a request for extra work is that you'd be glad to take a look at it, and you're sure the cost wouldn't be unreasonable. You might even state a figure if you're sure of your estimate. As a rule, you should make yourself available for add-on assignments so long as the client understands there will be add-on charges.

Protecting Yourself When Using Other Consultants

From time to time you may have to call in other consultants to help you on a project. The steps required to guard your interests depend largely on the people with whom you're working. Some are so aggressive that they draw clients away from you as soon as you turn around, whereas others are so scrupulous that they would never dream of approaching your clients for work.

One way of protecting yourself against your more aggressive colleagues is to maintain a high profile with the client. Although you have other people working on the assignment, let the client know that you alone are managing these people. Another way is to be the collector and disseminator of all information. Controlling the flow of information from the client to the other consultants, and vice versa, is vital to your interests. As long as you are monitoring and regulating the two-way flow, you can limit the free advice that might otherwise leak out of your organization. You can also detect any efforts by the other consultants to develop greater visibility with your client.

Personal Involvement

Self-protection brings up another problem common in consulting. When marketing themselves to prospects, consultants often use the word *I* more than they should. Clients come to expect a personal commitment from their consultants and assume they will do everything, even though some tasks can just as well be handled by less-trained and lower-paid staff.

Even when a client is willing to pay for a consultant's time, the consultant may not want to tie up so many hours or days on one client or on routine work. On the other hand, if the consultant allows others to become too involved with the client's work, they could become more prominent in the client's eyes than they should be. One solution is to involve your staff or associates early on in the marketing phase, directing the focus from *I* to *we* or *you*.

To avoid losing business, always talk to clients in a way that convinces them that you are controlling a team of staff and associates. Build the impression that the team would be just so many individuals without your guidance. And never give a staff member or associate complete control over information.

☞ Tips

If you have followed good marketing principles, you don't end a project only to find that you're out on the street looking for another. You have already set aside enough time and marketed yourself so that you're working on several projects at once and looking for more at the same time. In this way, you will never suffer from a shortage of work.

Good consulting is simply good business. The good consultant delivers a quality product at a fair price and makes a respectable profit. In many ways the consultant is the last of the true entrepreneurs, carrying on the best traditions of the American free enterprise system.

Appendix
Sample Contracts

As with a letter of agreement (see p. 215), a formal written contract may be prepared by either the client or the consultant. Review of the general form of a specific contract by competent legal counsel is recommended for both parties; it is recommended for Letters of Agreement as well.

A formal contract constitutes an agreement between a consultant and client governing a complex business transaction to be undertaken by the client but with detailed advice and supervision to be provided by the consultant. The consultant not only advises the client on the proper method of carrying out the transaction, or project, but is also given specific management authority over most of its aspects. This type of situation may be necessitated by the requirements of a third party, such as a lender or lessor, who believes the services of the consultant are necessary to the successful operation of the project.

Provision is made in the contract for compensating the consultant(s) based on the amount of work performed for the client with a minimum and maximum dollar amount each month.

The consultant also agrees to provide a minimum number of hours of service to the client and agrees that the amount of time to be spent in addition to this shall be at the sole discretion of the consultant. If disputes arise under the agreement, provision is made for arbitration in accordance with the rules of the American Arbitration Association.

To protect the reputation and good name of the consultant, the contract contains a provision declaring the uniqueness of the services to be provided by the consultant and the irreparable harm that would result to him or her if such services were not fully performed. It provides that equitable remedies, including injunctive relief and specific performance, may be obtained by the consultant if the contract is breached by the client. In such a situation, the rationale for this provision is to ensure that the consultant will continue to manage the client's project and thus fully protect the third-party investor.

SAMPLE BUSINESS CONSULTANT AND MANAGEMENT AGREEMENT

AGREEMENT made this _____ day of _____19XX, between [name of client],_____ (e.g., a Delaware corporation), hereinafter referred to as the "Corporation," and [name of consultant(s)], (both jointly and severally), hereinafter referred to as the "Consultants":

Recitals

The Corporation is presently in the process of negotiating [description of project, e.g. , to build or lease and to conduct and operate a general hospital at the following location]: It is the desire of the Corporation to engage the services of the Consultants to perform for the Corporation certain functions in the management and operation of [e.g., the hospital] and to consult with the board of directors and the officers of the Corporation and with the administrative staff concerning problems arising in the fields of [e.g., hospital management; fiscal policies; personnel policies; purchases of equipment, supplies, and services]; and other problems that may arise from time to time, in the operation of [e.g., a general hospital].

AGREEMENT

Term

1. The respective duties and obligations of the parties hereto shall commence on the date [e.g., that the Corporation enters into said lease].

Consultations

2. The Consultants shall make themselves available to consult with the board of directors, the officers of the Corporation, and the department heads of the administrative staff, at reasonable times, concerning matters pertaining to the organization of the administrative staff, the fiscal policy of the Corporation, the relationship of the Corporation with its employees or with any organization representing its employees, and in general, concerning any problems of importance concerning the business affairs of the Corporation.

Management Authority of Consultants

3. In addition to the consultation provided for in Paragraph 2 above, the Consultants shall be in complete and sole charge of the administrative staff of [e.g., the hospital]. The administrative staff of the hospital shall include all the employees of the Corporation directly or indirectly engaged in the affairs of the hospital other than the board of directors of the Corporation, the president, vice president, secretary and treasurer of the Corporation, and the medical staff of the hospital. The medical staff of the hospital is defined as those persons who are licensed by the State of Delaware to perform, and are performing, services as physicians, surgeons, nurses, physiotherapists, social workers, psychologists, psychiatrists, pharmacists, and other services of a professional standing in the healing arts and sciences.

Management Power of Consultants

4. The business affairs of the Corporation that affect, directly or indirectly, the operation of [e.g., the hospital], and which arise in the ordinary course of business, shall be conducted by the administrative staff. All the members of the administrative staff shall be employees of the Corporation; however, the Consultants shall have the sole and complete charge of the administrative staff, and shall have the absolute and complete authority to employ (on such terms and for compensation as they deem proper), discharge, direct, supervise, and control each and every member of the administrative staff. It is the intention of the Corporation to confer on the Consultants all the powers of direction, management, supervision, and control of the administrative staff that the Consultants would have if the members of the administrative staff were direct employees of the Consultants.

Business Manager

5. The Consultants, in their sole discretion, may employ, in the name of the Corporation, a business manager. If such a business manager is employed, he shall act as administrative assistant to the Consultants and as the chief administrative officer of the administrative staff. The business manager shall be under the direct control and supervision of the Consultants. The Consultants may, from time to time, delegate to the business manager as much of the Consultants' authority as they deem proper with respect to the employment, discharge, direction, control, and supervision of the administrative staff, and the Consultants may withdraw from said business manager, at any time the Consultants deem it expedient or proper to do so, any portion or all of the said authority theretofore conferred on the business manager.

Fiscal Policy

6. The Corporation recognizes the necessity for a sound fiscal policy in order to maintain and promote the solvency of the Corporation. To this end, it is hereby agreed by the parties hereto that the Corporation will establish reserve accounts for the following purposes:

   a. A reserve account for the payment of any and all taxes that may be charged against the Corporation by any governmental jurisdiction.

   b. A reserve account for the payment of all sums withheld from the salary or wages of the employees of the Corporation and for which the Corporation is chargeable under the laws of any and all governmental jurisdictions.

   c. A reserve account for the payment of all obligations due [name of lessor] pursuant to the terms and conditions of the above referred-to lease.

   d. A reserve account for the purchase of equipment necessitated by the wearing out or obsolescence of the equipment in use, or by the development of new equipment.

e. A reserve account for building maintenance and for the expansion of the physical facilities. The Consultants shall, from time to time, advise the board of directors of the amounts of corporate funds that should be deposited in each of said reserve accounts. This determination on the part of the Consultants shall be based on the principles of sound business management and the availability to the Corporation of said funds. The Corporation agrees to deposit corporate funds in said reserve accounts pursuant to the recommendations of the Consultants. The reserve accounts shall be deposited in one or more national banks, or branches thereof, located within [county and state]. All checks, drafts, or other instruments by which funds are withdrawn from said reserve accounts, in addition to any other signature that may be required, shall bear the signature of one of the Consultants.

Consultants to Act as Agents

7. From time to time, the Corporation may deem it advisable to enter into agreements with [e.g., insurance companies, prepaid medical plans, and other firms and associations that pay all or part of the expenses incurred or to be incurred by the hospital patients for the care and treatment afforded them while patients in the Corporation's hospital]. With regard to said agreements, the Consultants shall be the exclusive agent of negotiating the terms and conditions of the said agreements. However, the Consultants shall not bind the Corporation to said agreement without first obtaining the approval of the terms of said agreements from the board of directors of the Corporation.

Authority to Contract

8. From time to time, the Corporation may wish to expand the physical facilities of [type of facility] or remodel or modify the same. If the costs to be incurred by the Corporation for such expansion, modification, or remodeling are less than $_____, then the Consultants may contract for the performance of the same in the name of the Corporation under the authority given them in Paragraph 4 above; however, if such expansion, modification, or remodeling is to be of such extent that the cost to be incurred by the Corporation for the performance thereof is $_____ or more, then the terms and conditions of said contracts for said expansion, modification, or remodeling shall be negotiated by the Consultants, and the Consultants shall be the exclusive agents of the Corporation to said contracts without first obtaining the approval of the terms and conditions of said contracts from the board of directors of the Corporation. The provisions of this paragraph shall apply with equal effect to the purchase of equipment and supplies.

Employment of Certified Public Accountants

9. It is understood and agreed by the parties hereto that the services to be performed by the Consultants do not include the auditing of the books of the Corporation or of [name of project], the preparing of any financial statements, the preparing of any tax returns or other documents required to be prepared by any governmental body having jurisdiction to tax, or any other acts or services normally performed by public accountants. The Consultants may engage, hire, retain, and employ, in the name and for the account of the Corporation, one or more, or a firm of, certified public accountants to perform for the Corporation the services denoted above in this paragraph. Said accountant or accountants may be employed, hired, engaged, and retained on such terms and conditions and for such compensation as the Consultants deem reasonable. [E.g., it is understood by the Corporation that the Consultants are partners of a firm of certified public accountants known as (name of firm). It is specifically agreed that the Consultants may be, and the Consultants are, hereby authorized to employ said partnership, or its successors in interest, to perform for the Corporation the services denoted above in this paragraph, and the Consultants may obligate the Corporation to pay to said partnership, or its successors in interest, a reasonable amount for the performance of said services.]

Employment of Assistants

10. If it is reasonably necessary for the Consultants to have the aid of assistants or the services of other persons, companies, or firms to properly perform the duties and obligations required of the Consultants under this agreement, the Consultants may, from time to time, employ, engage, or retain the same. The cost to the Consultants for said services shall be chargeable to the Corporation, and the Corporation shall reimburse and pay over to the Consultants said costs on demand.

Limited Liability

11. With regard to the services to be performed by the Consultants pursuant to the terms of the agreement, the Consultants shall not be liable to the Corporation, or to anyone who may claim any right due to his or her relationship with the Corporation, for any acts or omissions in the performance of said services on the part of the Consultants or on the part of the agents or employees of the Consultants, except when said acts or omissions of the Consultants are due to their willful misconduct. The Corporation shall hold the Consultants free and harmless from any obligations, costs, claims, judgments, attorneys' fees, and attachments arising from or growing out of the services rendered to the Corporation pursuant to the terms of this agreement or in any way connected with the rendering of said services, except when the same shall arise due to the willful misconduct by a court of competent jurisdiction.

Compensation

12. The Consultants shall receive from the Corporation a reasonable monthly sum for the performance of the services to be rendered to the Corporation pursuant to the terms of this agreement; however, in no event shall the compensation paid to the Consultants by the Corporation be less than $_____ per month nor more than $ _____ per month. The Corporation and the Consultants, by mutual agreement, shall determine the compensation to be paid the Consultants for any particular month by the fifteenth (15th) day of the next succeeding month. The final determination of the monthly compensation shall be based on the reasonable value of the services rendered by the Consultants, and within the range prescribed above in this paragraph. If the Corporation and the Consultants fail to agree on said compensation within the said fifteen (15) days, the amount of monthly compensation due the Consultants shall be determined by arbitration pursuant to the provisions of Paragraph 14 below. Anything contained in this agreement to the contrary notwithstanding, the minimum monthly remuneration of $_____ shall be paid to the Consultants on the first of every month during the term of this agreement and the acceptance of said minimum amount by the Consultants shall not in any way diminish, affect, or compromise their rights to additional compensation as provided for herein.

Minimum Amount of Service

13. The Consultants shall devote a minimum of _____ hours per month to the affair of the Corporation. Anything to the contrary notwithstanding, the Consultants shall devote only so much time, in excess of said _____ hours, to the affairs of the Corporation as they, in their sole judgment, deem necessary; and the Consultants may represent, perform services for, and be employed by such additional clients, persons, or companies as the Consultants, in their sole discretion, see fit.

Arbitration

14. Any controversy or claim arising out of or relating to the compensation to be paid by the Corporation or the Consultants for the services rendered by them pursuant to the terms of this agreement shall be settled by arbitration in accordance with the rules of the American Arbitration Association and judgment on the award rendered by the arbitrator or arbitrators may be entered in any court having jurisdiction thereof. Any part to this agreement may submit to arbitration any said controversy of claim.

[The following paragraph may be used where two Consultants are a party to the agreement.]

Failure to Act by One Consultant

15. It is understood and agreed that any direction or consultation given or service performed by either one of the Consultants, pursuant to the provisions of this agreement, shall constitute the direction or consultation or the performance of service of both of the Consultants. If, for any reason, one or the other of the Consultants is unable or unwilling to act or perform pursuant to the terms of this agreement, such event shall not void this agreement or diminish its effect, and the performance on the part of the other Consultant shall constitute full and complete performance of this agreement on the part of the Consultants.

Legal and Equitable Remedies

16. Due to the uniqueness of the services to be performed by the Consultants for the Corporation, and due to the fact that the Consultants' reputation in the community as business managers may be affected by the financial success or failure of the Corporation in the operation of the [project], in addition to the other rights and remedies that the Consultants may have for a breach of this agreement, the Consultants shall have the right to enforce this contract, in all of its provisions, by injunction, specific performance, or other relief in a court of equity. If any action at law or in equity is necessary to enforce or interpret the terms of this agreement, the prevailing party shall be entitled to reasonable attorneys' fees, costs, and necessary disbursements in addition to any other relief to which he may be entitled.

Right to Manage

17. Except as specifically provided to the contrary herein and to the greatest degree allowable under the Corporation Code and other laws of the State of Delaware, it is the intent of the Corporation to confer on the Consultants the exclusive and absolute right to manage and direct all the business affairs of the Corporation that in any way concern the operation of [project] and that arise in the ordinary course of business of [project]. Should any one or more of the provisions of this agreement be adjudged unlawful by any court of competent jurisdiction, the remaining provisions of this agreement shall remain in full force and effect. Further, should one or more of the provisions of this agreement be adjudged invalid by a court of competent jurisdiction, such determination shall have no effect whatsoever on the amount or amounts of compensation to be paid to the Consultants pursuant to the terms of this agreement.

Governing Law

18. This agreement shall be binding on and shall be for the benefit of the parties hereto and their respective heirs, executors, administrators, successors, and assigns, and shall be governed by the laws of the State of _____.

Executed at [name of State] on the day and year first mentioned above.

_____

CLIENT
[typed name of client]

_____

By [signature]
[typed name and designation of person signing]

_____

CONSULTANT(S)
[typed name of consultant(s)]

_____

[Signature]
[typed name and designation of person signing]

SAMPLE FIXED-PRICE SERVICE CONTRACT

AGREEMENT

THIS AGREEMENT is made, this _____ day of _____, 19XX by and between _____ , hereinafter referred to as the "University" and _____ , a California Corporation, hereinafter referred to as the "Contractor."

WITNESSETH:

WHEREAS, the University desires to develop and conduct a training program for its personnel and the personnel of such other eligible education agencies as may become participants in this program; and

WHEREAS, the purposes of said training program are to:

Upgrade the managerial and technical skills of career counseling and placement personnel; and increase the professional stature of career counseling and placement personnel; and provide a cadre of trained professionals appropriate materials to continue further training as required with minimum funding support needed; and provide a vehicle for the ongoing assessment of in-service training needs of career counseling and placement personnel.

WHEREAS, the Contractor is particularly skilled and competent to conduct such a management training program; and

WHEREAS, funds for this contract are budgeted for and included in federal project plan approved under _____ , and as described in the program prospectus identified as Grant _____ , which is hereinafter referred to as the "Project"; and

WHEREAS, said Project was approved [date] and project expenditures approved on [date].

NOW, THEREFORE, it is mutually agreed as follows:

1. The term of this Agreement shall be for the period commencing [date], continuing to and until [date].

2. The Contractor agrees to develop and conduct a training program consisting in part of a series of three workshop session presentations. Each of said workshop presentations shall be of eight hours' duration and shall be conducted at [place]. The aforesaid training program shall be developed and conducted by the Contractor in accordance with the project prospectus submitted by the University for funding under _____ and in a particular with the "attachment" to said program prospectus, which is marked Exhibit "A," attached hereto and by reference incorporated herein.

3. The aforesaid workshop presentations shall include three days of intensive training using an approach that has demonstrated considerable success working with career counseling and placement personnel of this type. Specific workshop topic coverage shall include the following:

   a.

   b.

   c.

4. The aforesaid training workshop will be conducted during the contract term in accordance with a schedule mutually agreed upon by the University and the Contractor.

5. In connection with the conducting and development of the aforesaid training program, the Contractor agrees as follows:

   a. The Contractor will plan for and prepare such necessary materials as are needed to conduct the various program sessions as described. Such material preparation and development will include the preparation of participant resource material, development of worksheets, orientation materials, participant guides and handbooks. All materials developed will reflect the highest standards of quality applicable to education material development state of the art.

   b. The contractor will provide expert session facilitation staff as follows:

   A minimum of one (1) expert staff for the first twelve (12) participants in attendance at each session; further, the Contractor will provide one (1) additional expert staff for each additional twelve (12) participants in attendance at each session to a maximum of 48 total participants per session.

   c. The Contractor will regularly consult with designated personnel of the University for the purpose of monitoring program progress and planned activities so as to improve and strengthen the overall program.

6. The Contractor further agrees to:

   a. Furnish the University on or before [date] with a final report. This report will describe all relevant aspects of program activity and will be in such style and format as to comply with the requirements of the enabling grant.

   b. Prepare appropriate pre-session and post-session participant testing materials to enable the ongoing assessment of the overall program activities. The Contractor shall collect, analyze, and interpret these findings as an integral part of the program development and conduct activity.

   c. Conduct, within four to six months after the conclusion of the workshop presentation, a post-test follow-up survey that will seek to discover what difficulties, if any, the participants in the program have encountered in applying the principles developed in the workshop training activity to career counseling and placement problems. A component of the follow-up survey will probe for participant attitude and individual assessment of the relevancy of the workshop training activity and the topic material in the context of program administration experience during the intervening period.

    d. Furnish the University with copies of all written and visual materials produced for distribution to the workshop participants. The Contractor will retain no proprietary rights to such materials, said rights being vested to the University.

7. The University agrees as follows:

    a. To designate one of its staff members as project director to represent the University in all technical matters pertaining to this program.

    b. To arrange the necessary pre-program advertisement and participant notification so as to encourage participation.

    c. To provide or otherwise arrange for facilities that are adequate to conduct the workshop sessions.

    d. To limit session attendance, exclusive of Contractor staff, to the maximum eligible number of _____ participants plus up to three (3) additional nonparticipating persons.

    e. To make the necessary arrangements with the participating educational agencies to make personnel available as participants in all specified training activities.

    f. To arrange for the use on an as available basis of University instructional equipment, including 16mm slide projectors, tape recorders, and/or related audiovisual equipment, as requested by the Contractor in response to program requirements.

       The University agrees to provide competent personnel to operate all such equipment. The University will provide adequate maintenance and care of such equipment and will provide operational assistance to the Contractor as requested.

    g. To distribute to the program participants at the request of the Contractor, various project materials that are relevant to the program. Such materials may include training session handout material, descriptive information, questionnaires, and announcements.

    h. To provide or arrange for assistance to the Contractor at training session locations as mutually agreed in connection with facility arrangement, scheduling, and other matters pertaining to the successful conduct of the program.

8. It is expressly understood and agreed by both parties hereto that the Contractor, while engaging in carrying out and complying with any of the terms and conditions of this contract, is an independent Contractor and is not an officer, agent, or employee of the University.

9. The Contractor shall provide worker's compensation insurance or self-insure his services. He shall also hold and keep harmless the University and all officers, agents, and employees thereof from all damages, costs of expenses in law, or equity that may at any time arise or be set up because of injury to or death of persons or damage to property, including University property, arising by reason of, or in the course of the performance of this contract; nor shall the University be liable or responsible for any accident, loss, or damage, and the Contractor, at his own expense, cost, and risk shall defend any and all actions, suits, or other legal proceedings that may be brought or instituted against the University or officers or agents thereof on any claim or demand, and pay or satisfy any judgment that may be rendered against the University or officers or agents thereof in any such action, suit, or legal proceeding.

10. In consideration of the satisfactory performance of the Contractor, the University agrees to reimburse the Contractor in the amount of Fifteen Thousand Dollars ($15,000) in accordance with the following schedule:

30 May 19XX	$ 4,000.00
30 June 19XX	$ 5,000.00
30 July 19XX	$ 4,000.00
30 August 19XX	$ 2,000.00
	$15,000.00

IN WITNESS WHEREOF, each party has caused this agreement to be executed by its duly authorized representative on the date first mentioned above.

CONTRACTOR   UNIVERSITY

_____   _____

Name   Name
Title   Title

SAMPLE PRODUCT DEVELOPMENT AGREEMENT

Date

Name
Company
Address
City/State/Zip

Dear

1. This letter shall serve as an agreement between _____ (CLIENT) and _____ (CONSULTANT) governing the provision of professional consulting services by CONSULTANT for CLIENT relative to the development, marketing, and licensing or similar distribution of CLIENT information and technology. CLIENT has developed and will continue to develop unique and highly regarded proprietary information and concepts on _____ . CONSULTANT has developed and will continue to develop unique and highly regarded proprietary information and concepts on the marketing, and licensing of such information. It is the mutual intent of the parties to combine their unique information and capabilities through a professional consulting relationship in which CONSULTANT shall receive professional fees and commission income in exchange for the synergy which is created by the combining of efforts and knowledge.

2. The purpose of this agreement is to spell out the working and financial relationship between CLIENT and CONSULTANT regarding the development and marketing of certain proprietary products and services of CLIENT designed to assist third parties (LICENSEES) with _____ on their own behalf or on the behalf of others, such as the LICENSEES' clients or employees of organizations in which the LICENSEES have management responsibility.

3. These proprietary products and services would be based on technology already developed by CLIENT as augmented by proprietary concepts developed by CONSULTANT relative to the marketing of this type of technology and new proprietary concepts that might be developed by CLIENT or CONSULTANT alone or in combination as they relate to the development and marketing of information on _____ .

4. The intent of this working relationship is to provide the LICENSEES with a subscription and/or license service that would provide LICENSEES with a limited right to use such technology on terms and conditions to be determined by CLIENT.

5. It is the objective of the parties to this agreement to package and sell the above referenced technology to the LICENSEES and to profit, as described herein, in doing so.

6. While the specific nature and description of the offerings to be made to the LICENSEES is subject to broad change and interpretation based upon analysis and market research/response, it is intended that LICENSEES would be charged a subscription and/or license fee to use and be trained in the use of the technology so as to enable its use with and resale to parties who might become the clients or customers of the LICENSEES.

7. CLIENT shall undertake the development, modification, packaging, and promotion of the technology and marketing strategies for this proprietary concept with the professional consulting assistance of CONSULTANT at such times and places as determined appropriate. Each party shall provide the highest and best state of the art known in the execution of this agreement and shall provide best efforts to ensure the success of this venture. Both parties acknowledge that this agreement relates to a speculative venture and that no assurances of success, sales levels, or profits can be assumed or predicted.

8. All direct expenses and investment capital required for this venture shall be contributed by CLIENT and all revenues and profits earned from the venture shall accrue to CLIENT, except as noted in paragraph 9. In this regard, all charges for licenses, training fees, license renewal fees, related rights, and sales of services and products provided shall be paid to CLIENT under such names and business entities as CLIENT shall direct or establish.

9. CLIENT agrees to pay CONSULTANT for professional consulting services and efforts in connection with this venture as follows:

   a. A sum equal to _____ dollars ($XXX) per hour, which is equal to one-third of CONSULTANT's customary hourly consulting fee, said sum to be provided on an advance retainer basis as required by progress made; plus

   b. A sum equal to five (5) percent of gross sales to LICENSEES to include license fees, training fees, license renewal fees, subscription fees, related rights, products and services; to be paid monthly on the fifteenth (15th) day of the month for the prior month; for a period of five (5) years from the receipt of the first revenue from LICENSEES; plus

   c. Reimbursement for direct expenses incurred by CONSULTANT in connection with the provision of services to include travel and communication expenses, but not routine overhead expenses that CONSULTANT would normally incur in the operation of his business. Travel expenses are taken to include automobile mileage at_____ (XX) cents per mile, standard coach air travel, ground transportation, rental car expense, and daily travel per diem of _____ ($XXX) per day or the cost of hotel lodging plus _____ ($XX) per day, whichever is greater, whenever responsibilities require that CONSULTANT travel in excess of one hundred (100) miles from _____ . Such sums to be paid within ten (10) days of the receipt of an invoice for such expenses.

d. CONSULTANT has estimated that the planned scope of work on the part of CONSULTANT shall not exceed one hundred forty-six (146) hours of CONSULTANT professional time during the first ninety (90) days of this agreement. In the event that the activities included within the planned scope of work (as evidenced by a plan submitted to CLIENT on _____) should exceed this amount, additional hours expended by CONSULTANT shall be deducted from the commission payments due CONSULTANT under the terms of paragraph 9.b., above. Additional hours may be expended by CONSULTANT and not subject to such deduction from commission income due to an expansion in the scope of work requested by CLIENT or within the defined scope of work when expressly authorized or requested by CLIENT. CLIENT shall have the right to notify CONSULTANT in writing, at any time, that such authorization or request must be in writing from CLIENT to CONSULTANT.

10. This agreement shall remain in effect for a period of five (5) years from the date on which the first revenues are received from LICENSEES or six (6) years from its execution, whichever is greater, and may be terminated by either party upon thirty (30) days written notice at any time commencing with the sixth (6th) month following the provision of the first fifteen (15) hours of professional consulting services by CONSULTANT. In the event of termination of this agreement, CLIENT agrees to continue to pay CONSULTANT commission income due for a period of time equal to the number of months from the date of execution of this agreement until its termination or six (6) months following the receipt of the first five thousand dollars ($5,000) of gross receipts from the LICENSEES, whichever is greater.

11. CONSULTANT shall have a reasonable right to inspect the books of account and records of CLIENT, at CONSULTANT expense, as they pertain to the payment of commissions due under the terms of paragraph 9.b., above. In the event that a discrepancy of one thousand dollars ($1,000) or more is determined as a result of such inspection, if any, CLIENT agrees to pay for the costs incurred for such inspection of records.

12. This agreement pertains only to activities and revenues related to the licensing or subscription sales of licenses, training, license and subscription renewal fees, products and services to the LICENSEES, as herein defined. CONSULTANT shall not receive a percentage commission on sales of CLIENT that are obtained through the regular and ongoing activities of _____.

13. This agreement shall be binding upon and inure to the benefits of the parties hereto and their respective heirs, assigns, successors, executors, administrators, and personal representatives.

14. This agreement shall be governed by the laws of the State of _____.

15. No waiver of any of the provisions herein shall be deemed or shall constitute a waiver of other provisions of this agreement.

16. In the event of a dispute between the parties hereto on any matter governed by this agreement, either party shall have the right to request that a resolution of the dispute and a determination of rights and remedies of the parties shall be determined by a process of binding arbitration under the rules and regulations of the American Arbitration Association.

17. Should CLIENT not sign and deliver a copy of the signed agreement to CONSULTANT on or before _____ , this agreement shall become voidable at the option of CONSULTANT.

Sincerely,   Accepted for _____

_____   Date   _____

Name of Consultant

SAMPLE MARKETING AGREEMENT

Date

Name
Company
Address
City/State/Zip

Dear

This letter shall serve as an agreement between _____ (CLIENT) and _____ (CONSULTANT) governing the provision of professional marketing consulting services for CLIENT by CONSULTANT relative to the promotion of _____ .

CONSULTANT shall prepare copy and rough mechanicals (suitable for use by professional typesetting and graphics arts personnel or clerical personnel, as appropriate, to develop camera-ready copy) for the following:

1. A letter to _____ seeking their cosponsorship of the seminar;

2. A direct mail brochure for _____ designed to obtain registrations for the seminar;

3. Two (2) advertisements for use in _____ newspapers and/or magazines to advertise the seminars for the purpose of obtaining registrations; and

CLIENT shall provide to CONSULTANT data, documents, and information in verbal and written form, as required and appropriate, to enable CONSULTANT to successfully complete the above responsibilities.

CONSULTANT shall complete the assigned tasks on a schedule consistent with the responsibilities involved and in accord with

CLIENT requirements, as mutually agreed.

CLIENT and CONSULTANT both understand that the promotion of a seminar is a speculative venture and that no assurances can be made as to the effectiveness of the promotional effort relative to the number of cosponsors or participants obtained or attending or revenues obtained from such participants.

CONSULTANT shall provide the above described services for a fee of _____ ($X,XXX) plus direct expenses for travel and communication, if any, incurred by CONSULTANT. The provision of additional services above and beyond those specified above, if any, that may be requested shall be invoiced at the rate of _____ dollars ($XXX) per hour.

CONSULTANT shall provide services on an advance retainer arrangement. Under such an arrangement, CLIENT shall advance sums to CONSULTANT prior to the provision of services and CONSULTANT shall charge against such advance, providing a statement of account not less frequently than twice monthly. Upon conclusion of the consultation, funds advanced and not used shall be returned.

In the event that CLIENT elects to terminate this agreement, CLIENT shall provide at least thirty (30) days written notice to CONSULTANT and shall be responsible for any and all costs incurred to date and experienced in the winding down of the project, if any.

If the terms of this agreement meet with your acceptance, please indicate same by signing below in the space provided and return a signed copy of this agreement along with your initial advance retainer deposit.

Sincerely,   Accepted for _____

_____   Date   _____

SAMPLE FINANCIAL CONSULTING AGREEMENT

Date

Name
Company
Address
City/State/Zip

Dear

This letter shall serve as a letter of agreement between _____ (CLIENT) and _____ (CONSULTANT) governing the provision of professional financial consulting services for CLIENT by CONSULTANT.

CONSULTANT shall provide such consulting services as determined appropriate and as specifically requested by CLIENT.

CLIENT agrees to compensate CONSULTANT on an advance base retainer arrangement. Under the terms of such an arrangement CLIENT will provide CONSULTANT with a check in the amount of _____ ($XXX) per month on or before the first day of each month (except for the first month, _____ , when payment shall be due on or before the tenth day of the month). In exchange for this compensation, CONSULTANT shall provide up to six (6) hours per month consultation. Additional time expended by CONSULTANT shall be invoiced at the rate of _____ ($XXX) per hour and CLIENT shall provide payment to CONSULTANT within ten (10) days of the date of such invoices.

CLIENT agrees to reimburse CONSULTANT for direct expenses specifically incurred as a result of providing such services to CLIENT, to include travel and communications within ten (10) days of the date of an invoice for such expenditures. Travel expenses, if any, shall be invoiced as follows:

Air Travel: Standard Coach Rates
Per Diem: $XXX per day or $XX plus the cost of hotel lodging, whichever is
               greater, for any travel in excess of 50 miles from _____ .
               Partial day per diem (where no hotel room is required) at $XX.
Ground Travel: Personal car mileage at $0.XX/mile and rental cars and public
               conveyance at actual charges incurred.

CLIENT may terminate this agreement upon thirty (30) days written notice and the agreement shall otherwise be terminated on _____ .

If the terms of this agreement meet with your approval, please indicate same below by your signature and return a copy for my files.

Sincerely,   Accepted for _____

_____   Date
                                         _____

SAMPLE PRESENTATION ENGAGEMENT LETTER

Date

Name
Association
Address
City/State/Zip

Dear

    Thank you for your letter of_____. I am looking forward to participating with you at the _____ Annual Meeting. This letter shall serve as an agreement between the Association (XXX) and _____ (YYY) governing the presentation.

    YYY shall undertake the development and delivery of a presentation for XXX at the Annual Meeting on _____ evening, _____ at the_____ _____ Hotel of a duration and on a topic to be determined. If desired, YYY shall also make himself available to handle questions and answers on the presentation topic or related subjects. XXX agrees to inform YYY not later than _____ of the particulars concerning the duration and topic of the presentation as well as the number of individuals expected to attend the presentation.

    In consideration of the above, XXX agrees to pay YYY a sum equal to _____ dollars ($XXX) plus round-trip standard coach air fare at rates prevailing on _____, said sum due and payable not later than _____.

    If the terms of this agreement meet with your acceptance, please signify same by signing below in the space provided and return a copy of this letter for my files.

    I look forward to being with you on _____.

Sincerely,

_____   Accepted for _____

                                   By   _____

                                   Date   _____

There are certain situations in which the engagement is of such limited duration and/or the time between scheduling an appointment and providing the consulting service is so short that entering into a contract between the parties is impractical. Yet the consultant may still want to inform the client of the terms and conditions under which he or she is willing to provide services. In such a case, the *engagement letter* may be utilized.

It is a good idea to provide your client with a letter that acknowledges the engagement you and the client have agreed upon. The engagement letter should contain several features. Chief among them are the following:

1. Acknowledgement of the time and place of the first formal/work meeting
2. Specifications of the purpose of the first meeting and purpose of the consultation in general
3. An indication of the time or duration that you expect will be involved in the consultation, or a statement as to why it is not possible to provide such an estimate
4. A communication as to what the fee will be for the service to be provided, if possible, or an indication of the basis on which the fee will be charged
5. Specification of the payment arrangements as well as the invoice schedule

In the past, consultants have tended to be satisfied by just telling clients when the invoice would be sent, leaving so-called "trade custom" to govern when payments would be made. With trade custom increasingly turning into 60 to 90 days or more, it's a good idea to inform the client and obtain his or her approval for a more reasonable period of time between invoice date and payment date.

SAMPLE ENGAGEMENT LETTER

[letterhead]

[date]

John Q. Doe, President
Doe Industries
1234 Main Street
Anytown, Anystate Zip

Dear Mr. Doe:

This letter will confirm our telephone conversation of this morning. It is my understanding that we will meet for a full day on May 19th at your office for the purpose of developing a proposal for the sale of your widgets to XYZ industries. I will plan to arrive at 8:30 AM.

Please be advised that the fee for my services is [amount] a day. It is my policy to work on an advance retainer basis. Under such an arrangement, my clients deposit with me [amount], and I invoice against the retainer that has been deposited. Funds deposited that are not utilized are returned.

Due to the short time between now and the time of our meeting, you may either forward your check for [amount] in advance of our meeting or plan to pay for the services provided at the time of the consultation.

I look forward to working with you next week on what should prove to be a most interesting project.

Sincerely,

Consultant

SAMPLE SHORT-TERM CONSULTATION LETTER

Date

Name
Company
Address
City/State/Zip

Dear

I am writing to confirm our appointment for a consultation. It is my understanding that we will be meeting at my office on Friday, _____ at 10:30 AM.

The fee for my services, on an initial consultation basis of this type, is _____ dollars ($XXX) per hour. It is my policy to work on an advance retainer basis. Under such an arrangement, my clients deposit funds in advance and I invoice against such deposits. Funds deposited but not used are returned following the completion of our work. Due to the short time between this letter and our meeting and the limited duration of the consultation, an advance retainer will not be required; however, you may plan on providing me with a check in payment of the services at the time of our meeting.

I am enclosing a copy of my _____ as well as some other information that I think may be useful for you.

I look forward to working with you, and if I may be of assistance prior to that time, please don't hesitate to let me know.

Sincerely,

Consultant

SAMPLE SUBCONTRACTING AGREEMENT

CONSULTING AGREEMENT

The _____ was formed to serve the continuing and specialized education of technical and other professional groups and individuals. Through its unique programs of publishing seminars and workshop offerings, the _____ provides quality education tailored to the specialized needs of professionals in a real-world, performance-oriented environment. In furtherance of this work, the president of the _____ (hereinafter called the President) desires to utilize the expert assistance of _____ (hereinafter called the Consultant) in the field or fields in which the Consultant has professional qualifications.

A. Character and Extent of Services

    1. It is the mutual intent of the parties that the Consultant shall act strictly in a professional consulting capacity as an independent contractor for all purposes and in all situations and shall not be considered an employee of the _____ (hereinafter called the Company).

    2. The Consultant reserves full control of his activities as to the manner and selection of methods with respect to rendering his professional consulting services to the Company.

    3. The Consultant agrees to perform his activities in accordance with the highest and best state of the art of his profession.

    4. The Consultant is an independent contractor and shall provide worker's compensation insurance or self-insure his services. He shall also hold and keep blameless the Company, its officers, agents, and employees thereof from all damages, costs, or expenses in law or equity that may at any time arise due to injury to or death of persons, or damage to property, including Company property, arising by reason of or in the course of performance of this agreement; nor shall the Company be liable or responsible for any accident, loss, or damage, and the Consultant, at his own expense, cost, and risk, shall defend any and all actions, suits, or other legal proceedings that may be brought or instituted against the Company or officers or agents thereof on any claim or demand, and pay or satisfy any judgment that may be rendered against the Company or officers or agents thereof in any such action, suit, or legal proceeding.

B. Period of Service and Termination

    1. The period of service by the Consultant under this agreement shall be from _____ through _____ and may be renewed upon the mutual agreement of the parties hereto.

2. Either the Company or the Consultant may terminate this agreement by giving the other party thirty (30) days written notice of intention of such action.

3. The President reserves the right to halt or terminate the conduct of a seminar/workshop by the Consultant without prior notice or claim for additional compensation should, in the opinion of the President, such conduct not be in the interests of the Company.

C. Compensation

1. Upon the Consultant's acceptance hereof, the Company agrees to pay the Consultant according to the following schedule: [insert compensation rate or fixed fee and any allowance for or schedule of allowable expenses, if any].

2. In the event that the Company desires, and it is mutually agreed to by the Consultant, the Consultant's services may be used in the conduct of seminars/workshops not specifically identified in paragraph C.1. In such cases, the Company agrees to pay the Consultant on the basis of the following schedule:

[insert appropriate schedule]

3. In the event of special circumstances, variations to the fee schedule of paragraphs C.1. and C.2. will be allowed as mutually agreed to in writing by the parties hereto.

4. Notification: The Consultant will be notified by the President in writing to engage his participation in specific seminar(s) and/or workshop(s) to which the fee schedule of paragraphs C.1. and C.2. apply. Such notification will include a statement of the time(s) and place(s) of intended seminar/workshop conduct together with other information contributing to the successful conduct of the seminar/workshop sessions.

5. The Consultant, as an independent contractor, shall be responsible for any expenses incurred in the performance of this contract except as otherwise agreed to in writing prior to such expenses being incurred. The Company will reimburse the Consultant for reasonable travel expenses incurred with respect thereto.

[a specification of "reasonable" may be inserted here]

D. Method of Payment
1. Having proper notification, the Consultant shall be paid as provided for in paragraphs C.1 and C.2 hereof, on the basis of a properly executed "Claim for Consulting Service" form.
2. The "Claim for Consulting Service" form is to be submitted at the end of the calendar month during which consulting services are performed. Exceptions to this arrangement are allowed with the written approval of the President.
3. Payment to the Consultant will be made by check, delivered by certified mail postmarked no later than _____ days subsequent to receipt of the "Claim for Consulting Service" form as provided for in paragraphs D.1. and D.2.

E. Copyrights
1. The Consultant agrees that the Company shall determine the disposition of the title to and the rights under any copyright secured by the Consultant or his employee on copyrightable material first produced or composed and delivered to the Company under this agreement. The Consultant hereby grants to the Company a royalty-free, nonexclusive, irrevocable license to reproduce, translate, publish, use, and dispose of, and to authorize others to do so, all copyrighted or copyrightable work not first produced or composed by the Consultant in the performance of this agreement but which is incorporated into the material furnished under this agreement, provided that such license shall be only to the extent the Consultant now has or, prior to the completion or final settlement of this agreement, may acquire the right to grant such license without becoming liable to pay compensation to others solely because of such grant.
2. The Consultant agrees that he will not knowingly include any copyrighted material in any written or copyrightable material furnished or delivered under this contract without a license as provided in paragraph E.1. hereof or without the consent of the copyrighted material is secured.
3. The Consultant agrees to report in writing to the Company promptly and in reasonable detail any notice or claim of copyright infringement received by the Consultant with respect to any material delivered under this agreement.

F. Drawings, Designs, Specifications
   1. All drawings, sketches, designs, design data, specifications, notebooks, technical and scientific data, and all photographs, negatives, reports, findings, recommendations, data, and memoranda of every description relating thereto, as well as all copies of the foregoing, relating to the work performed under this agreement or any part thereof, shall be subject to the inspection of the Company at all reasonable times; and the Consultant and his employees shall afford the Company proper facilities for such inspection. Such materials further shall be the property of the Company and may be used by the Company for any purpose whatsoever without any claim on the part of the Consultant and his employees for additional compensation, and subject to the right of the Consultant to retain a copy of said material shall be delivered to the Company or otherwise disposed of by the Consultant, either as the Company may from time to time direct during the progress of the work, or, in any event, as the Company shall direct upon the completion or termination of this agreement.

G. Assignment

   The Company reserves the right to assign all or any part of its interest in and to this assignment. The Consultant may not assign or transfer this agreement, any interest therein, or claim thereunder without the written approval of the Company.

IN WITNESS WHEREOF, the parties have executed this agreement.
CONSULTANT   _____

                                    Company

_____   _____

Date _____   Date _____

Bibliography

This thoroughly revised and expanded bibliography contains six distinct sections, including:

Whenever possible, annotations have been provided to guide readers to material of particular relevance.

General Directories and Reference Works

It is well worth any consultant's time to become familiar with the following standard directories and reference works. They are available at most larger libraries. For publishers' addresses and telephone numbers, consult *Literary Market Place* or *Publishers Directory,* available at most public libraries (see their listings below).

All-in-One Business Contactbook. Karen Hill, ed. Detroit: Gale Research. Provides address, chief executive, and sales volume for approximately 10,000 U.S. companies. Telephone and fax numbers are also included.

America's Corporate Families™ and International Affiliates. Parsippany, NJ: Dun's Marketing Services. Annually. Lists U.S. companies with foreign affiliates and foreign companies with U.S. affiliates.

Annual Register of Grant Support. Wilmette, IL: National Register Publishing Co. Annually. Includes information on more than 3,000 private and public grant-giving agencies.

Business Organizations, Agencies and Publications Directory. 8th ed. Holly Selden, ed. Detroit, MI: Gale Research. A guide to approximately 24,000 new and established organizations, agencies, and publications concerned with international and U.S. business, trade, and industry.

Business Periodicals Index. Bronx, NY: H. W. Wilson Co. Monthly, with quarterly and annually bound cumulations. Indexes more than 350 journals on business and economics. Can access the information by subject areas. Also available online as WILSONLINE.

Business Publications Rates and Data. Wilmette, IL: Standard Rate & Data Service. Monthly. Provides advertising rates and other information about trade journals.

Business Rankings Annual. Brooklyn Public Library. Detroit, MI: Gale Research. Annually. Provides wage and salary rankings and a subject guide to business, industrial, and financial rankings.

Catalog of Federal Domestic Assistance. Washington, D.C.: Government Printing Office. Annually. Provides key information on more than 1,200 programs administered by 50 federal agencies. In loose-leaf format with regular updates.

City and State Directories in Print. Julie E. Towell and Charles B. Montney, eds. Detroit, MI: Gale Research. Organized geographically with title, key word, and subject indexes.

Corporate 500: The Directory of Corporate Philanthropy. Detroit, MI: Gale Research. Provides information on corporate funding programs.

Daniells, Lorna M. *Business Information Sources.* Berkeley, CA: University of California Press. Provides descriptions of basic business sources.

Direct Mail List Rates and Data. Wilmette, IL: Standard Rate & Data Service. Monthly. Lists all known direct mail lists. Provides information on list size, source, segmentation, price, and more.

Directory of Companies Required to File Annual Reports with the Securities and Exchange Commission. Washington, D.C.: U.S. Government Printing Office. Lists 13,400 companies by name only with industry classification and federal identification numbers.

Directory of Corporate Affiliations. Wilmette, IL: National Register Publishing Co. Annually. Described as a "who owns whom" directory; lists major U.S. corporations and their divisions, all companies listed on the New York and American Stock Exchanges, and Fortune 1000 and many privately owned companies.

Directory of Research Grants. Phoenix, AZ: Oryx Press. Annually. Provides information on more than 4,000 research grants from business, foundation, government, and private sources.

Encyclopedia of Associations. Detroit, MI: Gale Research. Annually. Published in three volumes. Provides information on more than 22,000 national and international organizations; considered the "bible" for accessing information on associations.

Encyclopedia of Business Information Sources. James B. Woy, ed. Detroit, MI: Gale Research. Includes more than 21,000 entries of directories, encyclopedias, databases, newsletters, indexing services, almanacs, and more of interest in the business field. Provides a good starting point to accessing business information.

F and S Index of Corporate Change. Cleveland, OH: Predicasts. Quarterly with annual cumulation. Indexes business literature related to corporate changes within U.S. public and private corporations.

The Fortune Directory. New York: Time. Annually. Provides information on the 500 largest U.S. industrial corporations and the 500 largest U.S. service corporations, including banks, financial and insurance companies, public utilities, and more.

The Fortune World Business Directory. New York: Time. Annually. Provides information on the 500 largest industrial companies with headquarters outside the United States, the 50 largest foreign banks, and the 50 largest industrial firms in the world.

The Foundation Directory. New York: Foundation Center. Biennially. Provides key information on approximately 5,100 of the largest foundations in the United States.

Foundations Grants Index. New York: Foundation Center. Annually. Provides information on grants of $5,000 or more awarded by approximately 470 major U.S. foundations.

International Organizations. Kenneth Estell, ed. Detroit, MI: Gale Research. Annually. Provides information on more than 9,000 international nonprofit membership organizations.

Lavin, Michael R. *Business Information: How to Find It, How to Use It.* Phoenix, AZ: Oryx Press. An excellent primer and basic reference book on accessing business and statistical information.

Literary Market Place. New Providence, NJ: R. R. Bowker Co. Annually. Provides detailed information on 15,000 companies or organizations in the publishing arena, including publishers in the United States and Canada, advertising and public relations firms, book clubs, agents, book manufacturers, and direct mail firms.

Lonier, Terri. *Working Solo Sourcebook: Essential Resources for Independent Entrepreneurs.* New Paltz, NY: Portico Press. Provides information on a variety of resources, such as professional associations, conferences and events, government agencies, educational opportunities, and more.

Manufacturing USA: Industrial Analyses, Statistics, and Leading Companies. Arsen J. Darnay, ed. Detroit, MI: Gale Research. Annually. Provides statistical profiles for 450 types of manufacturing; also lists the top 50 companies in each product category.

Million Dollar Directory/America's Leading Public and Private Companies. Parsippany, NJ: Dun's Marketing Services. Annually. Provides key information on more than 160,000 top businesses in the United States.

Moody's Manuals. New York: Moody's Investors Service. Annually. Published in eight volumes organized by type of manufacturing company and providing profiles of more than 15,000 companies and thousands of municipalities.

National Trade and Professional Associations of the United States. Washington, D.C.: Columbia Books. Annually. Provides information on more than 7,500 national trade associations; labor unions; professional, scientific, and technical societies; and other national organizations.

Newsletters in Print. Robert J. Huffman and John Krol, eds. Detroit, MI: Gale Research. Annually. A descriptive guide to more than 10,300 subscription, membership, and free newsletters, bulletins, and updates published in the United States and Canada and available in print or online. Describes the publication and provides audience, editorial policies, circulation, and price information.

Oxbridge Directory of Newsletters. New York: Oxbridge Communications. Annually. Lists more than 21,000 U.S. and Canadian newsletters, providing information on personnel, circulation, and more.

Principal International Businesses: The World Marketing Directory. Parsippany, NJ: Dun's Marketing Services. Annually. Provides information on more than 50,000 businesses located in more than 140 countries.

Publishers Directory. Linda S. Hubbard, ed. Detroit, MI: Gale Research. Annually. Includes information on 18,000 U.S. and Canadian publishers and 600 distributors.

Scientific and Technical Organizations and Agencies Directory. Margaret Labash Young, ed. Detroit, MI: Gale Research. Provides information on 15,000 organizations and agencies, including a description, address, and publication names.

Standard & Poor's Register of Corporations, Directors and Executives. New York: Standard & Poor's Corp. Annually. Provides information on 55,000 corporations and 500,000 officers and directors.

Standard Industrial Classification Manual. Springfield, VA: National Technical Information Service. Provides the SIC code number—the number used by most business references in their indexes—for any field or industry.

State and Local Statistics Sources. M. Balachandran and S. Balachandran, eds. Detroit, MI: Gale Research. A subject guide to data on business, financial, and other topics for cities and states.

Statistics Sources: A Subject Guide to Data on Industrial, Business, Social, Educational, Financial and Other Topics for the United States and Selected Foreign Countries. Jacqueline Wasserman O'Brien and Steven R. Wasserman, eds. Detroit, MI: Gale Research. Annually. Provides statistical information on more than 20,000 topics.

Thomas Register of American Manufacturers and Thomas Register Catalogue File. New York: Thomas Publishing Co. Annually. A comprehensive and detailed guide to products manufactured in the United States. Contains information on 148,000 manufacturers with cross-references to more than 110,000 brand names. Emphasis is on products rather than manufacturers.

Ulrich's International Periodicals Directory. New Providence, NJ: R. R. Bowker Co. Biennially. Provides information on more than 118,000 serials published throughout the world. Organized by subject headings with multiple indexes.

United States Industrial Outlook. Washington, D.C.: United States Government Printing Office. Annually. Covers 350 manufacturing and service industries, providing trends and outlooks for each.

Ward's Business Directory of United States Private and Public Companies. Detroit, MI: Gale Research. Annually. Provides basic information on approximately 130,000 business firms.

Who's Who in America. Wilmette, IL: Marquis Who's Who. Biennially. Provides biographical profiles of more than 75,000 noteworthy individuals in the United States.

Who's Who in Finance and Industry. Wilmette, IL: Marquis Who's Who. Biennially. Provides biographical profiles of more than 17,000 individuals in finance and industry in the United States.

The Working Press of the Nation. Volume 1: *Newspaper Directory.* Volume 2: *Magazine Directory.* Chicago: National Research Bureau. Annually. Lists newspapers and magazines with addresses, deadlines, personnel, and more.

Writer's Market: Where and How To Sell What You Write. Mark Kissling, ed. Cincinnati, OH: Writer's Digest Books. Annually. Provides lists of technical and professional journals as well as consumer journals and features a how-to approach to placing your work.

Consulting Directories and Reference Works

The following books list consultants or resources specifically for consultants. For publishers' addresses and telephone numbers, consult *Literary Market Place* or *Publishers Directory* (see General Directories and Reference Works section for full citations).

Bradford's Directory of Marketing Research Agencies and Management Consultants in the United States and the World. Centerville, VA: Bradford's Directory. Biennially. Includes more than 2,400 listings.

Consultants and Consulting Organizations Directory. James McLean, ed. Detroit, MI: Gale Research. Triennially. A reference guide to more than 17,000 companies and individuals in the consulting field. Also available online.

Directory of Consultants and Management Training Programs: Intended for Local NonProfit Organizations. Marvin L. Peebles, ed. Philadelphia, PA: MLP Enterprises.

Directory of Experts and Consultants in Biotechnology.

Directory of Experts and Consultants in Electronics.

Directory of Experts and Consultants in Energy Technologies.

Directory of Experts and Consultants in Environmental Science.

Directory of Experts and Consultants in Lasers and Physics.

Directory of Experts and Consultants in Plastics and Chemicals.

Directory of Experts and Consultants in Robotics and Mechanics.

All of the above-mentioned *Directories . . .* are published by Research Publications, Woodbridge, CT. Most are published biennially and are organized geographically by state with keyword indexes.

Directory of Management Consultants. James H. Kennedy, ed. Fitzwilliam, NH: Consultants News. Provides information on more than 850 consulting firms and individuals in the field.

Dun's Consultants Directory. Parsippany, NJ: Dun's Marketing Services. Annually. Lists approximately 25,000 consulting firms in a wide range of fields.

Management Consulting: ACME Annotated Bibliography of Selected Resource Materials. New York: Association of Management Consulting.

Research Services Directory. Piccirelli, ed. Detroit, MI: Gale Research. Includes information on research and development firms, contract laboratories, and consulting organizations.

Online Databases

This section lists several major business databases of interest to consultants. Consult a good business library for information on the growing number of business databases available online.

ABI/INFORM. Louisville, KY: UMI Data/Courier. Provides indexing to business-related material from more than 800 periodicals from 1971 to the present.

Consultants and Consulting Organizations Directory. Detroit, MI: Gale Research. Provides information on more than 17,000 consulting organizations and individual consultants. Updated annually.

Disclosure Database. Bethesda, MD: Disclosure. Provides an index to records filed with the Securities and Exchange Commission by publicly owned companies from 1982 to the present.

Dow Jones News. Princeton, NJ: Dow Jones & Co. Provides business news and stock quotes from 1979 to the present. Updated continuously.

Grants. Phoenix, AZ: Oryx Press. Provides information on grants by federal, state, and local governments as well as private organizations.

Thomas Register Online. New York: Thomas Publishing Co. Provides key information on approximately 150,000 United States companies. Updated semiannually.

Trade and Industry Index. Foster City, CA: Information Access Co. Provides comprehensive indexing of approximately 300 business periodicals and selective indexing of approximately 1,200 other magazines and newspapers.

WILSONLINE: Business Periodicals Index. Bronx, NY: H.W. Wilson Co. Provides access to 300 business periodicals.

Consulting Newsletters and Journals

This section lists several commercially available publications of interest to consultants. The list by no means includes all of the newsletters or journals published in the field. Many of the associations serving the consulting profession (see Chapter 2) publish newsletters available only as a membership benefit. Whenever possible, these have been mentioned with the association's listing in Chapter 2.

Consultants News. Monthly newsletter. James H. Kennedy, ed. Fitzwilliam, NH: Kennedy & Kennedy. 603-585-6544. Oriented toward large-firm and management consulting. Provides information on management consulting and personnel changes in larger firms. Oldest newsletter published for the management consulting profession.

Consulting Opportunities Journal. Bimonthly newsletter. J. Stephen Lanning, ed. Clear Spring, MD: Consultants National Resource Center. 301-791-9332. Concentrates on marketing strategies and business opportunities for consultants; especially relevant for new consultants and those with limited professional experience.

Journal of Management Consulting. Quarterly journal. Gerald A. Simon, ed. North-Holland Publishers (P.O. Box 211, 1000 AE, Amsterdam, Netherlands).

Marketing Seminars and Conferences. Monthly newsletter. Paul Franklin, ed. Manhattan, KS: LERN. 800-678-5376. The definitive newsletter on the how-to's of promoting and operating seminars and conferences.

The Professional Advisor. Monthly newsletter. Bernard Hale Zick, ed. Kingwood, TX: SAC Management. 713-359-5955. Continuously published since 1978. Deals with strategies for marketing and managing a consulting practice. Includes surveys on consultant fees and incomes, and other data based on research.

Journal Articles

Articles on the topic of consulting appear frequently and in a wide range of professional and trade journals or magazines, from such publications as the *Economist* and *Canadian Banker* to *Training and Development Journal* and *Personnel.* To get a feel for what's being written on the topic or to find the complete citation for a specific article, consult the *Business Periodicals Index,* which is available at most good public libraries (see the reference in the General Directories and Reference Works section of this bibliography). You will need to check under the heading "business consultants" or, as appropriate, under headings specific to a consulting specialty, such as "personnel consultants" or "software development consultants."

Several major newspapers such as *The Wall Street Journal* and *The New York Times* also publish their own indexes, which list articles published in their newspapers on the topic of consulting. These indexes, the *Wall Street Journal Index* and the *New York Times Index* are also available at good public libraries. If you have access to a good business library, *Business Index,* published by Information Access Company, and available in microfilm, CD-ROM, and online, can also be helpful.

Books on Consulting

This section lists and, when possible, describes a wide variety of books on consulting. Some are aimed at the beginner and some at the experienced practitioner. At least several sources here can be valuable to any consultant. For publishers' addresses and telephone numbers, consult *Literary Market Place* or *Publishers Directory* available at most public libraries (see Directories and Reference Works section in this bibliography for full citations).

Ahoy, Christopher K. *Manual for Selection of Consultants.* Berkeley, CA: Comprehensive Facilities Management.

Allesch, J. *Consulting in Innovation: Practice, Methods and Perspectives.* New York: Elsevier Science Publishing Co., Inc.

Alston, Frank M. *Contracting with the Federal Government.* New York: John Wiley and Sons.

Arnoudse, Donald M. *Consulting Skills for Professionals.* Homewood, IL: Business One Irwin.

Barcus, Sam W., and Joseph W. Wilkinson, eds. *Handbook of Management Consulting Services.* New York, NY: McGraw-Hill.

Bell, Chip R., and Leonard Nadler, eds. *Clients and Consultants: Meeting and Exceeding Expectations.* Houston, TX: Gulf Publishing Co. Written for those who use or plan to use the services of an internal or external consultant.

Bellman, Geoffrey M. *The Consultant's Calling: Bringing Who You Are to What You Do.* San Francisco: Jossey-Bass.

Bennett, Roger. *Choosing and Using Management Consultants.* Woodstock, NY: Beekman Publishers.

———. *The Consultant's Malpractice Avoidance Manual.* Sarasota, FL: American Consultants League. A basic introduction to the issue of malpractice in consulting. Useful background reading but not sufficiently comprehensive to be authoritative on the subject.

———. *How to Become a Successful Consultant in Your Own Field.* Rocklin, CA: Prima Publishing. A well-written and interesting autobiography on how the author began his own consulting practice. A best-seller and good philosophical background reading for the new consultant.

———. *Profitable Book Publishing for the Consultant.* Sarasota, FL: American Consultants League. A complete how-to guide to publishing, from manuscript preparation through production, advertising, and distribution.

Block, Peter. *Flawless Consulting: A Guide to Getting Your Expertise Used.* San Diego, CA: Pfeiffer and Co. A how-to book, providing tips on what to do and say in different consulting situations.

Bly, Robert W. *Selling Your Services.* New York, NY: Henry Holt and Company, 1991, 349 pp. Proven strategies for getting clients to hire you or your firm.

Brennan, Gregory. *Successfully Self-Employed.* Chicago: Upstart Publishing Co.

Cafferky, Michael E. *Let Your Customers Do the Talking.* Chicago: Upstart Publishing Co.

Cannon, J. Thomas. *No Miracles for Hire: How to Get Real Value from Your Consultant.* New York: AMACOM. Provides guidance to managers on how to select and manage consultants.

Carmichael, Douglas R. *Guide to Small Business Consulting Engagements.* Fort Worth, TX: Practitioners Publishing Co.

Cohen, William A. *How to Make It Big as a Consultant.* New York: AMACOM. A practical guide to setting up a successful consulting business.

Connor, Dick. *Increasing Revenue from Your Clients.* New York: John Wiley and Sons. A self-teaching guide for professionals, providing strategies, skills, and techniques to establish profitable, long-term partnerships with clients.

Connor, Richard A., and Jeffrey P. Davidson. *Getting New Clients.* New York: John Wiley and Sons.

———. *Marketing Your Consulting and Professional Services.* New York: John Wiley and Sons.

Consultant's Library Editors. *The Successful Consultant's Guide to Winning Government Contracts.* Washington, D.C.: Bermont Books.

Cottle, David W. *Managing for Profitability.* High Tower. Available from Consultants Bookstore, Templeton Rd., Fitzwilliam, NH 03447.

Emery, Vince. *How to Grow Your Business on the Internet.* Scottsdale, AZ: Coriolis Group Books.

Franklin, Paul. *49 Proven Strategies for Selling Repeat Consulting Business.* Portland, OR: NTC Press. A practical how-to monograph.

Gray, Douglas. *Start and Run a Profitable Consulting Business.* Bellingham, WA: International Self-Counsel Press.

Greenbaum, Thomas L. *The Consultant's Manual: A Complete Guide to Building a Successful Consulting Practice.* New York: John Wiley and Sons.

Greenfield, Wendy M. *Successful Management Consulting.* Englewood Cliffs, NJ: Prentice-Hall. Provides guidance on consulting to newer and/or smaller, owner-operated companies.

Greiner, Larry E., and Robert O. Metzger. *Consulting to Management.* Englewood Cliffs, NJ: Prentice-Hall. An excellent book, well written and of particular value to management consultants.

Guttman, H. Peter. *The International Consultant.* New York: John Wiley and Sons. Provides a region-by-region survey of international consulting opportunities and an overview of issues faced while consulting in foreign countries.

Hameroff, Eugene, and Sandra Nichols. *The Successful Consultant's Publicity and Public Relations Handbook.* Sarasota, FL: American Consultants League. Provides techniques on marketing of consulting services.

Hand, D. J., ed. *The Statistical Consultant in Action.* New York: Cambridge University Press.

Harper, Malcolm. *Consultancy for Small Businesses: The Concept and Training the Consultants.* New York: Intermediate Technology Development Group of North America.

Hartman, Charles C. *100 Tips on Marketing and Selling Your Consulting and Professional Services.* Beltsville, MD: Charles Hartman.

Harvard Business School Career Guide Staff. *Management Consulting: 1991-1992.* Boston, MA: Harvard Business School Press.

Higgins, James M. *101 Creative Problem Solving Techniques.* The New Management Publishing Co. Available from Consultants Bookstore, Templeton Rd., Fitzwilliam, NH 03447. Helps you to take advantage of your own and your client's innate intuitive and creative abilities.

Hills, Curtis. *How to Save Your Clients from Themselves and Yourself from Them.* Phoenix, AZ: Olde and Oppenheim Publishers.

Holtz, Herman. *Advice, a High Profit Business: A Guide for Consultants and Other Entrepreneurs.* Englewood Cliffs, NJ: Prentice-Hall.

———. *Choosing and Using a Consultant: A Manager's Guide to Consulting Services.* New York: John Wiley and Sons.

———. *The Complete Guide to Being an Independent Contractor.* Chicago: Enterprise • Dearborn, a division of Dearborn Publishing Group.

———. *The Complete Guide to Consulting Contracts.* Chicago: Upstart Publishing Company, a division of Dearborn Publishing Group.

———. *The Consultant's Guide to Proposal Writing: How to Satisfy Your Clients and Double Your Income.* New York: John Wiley and Sons.

———. *The Consultant's Guide to Seminar Presentations: An Insider's Guide to Developing and Marketing Seminars as a Marketing Tool and Independent Profit Center.* New York: John Wiley and Sons.

————. *The Consultant's Guide to Winning Clients.* New York: John Wiley and Sons.

————. *How to Succeed as an Independent Consultant.* New York: John Wiley and Sons. Comprehensive and well written, containing useful information on how to establish and maintain a consulting business.

————. *Utilizing Consultants Successfully: A Guide for Management in Business, Government, the Arts and Professions.* Westport, CT: Greenwood Publishing Group. A guide to finding, negotiating, contracting, and working with consultants and service contractors.

Joseph, Richard A., Anna M. Nekoranec, and Carl H. Steffens. *How to Buy a Business: Entrepreneurship through Acquisition.* Chicago: Enterprise • Dearborn, a division of Dearborn Publishing Group.

Karlson, David. *Consulting for Success: A Guide for Prospective Consultants.* Los Altos, CA: Crisp Publications. A good primer for those interested in consulting.

————. *Marketing Your Consulting or Professional Services.* Los Altos, CA: Crisp Publications.

Kaye, Harvey. *Inside the Technical Consulting Business: Launching and Building Your Independent Practice.* New York: John Wiley and Sons.

Kelley, Robert E. *Consulting: The Complete Guide to a Profitable Career.* New York: Macmillan Publishing Co. A comprehensive book for the beginning consultant.

Kelly, Kate. *How to Set Your Fees and Get Them.* Visibility Enterprises. Available from Consultants Bookstore, Templeton Rd., Fitzwilliam, NH 03447.

Kemppainen, Rudolph. *Power Consulting: Using the Media to Expand Your Business.* New York: John Wiley and Sons.

Kennedy, James H., ed. *An Analysis of Management Consulting Business in the United States Today.* Fitzwilliam, NH: Consultants News.

————. *An Analysis of the Outplacement Consulting Business in the United States Today.* Fitzwilliam, NH: Consultants News.

————. *Fee and Expense Policies: Statement of 24 Management Consulting Firms.* Fitzwilliam, NH: Consultants News.

————. *How to Break One Hundred in the Consulting Game.* Fitzwilliam, NH: Consultants News.

————. *How Much Is a Consulting Firm Worth?* Fitzwilliam, NH: Consultants News.

————. *Public Relations for Management Consultants.* Fitzwilliam, NH: Kennedy Publications.

————. *Twenty-Five Best Proposals by Management Consulting Firms.* Fitzwilliam, NH: Consultants News. Includes actual proposals from the Consultants News list of 100 leading management consulting firms in the United States.

————. *What Clients Really Think about Consultants: 169 Turn-Ons in 4 Phases of the Engagement.* Fitzwilliam, NH: Consultants News.

Kennedy Publications. *The News Release Idea Book for Management Consultants.* Fitzwilliam, NH: Kennedy Publications.

Kirby, Jonell H. *Consultation: Practice and Practitioner.* Muncie, IN: Accelerated Development.

Kleiman, Carol. *The 100 Best Jobs for the 1990s and Beyond.* Chicago: Dearborn Financial Publishing.

Lant, Jeffrey L. *The Consultant's Kit: Establishing and Operating Your Successful Consulting Business.* Arlington, VA: VTNC. Well written and interesting reading for the beginner.

———. *How to Make at Least One Hundred Thousand Dollars Every Year.* Cambridge, MA: JLA Publications.

Lee, Robert J., ed. *Consultation Skills Readings.* Alexandria, VA: NTL Institute.

Lewin, Marsha D. *The Overnight Consultant.* New York: John Wiley and Sons.

Lippitt, Gordon L. *The Consulting Process in Action.* San Diego, CA: Pfeiffer and Co.

Mathieson, Michael. *Marketing on The Internet.* Gulf Breeze, Fl: Maximum Press.

Messina, James J., ed. *The Handbook of Readings for the Training of Consultants and Trainers.* Tampa, FL: Advanced Development Systems.

Metzger, Robert O. *Profitable Consulting: Guiding America's Managers into the Next Century.* Reading, MA: Addison-Wesley Publishing Co. Covers a broad range of topics—from building a practice to protecting your client relations and from working with international firms to working with family-owned local firms.

Moore, Gerald L. *The Politics of Management Consulting.* Westport, CT: Greenwood Publishing Group.

Nicholas, Ted. *The Corporate Forms Kit.* Chicago: Upstart Publishing Company, a division of Dearborn Publishing Group.

———. *The Business Agreements Kit.* Chicago: Upstart Publishing Company, a division of Dearborn Publishing Group.

———. *The Complete Guide to Nonprofit Corporations.* Chicago: Enterprise • Dearborn, a division of Dearborn Publishing Group.

———. *The Golden Mailbox: How to Get Rich Direct Marketing Your Product.* Chicago: Enterprise • Dearborn, a division of Dearborn Publishing Group.

———. *How to Form Your Own Corporation Without a Lawyer for Under $75.* Chicago: Upstart Publishing Company, a division of Dearborn Publishing Group.

———. *How to Form Your Own "S" Corporation and Avoid Double Taxation.* Upstart Publishing Company, a division of Dearborn Publishing Group.

———. *How to Publish a Book and Sell a Million Copies.* Chicago: Enterprise • Dearborn, a division of Dearborn Publishing Group.

———. *Secrets of Entrepreneurial Leadership: Building Top Performance through Trust and Teamwork.* Chicago: Enterprise • Dearborn, a division of Dearborn Publishing Group.

Payn, Ray. *Consultant's Little Instruction Book.* Las Vegas, NV: Mega Media Press.

Poynter, Dan. *The Expert Witness Handbook: Tips and Techniques for the Litigation Consultant.* Para Publishing. Available from Consultants Bookstore, Templeton Rd., Fitzwilliam, NH 03447.

Pyeatt, Nancy. *The Consultant's Legal Guide and Forms.* Sarasota, FL: American Consultants League. A basic but useful introduction to the legal environment in which consultants operate. Appropriate for the novice consultant in particular.

Radin, William G. *Billing Power!: The Recruiter's Guide to Peak Performance.* Cincinnati, OH: Innovative Consulting.

Ramsey, Dan. *The Upstart Guide to Owning and Managing a Consulting Service.* Chicago: Upstart Publishing Co.

Rudman, Jack. *Business Consultant.* Syosset, NY: National Learning Corp.

————. *Senior Business Consultant.* Syosset, NY: National Learning Corp.

Schiffman, Stephan. *The Consultant's Handbook: How to Start and Develop Your Own Practice.* Holbrook, MA: Bob Adams. An overview for the beginning consultant on finding clients, making presentations, pricing services, and organizing a consulting business.

Schrello, Don M. *The Complete Marketing Handbook for Consultants.* University Association. Available from Consultants Bookstore, Templeton Rd., Fitzwilliam, NH 03447.

Seiden, R. Matthew. *Breaking Away: The Engineer's Guide to Successful Consulting.* Englewood Cliffs, NJ: Prentice-Hall.

Shenson, Howard L. *The Consultant's Guide to Proposal Writing.* Portland, OR: NTC Press.

————. *The Contract and Fee-Setting Guide for Consultants and Professionals.* New York: John Wiley and Sons. Covers the business of consulting—from fee setting through proposal writing to drawing up the contract and issuing reports.

————. *How to Develop and Promote Successful Seminars and Workshops: A Definitive Guide to Creating and Marketing Seminars, Workshops, Classes and Conferences.* New York: John Wiley and Sons.

————. *How to Get More and Better Referrals: 73 Proven Strategies.* Portland, OR: NTC Press. Available from NTC, 123 NW 2nd Ave., Ste. 405, Portland, OR 97209.

————. *How to Get Quoted and Talked About by the Press.* Portland, OR: NTC Press. Available from NTC, 123 NW 2nd Ave., Ste. 405, Portland, OR 97209.

————. *How to Strategically Negotiate the Consulting Contract.* Portland, OR: NTC Press.

————. *Shenson on Consulting.* New York: John Wiley and Sons.

————. *The Successful Consultant's Guide to Fee Setting.* Sarasota, FL: American Consultants League. Written for both the experienced and new consultant, the book contains complete information on calculating overhead rates, determining fees, alternative methods of disclosing fees to clients, and reimbursement for direct expenses.

————. *77 Proven Strategies to Increase Seminar and Workshop Profits.* Portland, OR: NTC Press. Available from NTC, 123 NW 2nd Ave., Ste. 405, Portland, OR 97209.

————. *101 Proven Strategies for Building a Successful Practice.* Portland, OR: NTC Press. Available from NTC, 123 NW 2nd Ave., Ste. 405, Portland, OR 97209.

Smith, Brian R. *The Country Consultant.* Fitzwilliam, NH: Consultants News. Useful book for the solo consultant who will practice in a rural environment.

Steele, Fritz. *The Role of the Internal Consultant: Effective Role-Shaping for Staff Positions.* Melbourne, FL: Krieger Publishing Co.

Stryker, Steven C. *Principles of Professional Consulting.* Washington, D.C.: Bermont Books.

Tepper, Ron. *Become a Top Consultant: How the Experts Do It*. New York: John Wiley and Sons.

———. *The Consultant's Problem-Solving Workbook*. New York: John Wiley and Sons. A practical, how-to guide with sample forms, letters, contracts, sales-building pitches, and checklists.

———. *The 10 Hottest Consulting Practices*. New York: John Wiley and Sons.

Thomsett, Michael C. *The Consultant's Money Book*. Sarasota, FL: American Consultants League. Provides guidance on establishing a simple accounting system, proper recordkeeping, and accessible documentation.

Tyson, Kirk W. *Business Intelligence: Putting It All Together*. Oak Brook, IL: Leading Edge Publishing.

Ucko, Thomas. *Selecting a Consultant*. Los Altos, CA: Crisp Publications.

Weiss, Allen. *How to Maximize Fees in Professional Service Firms*. Summit Consulting. Available from Consultants Bookstore, Templeton Rd., Fitzwilliam, NH 03447. An excellent monograph on value-based fee setting. Of particular use to consultants with a few years under their belts.

———. *Million Dollar Consulting: The Professional's Guide to Growing a Practice*. New York: McGraw-Hill. A must read for every consultant, new or old.

Index

profit, 178–79
Field survey data, 170
Finance and purchasing
consultants, 62
Financial consulting
agreement, 215
Financial management, 14
Firm fixed-price contract, 187
First impressions, 148
Fixed-fee-plus-expenses
contracts, 187
Fixed-price contract, 179, 186–
87
sample, 205–8
with redetermination, 187
Flexibility, 161
Flowchart. See Functional flow
diagram
Follow-up consultation, 194
Foodservice Consultants
Society International,
29
Foresters of America, Inc.,
Association of
Consulting, 29
Foundation grants, 79–81
Franchise Consultants Interna-
tional Association, 29
"Free" consultation, 193–95
Free offer, 131–41
advertising campaign, 141–
45
development of, 133–34,
139–41
sample, 132
worksheet for, 135–38
Fringe benefits, 175
Functional flow diagram, 153–
54, 155, 156, 167
Funding, 151

G

General and administrative
expense, 181
General partnership, 18–19
Goals, 162
Government agencies, 77–81,
161, 179–81
government and foundation
grants, 79–81
information, 78
maximum labor rates and,
179
Grants, 79–81, 134, 151
Growth, 178

H

Harvard Business Review, 90
Healthcare Consultants,
American Association
of, 27
High-bids, 97
High-gain potential situations,
191

"Hotfoot" situation, 74–76
Hours, in workday, 173
*How to Get the Best Results
from Management
Consultants,* 24
*How to Strategically Negotiate
the Consulting
Contract,* 162, 185
Human relations
consultant, 61
skills, 52
Human resources
management, 16

I

IBM, 88
Image, 125, 148
Incentive contracts
cost-plus-incentive-fee, 189
incentive fixed-price
contract, 187
Income, average annual, 3
Incorporation, 19–20
Independent Computer
Consultants Associ-
ation, 30
Institute of Certified Profes-
sional Business
Consultants, 30
Institute of Management
Consultants, 24
Institute of Tax Consultants, 30
Insurance Management
Consultants, American
Association of, 27
International Association of
Business Communi-
cators, 26
International Association of
Merger and Acquisition
Professionals, 30
Internet, 40–47, 89–90, 122–
23, 169
sample Web pages, 41–43,
44–46
Interview
control of, 147–48
focus on problem, 150
inexperienced interviewer
and, 149–50
payment for first meeting,
149
Investment Management
Consultants Associ-
ation, 30

J

Jargon, 52
Journal articles, 105, 120–22

K

Kleiman, Carol, 1–2

L

Labor, estimating, 156
Labor rate, daily, 171–73
government client and, 179
Lawyer, 21–22, 47
Legal Nurse Consultants,
American Association
of, 27
Letter of agreement, 185–86.
See also Contract
Letters to the editor, 123
Liability, 22
Limited liability company, 20
Limited partnership, 18–19
Literary Market Place, 121

M

Mailing lists, 111
Malpractice, 22
Management Advisory
Service, 24–25
Management consultants, 61
Management Consultants,
National Association
of, 31
Management plan, 167–68
Marketing, 4, 14
direct, 129–46
advertising, 129, 141–45
client concerns, 129–31
free offer, 131–41
fees, 175–76
low-cost/no-cost techniques
directories, 110
Internet, 122–23
letters to the editor, 123
newsletters, 110–20
newsmaking, 124–25, 126
newspaper/magazine/
journal articles, 120–22,
128
public and professional
meetings, 109–10
requesting assistance in
research, 105–7
speeches, 107–9
teaching, 124
volunteering, 125
planning approach to, 102–4
Marketing agreement, sample,
213–14
Marketing consultants, 61
Market position, protection of,
9–10
Meetings, public and professional, 109–10
Merger and Acquisition
Professionals,
International
Association of, 30
Misdefining, 98
Motivation, 5